'This is a really excellent book – a fascinating examination no[...] about notions of creativity in education and most specifically i[...] of the whole history of the idea of creativity. Smith is erudite a[...] she tells, bringing to light the relevance of past thinking, repo[...] [...] [...] [...]ing [...] [...]king to present trends and attitudes. This is a key book for anyone researching English teaching but also essential reading for teachers wanting to understand more about creativity and learning and the rationale for bringing it into being in their own classrooms. Most importantly, its superb tracing of ideas historically provides a much-needed context for thinking about the idea of creativity today. And the thinking of today is brilliantly brought to life in the transcribed conversations in the 'playscript' of the third part of the book – absolute golddust in showing in action the ways in which teachers are grappling with the challenges and constraints they face in trying to enact own conceptualisation of the subject and learning within it.'

Barbara Bleiman, *English consultant at English and Media Centre (EMC), author of 'What Matters in English Teaching' (EMC)*

'This book presents a timely, compelling and important argument for the restoration of creativity to the curriculum for English. The history of English as a subject is deftly distilled, and followed by a thought-provoking series of research-informed scripts which present a range of opinions and perspectives on 'creative English'. This will be of interest across the English teaching community: an excellent resource to prompt discussion, reflection and creative practice.'

Dr Annabel Watson, *Senior Lecturer, University of Exeter; editor of 'A Practical Guide to Teaching English in the Secondary School' (Routledge)*

'Dr Lorna Smith's book has many major strengths and distinctive features. It covers vital areas connected with creativity and the history of English teaching. Her creative coverage of these topics is much needed at the moment, not just as an academic resource, but to generate wider public debate about creativity and English teaching. It is innovative in the way it uses scripted dialogue to promote wider and imaginative thinking about English teaching, creative pedagogy and English teaching's place in the wider culture. It is also a great summation of the current research/thinking in the field of creativity.'

Dr Francis Gilbert, *Senior Lecturer in Education, Head of the MA in Creative Writing and Education & course leader for PGCE English at Goldsmiths University; author and novelist*

Creativity in the English Curriculum

Creativity in the English Curriculum is essential reading for anyone involved or interested in the teaching of English, offering both a detailed history of how creativity has informed the tradition of teaching English, and how it should be used to position this teaching in the future.

Highlighting the need to promote creativity as a rich, intellectual pursuit, *Creativity in the English Curriculum* celebrates artistry in English past and present, and argues for its restoration to the curriculum. It emphasises that creativity is at the core of a humane education, not only through stimulating and enhancing the growth of the individual, but also through developing understanding of the importance of community, society and collaboration. Smith presents the historical relationship between curriculum policy and creativity, demonstrating that creativity has and always will be the life blood of teaching and learning.

Including dialogues between expert English teaching practitioners and leading professionals concerning the place of creativity in English, *Creativity in the English Curriculum* includes practical, research-informed ideas for effective creative practice for any English classroom. It is a must-read for teachers, educators, parents and guardians to prepare all learners for life in and beyond school.

Dr Lorna Smith leads the PGCE English course at the University of Bristol and is Chair of the NATE Initial Teacher Education working group. She was awarded the NATE Terry Furlong Award in 2020 for the research that underpins this book.

National Association for the Teaching of English (NATE)

The National Association for the Teaching of English (NATE), founded in 1963, is the professional body for all teachers of English from primary to Post-16. Through its regions, committees and conferences, the association draws on the work of classroom practitioners, advisers, consultants, teacher trainers, academics and researchers to promote dynamic and progressive approaches to the subject by means of debate, training and publications. NATE is a charity reliant on membership subscriptions. If you teach English in any capacity, please visit www.nate.org.uk and consider joining NATE, so the association can continue its work and give teachers of English and the subject a strong voice nationally.

This series of books co-published with NATE reflects the organisation's dedication to promoting standards of excellence in the teaching of English, from early years through to university level. Titles in this series promote innovative and original ideas that have practical classroom outcomes and support teachers' own professional development.

Books in the NATE series include both pupil and classroom resources and academic research aimed at English teachers, students on PGCE/ITT courses and NQTs.

Titles in this series include:

Teaching English Language 16–19, 2nd edition
A Comprehensive Guide for Teachers of AS and A Level English Language
Martin Illingworth and Nick Hall

Teaching English Language and Literature 16–19
Edited by Furzeen Ahmed, Marcello Giovanelli, Megan Mansworth and Felicity Titjen

Knowledge in English
Canon, Curriculum and Cultural Literacy
Velda Elliott

International Perspectives on English Teacher Development
From Initial Teacher Education to Highly Accomplished Professional
Edited by Andy Goodwyn, Jacqueline Manuel, Rachel Roberts, Lisa Scherff, Wayne Sawyer, Cal Durrant, and Don Zancanella

For more information about this series, please visit: https://www.routledge.com/National-Association-for-the-Teaching-of-English-NATE/book-series/NATE

Creativity in the English Curriculum

Historical Perspectives and Future Directions

Lorna Smith

Routledge
Taylor & Francis Group

LONDON AND NEW YORK

Designed cover image: Rosmarie Wirz / Getty Images, Jeanri Myburgh / EyeEm / Getty Images, Daniel Grill / Getty Images, krisanapong detraphiphat / Getty Images

First published 2023
by Routledge
4 Park Square, Milton Park, Abingdon, Oxon OX14 4RN

and by Routledge
605 Third Avenue, New York, NY 10158

Routledge is an imprint of the Taylor & Francis Group, an informa business

© 2023 Lorna Smith

British Library Cataloguing-in-Publication Data
A catalogue record for this book is available from the British Library

Library of Congress Cataloging-in-Publication Data
Names: Smith, Lorna, 1967- author.
Title: Creativity in the English curriculum : historical perspectives and future directions / Lorna Smith.
Description: Abingdon, Oxon ; New York, NY Routledge, 2023. | Series: National Association for the Teaching of English (NATE) | Includes bibliographical references and index.
Identifiers: LCCN 2022051704 (print) | LCCN 2022051705 (ebook) | ISBN 9781032152585 (hardback) | ISBN 9781032152592 (paperback) | ISBN 9781003243311 (ebook)
Subjects: LCSH: English language—Study and teaching (Secondary)—Great Britain. | Creative thinking—Study and teaching (Secondary)—Great Britain. | Language arts—Curricula—Great Britain.
Classification: LCC LB1631 .S644 2023 (print) | LCC LB1631 (ebook) | DDC 428.0071/2—dc23/eng/20230103
LC record available at https://lccn.loc.gov/2022051704
LC ebook record available at https://lccn.loc.gov/2022051705

ISBN: 9781032152585 (hbk)
ISBN: 9781032152592 (pbk)
ISBN: 9781003243311 (ebk)

DOI: 10.4324/9781003243311

Typeset in Bembo
by codeMantra

For English teaching practitioners of today and tomorrow:
be yours to hold the torch of English high.

Contents

Figures

Tables

Series Editor Foreword

Gary Snapper

When I was at school – between 1972 and 1976, in what we now call Years 5,6,7 and 8 – sets of the *Penguin English Project* book series and its sibling publications, the *Voices* and *Junior Voices* poetry collections, made frequent appearances in my English lessons.

These delightful anthologies of all kinds of writing (short stories, poems, autobiographical writing, extracts from plays and so on) and pictures (photos, drawings, cartoons, *etc.*) had titles like *I Took My Mind a Walk*, *Creatures Moving*, *Worlds Apart* and *That Once Was Me*. They were published by Penguin as part of its hugely influential, progressive imprint Penguin Education, and were designed to bring into the English classroom – in a move that was revolutionary for its day – high-quality, beautifully presented and illustrated, selections of literary writing designed to intrigue and delight children.

There were no comprehension questions in these anthologies, no attempts to specify what should be learnt from them. They were mainly composed of contemporary texts and photographs, with some intriguing older texts and folk writing mixed in. There was a strong emphasis on reflecting on personal experience – the experience of many kinds of people – and on autobiographical writing.

These books were treasure troves of creativity. They were intended to inspire creative teaching, creative learning and creative writing – and that is what I remember most vividly from English in those years: English teachers who encouraged us to read, to wonder, to imagine, to explore, to respond, and to create – to write about ourselves and the world around us, and to grow.

All those books – which could be found in most schools around the UK (and are still lurking at the back of the stock cupboards of many!) – were edited by Geoffrey Summerfield, an English teacher who went on to become Senior Lecturer in the Department of Education and English at the University of York, and eventually Professor at New York University. He was also the editor and co-author (along with David Holbrook and Reed Whittemore) of *Creativity in English (1968)* – a text which, as Lorna Smith suggests in this volume, was one of the key works to emerge from the influential Dartmouth Conference of 1966 (along with John Dixon's *Growth through English,* 1969), and perhaps the first major text to deal specifically with the topic of English and creativity.

Smith cites Summerfield's view of 'Creative English', which, he writes, is about promoting 'experiment, talk, enquiry, amusement, vivacity, bouts of intense concentration, seriousness, collaboration, and clearer and more adequate self-knowledge ', involving us in 'talk about our selves, our language, our behaviour, our attitudes and beliefs, and, when appropriate in recording such things in writing'.

It's fascinating to look at the Teachers' Handbooks to *Voices* (Summerfield, 1968) and the *Penguin English Project* for alternative expressions of this philosophy, as well as for more specific pedagogical advice of the time. One of the most striking of these is in the handbook to Stage One of the *Penguin English Project* (Radley *et al.,* 1972), in which Patrick Radley writes:

> In the English classroom we set up an artificial situation so that certain things can happen. The most important of these is 'being'. Only if we let the children 'be' shall we have created an atmosphere in which they have scope to find themselves and to respond fully to the world around them. This is no invitation to disorder; tyranny of any kind, by teacher or children, is going to cause distracting and irrelevant tensions. It is a plea for the making of classroom relationships from which there can arise the order based on mutual knowledge and respect.

He continues:

> Too many of us struggle still to test our powers of instruction by devising exercises for the children which we can measure or grade; and in this we are amply assisted by the country's examination system. But it is not possible to *mark* the Inner Light, and 'becoming oneself' is not a competitive process. How can children respond fully to that or this passage in a climate of tests and competition?'

Amongst his comments on individual poems, one that stands out is:

> I don't often advocate close textual examination, but a look at the way Morgan uses language in this poem could encourage some exciting work.

Such sentiments are strikingly different from those which seem increasingly to dominate discourses about English in schools today.

Even those of us who most regret the gradual shrinking of the role of creativity and personal response in the English curriculum that has taken place in the decades since this was written may feel slightly shocked by phrases such as 'I don't often advocate close textual examination', or somewhat queasy at the idea that the most important thing we can make 'happen' in the classroom is 'being'. But we may also feel a renewed thrill at the emphasis on 'self-knowledge', on 'becoming oneself', and on 'responding fully to the world around [us]' – and on the idea that not everything that is valuable in English can be assessed. This is a different kind of 'knowledge-rich' curriculum, which places children's authentic voices and social relationships at its heart and sees them as creative agents in making meaning.

In this book – a timely and significant contribution to the NATE series on the teaching of English – Lorna Smith admirably charts the growth of the idea of creativity in English during the formative years of the subject, and the shifts in government policy, since Summerfield's books were published, which have subsequently led to the almost complete removal of the idea from the official English curriculum. These shifts, she argues, in turn have reduced opportunities for the kind of creative teaching and learning – and possibly also 'being'? – which Summerfield – along with Harold Rosen, James Britton, John Dixon, David Holbrook and many others at the time – advocated.

She charts, too, the ways in which students' voices, concerns and creative agency have been relegated – through devaluation of the role of dialectal variety and authentic voice in favour of a prescriptive approach to Standard English and grammar; of extended, exploratory and expressive creative writing in favour of highly structured approaches and academic genres; and of pleasure, choice and range of reading in literature and popular culture in favour of a prescriptive approach to canonical literature.

Happily, Smith also reports that a reading of government policy does not tell the whole story, and that there are strong undercurrents of resistance. Using a notably creative method of presenting her findings, she shows that English teachers continue to believe in the power of creativity, even if it has been removed from the curriculum, and even if we are not always entirely sure what it is and what it looks like. Smith also valuably explores the ways in which we can keep creativity in English going, despite the policy context.

Novelist James Kelman, discussing linguistic, literary and cultural prejudice (Tait, 2008), once said:

They want to block your stories – and they will, if you let them.

This volume is an important rallying cry for English teachers: we must not let them.

Gary Snapper, *Lecturer in English Education, University of Oxford*

References

Dixon, J. (1969) *Growth through English* Oxford: Oxford University Press

Radley, P, *et al.* (1972) *Penguin English Project Stage One: Teachers' Handbook* London: Penguin

Summerfield, G. (1968) *Voices: Teachers' Handbook* Harmondsworth: Penguin

Summerfield, G. (1968) *Creativity in English: Papers Relating to the Anglo-American seminar on the teaching of English (Dartmouth College, New Hampshire, 1966): The Dartmouth Seminar Papers* Champaign, IL: NCTE

Tait, T. (2008), 'In his own words' (an interview with James Kelman), The Guardian, 12 April.

Acknowledgements

There are many voices that have shaped this book, and to these I am indebted.

To all those I have taught, both as a secondary English teacher and teacher educator, and to all colleagues I have ever had the privilege of working alongside: thank you. I have learnt everything from you.

To the colloquists who gave so generously of their time and ideas: thank you for your inspirational testimony, and thank you for all that you have done, and still do, for secondary English.

To friends, colleagues, reviewers, Dr. James Ogden, the librarians at the University of Bristol and Clifton College, and the team at Routledge whose kind input, comments and feedback helped bring this book to fruition: thank you for your guiding wisdom.

To Paul, Will and Alex: thank you for your constant encouragement and love.

Part I
The case for creativity

Introduction

'Nothing without the make-believe of a beginning'[1]

The term 'creative' is associated with making, developing, inspiration, artistry, originality, the imagination and working things out. To be recognised as 'creative' is usually taken as a compliment, and it has been suggested that 'creative' is the most consistently positive word in the English language (Williams, 1961). Yet the qualities and values that might be assumed to go hand in hand with creativity are not truths universally acknowledged, particularly in the field of education. Academic and professional literature (*e.g.* Craft, 2005; Ofsted, 2010; Bleiman, 2020) has continued to rehearse the same arguments for creative learning made by Plowden in *Children and their Primary Schools* (1967) over 50 years ago. The fact that the position has continually to be remade suggests that its position is vulnerable.

This seems particularly so in the field of English education in England. 'Creativity' is entirely absent from the current *National curriculum in England: English programmes of study* (DfE, 2014) (hereafter 'the National Curriculum' or 'the Curriculum'). Although the previous National Curriculum for English (DCSF/QCA, 2007) included creativity as one of its four core principles, and creativity *is* retained in other subject areas[2] of the current Curriculum, the exclusion of the term creativity (and any words containing the 'creat-' root) appears to be a particularly stark indicator that creativity is out of favour where English is concerned.

Since I have been involved in secondary English teaching in England throughout my professional life, with creativity underpinning my work throughout, I was troubled when the current 'creativity-less' Curriculum was first published. I wondered how English might manage *without* creativity: how might the subject be affected? And what would be the impact on English teachers? These questions prompted the research that is presented in this book. The project led not only to a deep understanding of the views of expert English teachers in England, but an enhanced appreciation of the centrality of creativity to effective first-language (L1) teaching. I hope that it may be of value to educators and researchers in English education in England, whether primary or secondary, other English-speaking jurisdictions in the UK and beyond, and also to first language teachers in the wider world.

Connecting the personal with the policy

Before I begin, I want to acknowledge that I am writing from a position of several biases. I am a lover of language, seeing language as humankind's most important invention; I am a natural optimist, with an idealist, constructionist perspective; I hold that creativity is important not only to English but to education more widely, and believe it

DOI: 10.4324/9781003243311-2

is a huge error of judgement to write creativity out of the Curriculum. My position and my prejudices have been determined by my lived life; what I see is illuminated 'by their light' (Gadamer, 1975/2004: 360). The metaphor is important: it emphasises that one's experiences *elucidate* what we seek to understand, so that far from trying to suppress what led me to embark on this inquiry, they need to be foregrounded.

Given that research is often prompted by a *personal* story in a *public* context (Jessop, 2019) – in this case, the context of public education policy – this book accordingly begins with the story of my own experience of that policy. My 30-plus-year career in the field of English education in England, first as a secondary classroom English teacher and then as an English teacher educator has, coincidentally, spanned the life of the National Curriculum. Yet the singular determiner 'the' is a misnomer: there have been six versions of the Curriculum to date, and one unpublished. This means that my career has necessitated reflecting upon the changes between each iteration on multiple occasions.

I recall poring over the initial draft, *English for ages 5–16* (Cox, 1989), during my Post Graduate Certificate in Education (PGCE) studies, inspired by its twin aims of contributing 'to the personal development of the individual child' (Cox, 1989: 59) and preparing them for the adult world; I remember the challenges of putting the new Curriculum into practice during my probationary year (as it was then known) in a school in the south west of England. There, I worked under an inspirational Head of Department who believed that English could be taught exclusively through literature. He encouraged us to read fiction extensively with our classes and to experiment in our wider practice. So, in the days before Health and Safety concerns proscribed such activity, I took my mixed-attaining classes to sit under a tent of cherry-tree blossom in the school grounds, or to the churchyard down the road (having first phoned the vicar for permission) to write poetry. I would type up learners'[3] work for an anthology which we then discussed in class as if it were published literature. I encouraged them to write for other audiences – one won a national letter-writing competition. We were early adopters of email, using it to correspond with a partner school in Australia. I revised punctuation conventions by pairing my Year 8 class with a primary school class and getting them to design a bespoke 'Mr Men'–style book with an animated punctuation symbol as the lead character and a narrative tailored to the interests of the buddy pupil. Although I did not refer to it in such terms at the time, I came to define my approach as 'creative'. My learners enjoyed English; they did very well in examinations, too. These experiences had a fundamental impact on my future practice.

I stayed at this school for ten years and served a spell as Head of Department myself. The 1990s were dynamic in terms of curriculum change. Cox's Curriculum was challenged almost immediately for being insufficiently rigorous, but Pascall's (DfE/WO, 1993) reactionary mooted replacement prompted a wave of complaints from teachers and academics and was shelved. However, a new iteration was published in 1995 (DfE/WO), followed by another in 1999 (DfEE/QCAa). Thus, in the first decade of my career, I worked with the first three published and the one unpublished Curricula, each with a slightly different perspective on the place, role and substance of English. While the prevailing narrative in education management became increasingly tied to standards agendas, creativity simultaneously became 'something of a catchphrase' (Dymoke, 2011: 144) – 'catchphrase' suggesting that while creativity was being promoted, it was perhaps rather tokenistic. Nevertheless, I continued to seek to develop my practice, building on my earlier creative work.

When the fourth Curriculum (DfES/QCA) was launched in 2004, I was teaching PGCE student teachers and undergraduates in Education Studies; when the fifth (DCSF/QCA, 2007) followed three years later, I was leading the PGCE English programme at a post-1992 university, and saw it as my mission to nurture a new generation of creative English teachers. I was two years into my present post as the coordinator of the PGCE English programme at a Russell Group university when the current Key Stage 3[4] Curriculum for English was introduced in 2013, followed by KS4 (DfE, 2014).

Its aims appear not unlike those of Cox:

> A high-quality education in English will teach pupils to speak and write fluently so that they can communicate their ideas and emotions to others and through their reading and listening, others can communicate with them.
>
> (DfE, 2013: 13)

However, it continues with a list of requirements that belie the similarities. The emphasis on canonical English literature and technical accuracy, decontextualised grammar and spelling, does little to promote personal development and arguably stymies creative opportunities, with a 'naming of parts'-style knowledge (Brindley, 2015: 45) foregrounded rather than personal growth.

I feared that the formal tenor and prescriptive content of the revised Curriculum, together with ever-increasing pressure on both teachers driven by accountability and performance tables and on young people driven by societal pressures, could change what happens in English lessons. This was compounded when some of my student teachers were required to 'teach to the test' and asked to practice GCSE[5]-style questions with early KS3 learners at the expense of broader, creative, age-appropriate content. I heard anecdotes suggesting several schools had reduced creative writing to training learners to memorise passages to regurgitate in an examination, requiring only slight variance according to the question ('The grey clouds lumbered across the sky' or 'The silver clouds scudded across the sky'?).

I realised that English teachers adopting such practice were resigned to 'curricularization' (Kress *et al.*, 2004: 152). A picture emerged that suggested the marginalisation of creativity was delimiting the English offer in secondary classrooms at the expense of the teacher, the learner and the subject itself, a hunch confirmed by subsequent research. An increasing number of teachers were choosing to leave the profession, feeling overwhelmed by policy changes, undervalued (Smith, 2017) and despairing their loss of agency (Rosen, 2015; Londesborough *et al.*, 2017). The Covid pandemic exacerbated the exodus, while at the same time fewer people are now applying to become teachers (UCAS, 2022). The wellbeing and overall happiness of British students have fallen dramatically since the introduction of the current Curriculum (PISA, 2019). Many learners no longer see the English classroom as a place to enjoy reading and fewer read for pleasure outside the classroom (Videbaek, 2020); numbers sitting A level English Literature (traditionally a subject for those who 'love' reading) decreased by 35% between 2012 and 2022 (Noble, 2022). This cannot but have an adverse impact on the subject, as fewer students go on to study English at University, leading to fewer academics researching and developing the subject, and there will be commensurately fewer who choose to train to teach.

All this led me beyond English, to ask broader questions about the remit and impact of the education system. The Latin root 'educare' means 'to lead' (www.oed.com) which suggests that to educate is to develop, to nurture: education is about *becoming* – there is an implicit emphasis on cultivating the whole child that is reminiscent of Cox's primary aim of promoting individual development, personal growth. The Oxford English Dictionary emphasises the cultural and moral dimensions: education is 'The culture or development of personal knowledge or understanding, growth of character, moral and social qualities, etc., *as contrasted with* the imparting of knowledge or skill' (*ibid*, my emphasis). In a similar vein, Biesta defines education as 'a human event of communication, meaning making and interpretation' (2015: 11). It is this definition that I have chosen to adopt for this book because of the import given to 'human' (humanism is the philosophy underpinning early English policy documents), 'communication' and 'meaning' (both of which rely on language), 'making' (a synonym for 'creating') and interpretation (which is core to understanding). The perspective has been given fresh prominence through the *Futures of Education: Learning to Become* (UNESCO, 2019) initiative which seeks to 'reimagine' knowledge, education and learning to enable humanity to meet the imagined and as-yet-unimagined challenges of the future.

However, a more prosaic definition of education – one that departs from its etymological roots – has been adopted by the Department for Education (DfE). In a speech to the Education Reform Summit the year after the current Curriculum was published, Nick Gibb MP (then Schools Minister) stated, 'Education is the engine of our economy' and went on, '… most important of all, we must ensure that more people have the knowledge and skills they need to succeed in a demanding economy' (2015: n.p). Granted, Gibb went on to discuss the importance of nurturing an appreciation of culture and of preparing children for adult life but – in striking contrast to the OED definition – he suggested that ensuring young people have the 'knowledge and skills' for work is the *prime purpose* of education (*ibid*), termed the 'cause-effect' (Biesta, 2015: 11) notion of education, as it assumes certain inputs ('knowledge and skills') will result in corollary (economic) outputs.

This is notwithstanding the problem that 'knowledge' is itself ill-defined: 'the meaning of knowledge is at best implicit and at worst virtually empty of content' (Young, 2009: 193). And to ask what 'being educated in English' means (Wilson, 1972: 9) is not necessarily rhetorical, although Victoria Elliott (2020) and Robert Eaglestone (2021) have both recently made excellent attempts to present answers. Brindley describes a 'knowledge dichotomy' (2015: 46) through which English is concerned with the knowledge decided by 'policy committees' (*ibid*) which is measurable and accountable, *and* knowledge borne of 'self-reflexivity' (*ibid*) – personal growth – which is not. The two knowledges are equally valid but are in competition with each other, creating a challenge for English teachers who are required by the Teachers' Standards (DfE, 2011) to teach both.

The problem has been recently compounded by the publication of the Core Content Framework (CCF) (DfE, 2019a) and the Early Career Framework (ECF) (DfE, 2019b). Intended to provide structured pedagogical guidance for new teachers, neither includes the terms 'creative' or 'creativity'. This presents a situation where creativity is absent from both the current Curriculum (which stipulates *what* to teach) and new direction on *how* to teach.

I am not suggesting that the economy should be ignored, but I do wish to question the absence of creativity in current policy, and what this means for subject English, those who teach it and those preparing to teach it. This book examines how the idea of creativity in English is interpreted by subject experts today, and whether (or to what extent) this reflects how the relationship between English and creativity in England has been seen over the years, recognising how understanding what is happening in the present in the light of the past might inform the future. Ultimately, it aspires to help create positive change in secondary English education and inform the development of what will be the seventh Curriculum, but in the shorter term it is intended to inspire dialogue between all those interested in English teaching, and present ideas, perspectives and ambiguities they may not otherwise encounter and from which new knowledge can emerge. In this way, the book offers everyone in the profession a secure perspective from which to orientate their work, develop confidence in a creative pedagogy and continue to flourish.

Notes

1 George Eliot (1876) *Daniel Deronda*, Chapter 1.
2 Art and Design, Computing, Design and Technology, Mathematics and Music (DfE, 2014).
3 I debated whether to label the children 'pupils' (the term used in Curriculum documents), 'students' or 'learners'. I settled on 'learners', a learner being defined as one who acquires knowledge or skills through study, experience or teaching (www.oed.com), although I occasionally use 'student' or 'pupil' if relevant to the policy document discussed. The word 'pupil' originally meant an orphan or ward, which has uncomfortable connotations of powerlessness, while 'student' is simply a description of one who studies. I interpret 'learner' as carrying with it a greater sense of agency and so is appropriate to my argument about creativity; it also to some extent 'flattens' the hierarchy between teacher and child because, as I go on to show, a creative teacher is a learner too.
4 Key Stage 3 in England is intended for school years 7–9, i.e. for students aged 11–14; Key Stage 4 is for school years 10–11, i.e. students aged 15–16.
5 General Certificate of Secondary Education, usually taken in the academic year in which learners turn 16.

1 What is creativity and why does it matter?

1.1 Introduction

It is helpful to consider why creativity has become such a contentious term where subject English is concerned, especially since English and creativity are popularly closely associated: it was Chaucer – 'the father of English poetry' (Dryden, 1700, n.p.) – who provides the first recorded use of the term 'create' (OED.com) in *The Parson's Tale*: 'Al be it so that God hath creat alle thynges / In right ordre, and no thyng withouten ordre' (c. 1390: 218). The removal of 'creativity' from the National Curriculum is evidence that its story is no simple one, and an exploration of the literature begins to reveal some of the complexity.

The purpose of this chapter is to tell that story from the beginning and provide the context for what follows. 'Context' is from the Latin *contexere* meaning 'to weave together, to connect' (OED.com), which emphasises that knowledge is woven into (and so cannot be separated from) its context. It is therefore important to ground a discussion about creativity in subject English within the wider field. This involves asking broader questions: what *is* creativity? How has creativity been understood in education policy in England? What is the effect of that policy on contemporary English practice? The chapter highlights key positions, arguments, contradictions and challenges.

The chapter begins (Section 1.2) with a broad-brush history of creativity, showing how it has been variously understood across psychology, art and design theory, literature and education. Section 1.3 goes on to provide context specific to the chapters that follow by exploring the contentious position of creativity in education policy in England at three salient points over the last 50 years, starting with the 1960s (when the debate rose to prominence), through to a renewed interest in creativity in the 1990s, to a resurgence in the 2000s. Section 1.4 provides an overview of the literature summarising the current debate around creativity in the secondary English classroom context, as a precursor to explaining how this book contributes to that dialogue.

1.1.1 Opening questions

Before you continue your reading of this chapter, pause to consider these questions:

- What is your own definition of 'creativity'? Note it down. You will be invited to return to this definition at various points through the book.
- What values do you associate with creativity?

DOI: 10.4324/9781003243311-3

- What hallmarks of creativity might be apparent in a school that could indicate whether creativity is promoted and valued (or not) in that setting? What hallmarks of creativity might be apparent in an English department or English classroom?

1.2 The contested notion of creativity

A broad review of the literature of creativity across various fields provides both a sense of the ambiguity of the term, and hence how potentially awkward it is to apply in practice in education; it also – paradoxically – highlights the interconnectedness of creativity and subject English. The main movements in the history of the concept of creativity are explained in roughly chronological order – although this is not to suggest that the story is a simple linear narrative, nor complete: notions of creativity themselves are in fact constantly being (re)created (Chappell, 2018).

1.2.1 Big C Creativity: from Gods and geniuses to the hard graft of the great artists

Creativity was initially understood to be the preserve of deities: different faiths have different creation stories to explain the genesis of the world and everything in it. Chaucer's Parson, a Christian, speaks of a powerful creator God; the Qur'an describes God as the 'Originator' (Chp. 35:1); Brahma is the Hindu god of creation (together with his wife, Saraswati, goddess of knowledge, music, arts, wisdom and learning); the Greeks saw Zeus as their creator-God.

Yet philosophers gradually came to allow that humans have creative ability too, albeit elite humans, and perhaps as a divine gift: for Plato, inspiration was a gift from the Muses (Pappas, 2014). Tasso, working in sixteenth-century Italy, suggested that since nature was the art produced by God, artists should be envisaged as creators too: 'There are two creators, God and the poet' (*in* Williams, 1961/2011: 22). This notion idea took off during the Romantic period: for instance, Coleridge saw 'the living Power and prime Agent' as '[t]he primary Imagination' which gave him a quasi-divine creative power, 'the infinite I Am' (1817: n.p.).

The view that it is only the 'greats' – born with an inspired (or God-given) combination of spontaneous insights, imagination and skills – that are truly creative is now rare (Sternberg, 1999; Scruton, 2000). A more contemporary view is that creativity is as much a result of nurture as nature, and that nurturing creativity is hard work. Matisse argued that it is a 'mistake' to ascribe creativity to inborn talent: creativity takes 'effort' and 'courage' (1954, n.p.). He described an artist as one who combines vision *with application* to produce something beautiful. The sense of the sheer exertion needed for creativity is reinforced by Koestler, who describes having to 'wrench [...] away from the known to create the unknown' (1959, n.p. *in* Lytton, 1971: 15), the violence of his choice of verb suggesting that creativity can be a painful process; for Spender, writing a poem depends upon inspiration but takes 'sweat and toil' (1946, n.p. *in* Lytton, 1971: 18). This recognition that creativity is effortful and requires resilience counters suggestions from some quarters that it is merely 'light relief' (Claxton, 2006: 351) or an easy, sugar-coated appendage (Hodgson and Wilkin, 2014).

Creativity can also be an involved process – Wallas (1926) lays down the stages he believes necessary to reach a creative destination: preparation, incubation, illumination and, ultimately, verification. Lytton (1971) uses a mountaineering metaphor to sum up how both physical *and* complex the imaginative thinking required can be, the product arrived at on reaching the summit; while Summerfield describes 'the state of mind' of a 'good artist' as one which 'includes absorption, curiosity, persistence, inquisitiveness, tentativeness, experimentation, and exhaustion' (1968: 23). Similarly, Sternberg implies that the creative act takes vision, strength and determination: he presents the view that creativity is 'sculpted' out of 'imagination, originality, genius, talent, freedom and individuality' (1999: 17). These suggestions that creativity can be developed independently imply that it may therefore also be taught, with the support of peers or more experienced others.

The renowned creatives cited above (Matisse, Spender, Summerfield) are associated with the aesthetic (painting and poetry), but creativity gradually came to have wider connotations, so that a great – or 'Big C' (Craft, 2001) – creative may be anyone whose work is influential or publicly recognised. Creativity therefore bridges science and the arts. Einstein well recognised science as a creative exploration: 'The greatest scientists are artists as well' (1923 *in* Calaprice, 2000: 245); the philosopher and academic Bertrand Russell described mathematics as having 'supreme beauty... like that of a sculpture' (1919: 60). It has been proposed that there are 'domain differences' between creative people, so that while Einstein and Russell might have 'greater flexibility in the intellectual sphere', the artist might have 'greater flexibility in the emotional or affective sphere' (Stein, 1953: 313), a position acknowledging the importance of creativity across domains.

1.2.2 The interdependence of creativity and culture

Any debate about creativity presupposes that it cannot exist in a vacuum (Jones, 2009). Creative outputs have to be acknowledged as valuable (Robinson, 2007; Chappell *et al.*, 2019), and therefore creativity should be conceptualised as a sociocultural entity (Loi and Dillon, 2006). The German philosopher and hermeneutist, Gadamer, describes the relationship between culture and creativity. He begins his seminal work *Truth and Method* with a discussion of the crucial importance of culture, which he defines as 'the concept of self-formation, education, or cultivation' (1975/2004: 8), to us all. We are each rooted in our culture; through culture, humans grow, learn, bond with each other. For Gadamer, culture is not an optional extra, an affectation adopted by cultural elitists, but the very foundation of knowledge and understanding, fundamental to human existence.

Gadamer emphasises the importance of culture through exploring the concept of 'Bildung', a complex term that is impossible to render precisely into English (Biesta, 2006). While 'bildung' is commonly understood as a synonym for 'education' or 'formation' (as in the term Bildungsroman), Gadamer argues that the term should be understood as Goethe saw it, 'cultivating oneself' (1975/2004: 9) – enculturation – and I further suggest that the close association between culture, art and education is captured and emphasised through the rich complexity of the word itself: a 'bild' is an image, suggesting 'bildung' is built on images. Gadamer explains that our memories are a collection of images, but because it is beyond the capacity of our brains to remember everything, we forget what is not valuable and only remember what *is* valuable. We each pass on what we value to our children. Culture acts as our collective memory: it is the continuous passing on of what we collectively value from one generation to another. Culture (like history) is therefore constantly being made and remade. In the daily drama that is human existence, each new character has a greater store of culture on which to create their own performance; yet 'the essential nature of the historical spirit consists not in the restoration of the past but in *thoughtful mediation with contemporary life*' (1975/2004: 161, emphasis original). In other words, culture is ever-changing and dynamic, created and recreated and essential to our being.

According to this view – that it is through our creative outputs that these precious images are passed on – any *judgements* about creativity and how it is valued are therefore based within the embedded sociocultural context. The difficulty lies in who does the valuing and how that value is acknowledged (Burnard, 2006; Craft, 2006; Dymoke, 2011).

On the one hand, cultural conservatives see 'culture' as the art produced by the Big C/high culture creatives. Unlike Gadamer, they see culture as not a universal entitlement but, rather, a rarefied offering for the select few who can properly appreciate it. In this exclusive and purist view – associated in the field of English literature with TS Eliot's famous assertion that the function of literary criticism is 'the common pursuit of true judgement' (1923: n.p.) – a self-appointed hierarchy make judgements about what is culturally significant on behalf of the majority. Ironically, a school English curriculum built around an elitist literary canon would necessarily be inaccessible to most learners.

Cultural democrats, on the other hand, follow Gadamer in suggesting that the cultural value ascribed to a product of creativity is flexible and fluid because society and culture are undergoing constant change. It is difficult to know which of today's creations will be valued in the future and which rejected: Bach was seen as no more than a proficient composer in his days (Bannerman, 2008), while Van Gogh was dismissed by contemporary critics and sold only one painting during his lifetime (Jones, 2009). This point about the sales-worthiness of a painting emphasises that the monetary value of a created work does not necessarily reflect its aesthetic or cultural value. Yet the Big C artists are revered – and so their work becomes expensive – *because* their art became culturally significant in their respective canons (Green and Cormack, 2008).

With near-universal education in the Global North, the concept of the canon is now understood more broadly, such that 'high culture' and 'low culture' labels have become increasingly difficult to apply. The distinction between them is superficially obvious but hard to defend (Fleming, 2010) due to the challenge of identifying distinguishing criteria and even the problem of identifying what is 'art'. For example, highly successful creative people such as the Beatles – whose pop (popular) music is by definition low culture – are now recognised as part of the canon (Collins, 2020).

The relationship between creativity and culture is, therefore, complex, value-laden and disputed, a notion exacerbated by the fact that many of the examples I have cited thus far concern western white men. This is not intentionally to exclude women, people of colour, or those of the Global South: indeed, I advocate that culture is and cultures are 'desirably diverse and internally plural' (Hodgson and Harris, 2022: n.p.). Rather, it is a result of western white men writing largely about the culture produced by western white men, and these texts becoming seminal in the field, and highlights the difficulty of ascertaining who does the valuing and how it is acknowledged. In a globalised world with an ever-present need to fight injustice, careful consideration of which notion or notions of culture prevail in English policy documents is crucial. Parts II and III of this book go on to explore how 'culture' is presented and understood in the policies, and whether different notions might be held in parallel.

1.2.3 Making it personal

While Big C creatives make transformational 'knight's move[s]' (Haste, 2008: 97) that advance human understanding, there is another view of creativity at the opposite end of the scale: 'little c' creativity (Craft, 2001: 45) or 'ordinary creativity' (Carter, 2004: xviii) that has an impact at a personal level. They suggest we can not only appreciate the aesthetic creative outputs of others *but be creative ourselves* and so, through individual aesthetic experience, grow as individuals.

Little c also goes beyond the aesthetic: it describes the creativity latent in humans to enable people to cope with the everyday. It is 'possibility thinking' (Cremin *et al.,* 2006: 108), a notion of creativity that enables us to solve problems, find alternative ways to do things; and is thereby essential to a full life (Seltzer and Bentley, 1999). The term 'little c' might be a more economical way of expressing what have been termed 'clusters' of creative capacities: 'originality, fluency and volume of ideas, adaptive flexibility, spontaneous flexibility, expressional fluency, sensitivity to problems' (Barron *et al.,* 1997: 12) and 'flexibility, critical evaluation, taking multiple perspectives, and exploring non-obvious connections' (Haste, 2008: 96). And it is not a new idea – over a century ago, Dewey noted,

> Only silly folk identify creative originality with the extraordinary and fanciful; others recognise that its measure lies in putting everyday things to use which had not occurred to others.
>
> (1916: n.p.)

In this view, creativity refers to an individual's relationship with the world – one that is constantly evolving – and is about the interplay between what is known and unknown. Piaget (1953) presented a slightly different angle, when he yoked together intellect and creativity, suggesting intellect refers to logic and factual knowledge, while creativity refers to the 'emotional, imaginative, spontaneous and productive' (Banaji and Burn, 2010: 51), the one being seen to enrich the other. It could be said here, then, that creativity is synonymous with learning – the term 'creative thinking' perhaps being an oxymoron, as to think is to be creative – and that such thinking is necessary to help us make responsible, informed choices necessary for the functioning of a democratic society.

One difficulty with the little c view is that it is 'self-endorsed' (Banaji and Burn, 2010: 32), which sits uncomfortably with the notion that creativity brings something particularly special to our lives. Some critics question the very premise of little c creativity, arguing that since it is the tension between the mundane and the exceptional that is at the heart of creative encounters (Negus and Pickering, 2004), little c creativity is by definition *un*exceptional. Others equate 'little c' to 'vulgar creativity' – deliberately referencing the dual connotations of vulgar as 'ordinary' and 'crude' (Slocum, 2014: n.p.).

Further, the binary Big/little c categorisations are perhaps insufficient to describe the full range of creative activity. Kaufman and Beghetto (2009) offer a Four Cs model, whereby 'mini-c' creativity (typically exhibited by learners in school) is the preparation stage for little c, 'everyday' creativity, while 'Pro-c' (professional) creativity describes those who make their living through their creative practice (a category which might include teachers) but will never achieve Big-C eminence.

Nonetheless, the little c (and mini c) perspectives reinforce the point that creativity is fundamental both to the full development of individuals and to learning, and it is this that makes the removal of creativity from the Curriculum intriguing and concerning.

1.2.4 Community and collaboration

The positions outlined thus far largely describe creativity as generated by individuals. However, in tune with the notion that creativity is a sociocultural phenomenon, is the idea that creativity happens when humans are in dialogue with each other, communicate, work together. Countering the view that creativity is the result of work by 'autonomous agents' (Knoop, 2008: 122) – Philip Pullman, for instance, celebrates *individual* acts of creativity in his Isis lecture (2003) – is a significant body of literature (*e.g.* Sternberg, 1999; Craft *et al.*, 2008; Littleton and Mercer, 2013; Chappell 2018; Chappell *et al.*, 2019) that argues creativity develops within a community and is dependent on collaboration. Csikszentmihalyi suggests 'Most of the things that are interesting, important, and human are the result of creativity' (1990: 139), the inclusion of 'human' emphasising it is an endeavour *for* and *by* each other, while John-Steiner's *Notebooks of the Mind* (1997) highlights the extent to which sociocultural connections (whether deliberate or accidental) are necessary to inspire creativity; she goes on in *Creative Collaboration* (2006) to emphasise the importance of partnerships, friendship groups and communities. Given that schools are communities that offer opportunities for collaborative interplay, this view is particularly pertinent for educators.

Sternberg (1999) suggests that one reason for the interdependence of creativity and community is that ideas borne of creativity need an audience. He identifies three intellectual abilities as important for creative production: the 'synthetic' ability to see a problem in a fresh light, the 'analytic' ability to realise ideas that are worth following through and the 'practical-contextual' ability *to explain and defend those ideas to others* (Sternberg, 1999: 11). In other words, the combination of certain intelligences and motivations may well result in creative outputs, but these are worth little if one is unable to convince others that they are worth acting on. By extension, creativity is important for leadership (Sternberg, 2008) – society depends on the creativity of its chiefs. Leaders are not only those who have the best ideas, but are best able to talk other people into following them. It is interesting to consider this in an educational context where teachers might be seen as leaders; good teachers accordingly are creative, and this understanding empowers their work with learners (Cremin and Barnes, 2018).

It is not always top-down, however. The notion of socially responsible creativity is explored in Feldman's essay *Creativity and Wisdom: Are They Incompatible?* which argues that humans have a 'transformational imperative' (2008: 81) – a tendency to become dissatisfied with the world as we know it and seek to change it through creative efforts. This idea of people working something out together has elsewhere been termed 'interthinking' (Littleton and Mercer, 2013), the coinage highlighting the active and collaborative way that humans solve problems through dialogue 'inter' – between – one another. Biesta suggests that it is this very 'gap between the teacher and the learner' (2004: 13) through which learning happens, the 'gap' providing opportunities for participation and coordination.

Nevertheless, the literature acknowledges that humans do not always capitalise on creative interplay – it is often stymied at both personal and institutional levels. For instance, a popular dictionary defines creativity as 'The use of imagination or original ideas to create something; inventiveness', providing the example, 'firms are keen to encourage creativity' (www.oxforddictionaries.com), putting creativity solidly in an economic context, and implying that a collaborative workforce is necessary for economic success in a post-industrial society. However, it has been pointed out that the irony is twofold: on the institutional level, if employers *demand* creativity, they are potentially thereby limiting their choice of employee (not all potential applicants will see themselves as creative, so will not apply for a role for which they are qualified); equally, job security is not necessarily enhanced by developing a creative, flexible workforce – employees who can see ways of streamlining a production line will not necessarily pass on their idea to their employer and thereby render themselves redundant (Banaji and Burn, 2010). This reinforces the suggestion that the settings we inhabit constantly both encourage and *dis*courage creativity (Knoop, 2008).

1.2.5 Considering the ethics of creativity

A related contemporary economic question is to ask how far a consumer's wish for a newly minted product is at the expense of sustainability? If we continue to want what is freshly created, we are in danger both of ignoring all that has been carefully created in the past (thereby missing what might be of aesthetic and cultural value) and using up unrenewable resources (Craft *et al.*, 2008). There cannot but be 'collateral damage' (Rowson, 2008: 85) if the imperative is ever to seek the new.

Further, it is worth touching on the paradox that not all that is new is universally understood to be 'good'. Sometimes acting creatively means breaking away from received wisdom, as the sixteenth-century Italian polymath Galileo – whose world-changing ideas were rejected by many of his contemporaries – might have attested (Sharratt, 2006). Sometimes what is created causes harm: humans have created weapons as enthusiastically as they have things beautiful, benign and progressive. An invention used generally constructively – the internet – was initially funded by the US Department of Defense for military purposes (Couldry, 2012) and so has arguably *de*structive roots, and there are thousands of examples of it having been subverted by those acting harmfully or illegally: paradoxically, an artefact produced by extremists to wage terror may be of 'value' to its makers only through creating devastation.

These arguments reinforce the idea that creativity is a term laden with values (Whittemore, 1968). To reiterate, what is not clear is *whose* values and who is qualified as arbiter (Burnard, 2006; Craft, 2006; Dymoke, 2011). Thus, we should use our creativity wisely: creativity should not simply be associated with novelty but with 'trusteeship' (Craft *et al.*, 2008: 172) of each other and our world. Chappell and Craft (2011) propose the notion of Wise Humanising Creativity (WHC) through which creativity is 'generated by an inside-out/outside in dialogue' (Chappell, 2018: 6) involving individuals and communities searching for new possibilities, a theory which has subsequently been developed into New Materialism, a 'post-humanising' notion of creativity that sees places, spaces and objects as equal 'actants' (Chappell, 2018: 9) to humans in the world. The argument that humanity is 'enmeshed' (*ibid*) in a greater whole is also posed by

Osberg (2010) and Facer (2019), both of whom suggest it is our duty to use our creative talents carefully to safeguard ourselves and the planet. Accordingly, creativity is not an end in itself, but a means to a greater end: one that is about nothing less than survival of Earth. In such a context, the claim that 'creativity is a much a decision about and an attitude toward life as it is a matter of ability' (Sternberg, 2003: 98) takes on real magnitude.

Given our collective reliance on creativity, then, it is of fundamental importance to explore the extent to which these notions are acknowledged and represented in English policy documents. Key to this research is therefore to ask not only whether they engage with 'What is creativity?' but with 'Creativity for what?'

1.2.6 Towards 'creativities'

As shown, the literature presents multiple definitions of 'creativity', indicating that creativity is multi-faceted, 'a fuzzy concept' (Fryer, 2012: 21) understood in so many different forms that it effectively resists a definitive definition. It is applied to the arts and the sciences, to great achievements and to everyday life, to individuals and to community, and is essential to our continued existence. It may not be too much of an exaggeration to suggest that there are as many definitions of the term 'creativity' as there are people who use it, such that the plural coinage 'creativities' (Han and Marvin, 2002: n.p; Sternberg, 2005: n.p; McCallum, 2012: 20) is perhaps more helpful than a single abstract noun to convey the range of meanings.

In his book *Creativity and Learning in Secondary* English (2012), McCallum reiterates ideas rehearsed above: that creativities are central to the freedom and growth of both individuals and societies and, that it is '[o]ur impulse' (2012: 32) to create and, accordingly, to learn. It would therefore appear self-defeating for a Curriculum whose *raison d'etre* is to facilitate learning (DfE, 2014) to deny students that learning by removing creativity from the equation. The fact that it *has* been removed indicates that the curriculum policy field must itself hold conflicting views on creativity – as neatly summarised by Marshall: 'We appear uncertain as to its value, unable to decide whether it is a good or bad thing' (2001: 116). It is therefore to the literature on creativity in the educational policy context that we now turn, looking to see where the emphasis lies and what the tensions are.

1.3 'Creativities' in education policy

A discussion of education policy unavoidably involves discussion of politics. The literature exploring the ambiguous and often fraught connections between creativity and education policy reveals the friction between educationalists of different constituencies and politicians of differing hues. The relationship is made more complex given that neither of the two major political parties that have governed England over the 120 years covered in this book (the Conservatives and Labour) has a fixed definition of creativity. Notions vary according to the policy context, which is itself dependent on the socio-political context; and the place of creativity *in* education is directly connected to how the purpose *of* education is construed, which is also not fixed[1]. An added challenge for researchers is that criteria vary from study to study (Craft, 2001; Blamires and Peterson, 2014).

These tensions are played out in policy and practice. This section explores how some of the constructs of creativity (or 'creativities') in education as outlined above have shifted over recent decades according to political vicissitudes. Significant moments of the 1960s, 1990s and 2000s are highlighted to illustrate the different perspectives and to set the context for the following section on subject English.

1.3.1 The 1960s – creativity (re)discovered: from Pestalozzi to Plowden

Although many today associate education policy of the 1960s with the child-centred, personal growth models of creativity that provoked the culture wars ultimately leading to the current impasse, a creative approach to education is not a modern innovation. Sir Henry Wotton, author, diplomat and politician, writing in the sixteenth century, suggested that the first step of a teacher should be 'to discern the natural inclinations and capacities of children' (n.d. *in* BoE, 1937: 8). Two hundred years later, the Swiss educational reformer Pestalozzi likewise advocated a creative, nurturing, child-centred pedagogy, arguing that learning happens through the 'head, hand and heart' (https://www.jhpestalozzi.org/). These child-centred ideas were advanced in early pedagogical settings, including the progressive Home and Colonial [Teacher] Training College established by Elizabeth Mayo in 1836 (Gillard, 2018). However, they were not then widely embraced, suggesting that they attracted suspicion in some quarters even then.

Instead, the stereotype holds of children learning by rote in a manner caricatured by Dickens' Mr Gradgrind, whose 'little pitchers' were to be 'filled… full of facts' (1854: n.p.) – the 'facts' being the products of the Big C creatives of the past (and presumably it was for the 'facts' that the parents of Gradgrind's pupils paid their fees). Ironically, there were few opportunities for the little pitchers themselves to be creative. The received view (Jones, 2009; Medway *et al.*, 2014) is that this fixed, knowledge-based curriculum was favoured in English schools from the Victorian era up to and including the 1950s (although I go on to challenge this view in Part II).

Change at primary level came upon the election of Harold Wilson's Labour government in 1964 on a manifesto that included the abolition of selective education (Medway *et al.*, 2014). The change – even 'revolution' (Cooper, 1981: 125) – resulted from two key events: the gradual introduction (in most local authorities) of a new comprehensive system which ended the 11+ tests that divided the grammar school sheep from the secondary modern goats, thereby freeing primary teachers from stultifying test preparation; and the publication of *Children and their Primary Schools* – more commonly known as The Plowden Report (1967). Bridget Plowden, chair of the Central Advisory Council for Education, was influential in showing teachers an alternative and, implicitly, creative pedagogy through which the development of the whole child is promoted, not merely their intellectual capacity. The Report is variously interpreted as representing the 'first wave' (Craft, 2002 *in* Craft, 2005: 11) and the 'high water mark' (Sugrue, 2010: 107) for progressive primary education, this oceanic imagery indicating that some commentators see it as the start of refreshing change while others, less optimistically, see it as its apogee.

Plowden eschewed a knowledge-based curriculum. Building on the Hadow Report that had advocated 'a humane and general education' (1926: xx) but was practised in only few primary schools (Kogan, 1987), Plowden promoted a curriculum where teachers work in 'artistic interaction' (Kogan, 1987: 14) with their pupils. The ambitious aim was both to support individual development and promote a fairer society.

This corresponded with ideas simultaneously resurging in the secondary context that championed a child-centred, personal growth curriculum on the premise that 'literacy *depends upon* creative living' (Holbrook, 1968: 2, my emphasis).

Plowden's recommendations – the 'revolutionary' impact on subject English (1967: 210) is discussed further in Chapter 3 – were seen as ground-breaking (Sugrue, 2010) and were welcomed by a Labour government keen to make a difference after over a decade of Conservative rule in a country still recovering from the Second World War. It acted upon the Report's recommendations. Government policy therefore had a direct impact on the ushering in of a child-centred, personal growth view of creativity in the primary classroom.

The resulting recommended model, encouraging imaginative approaches ('imaginative' appears 23 times in the Report), aimed to foster experimental, open-ended approaches across the curriculum. However, difficulties sometimes arose in applying the recommended practice to formal classroom settings, perhaps because confidence, creativity and independence are best developed *outside* these constraints: schools – given the importance they place on adhering to rules – were simply not generally set up to promote creativity (Lytton, 1971; Benson, 2004; Hodgson and Wilkin, 2014). Accordingly, despite government support, primary schools were not always able to promote creativity in the ways Plowden recommends.

Furthermore, some commentators were wary of the changes. Because child-centred, creative approaches are, by definition, not prescribed or controlled by policy-makers, those in the establishment viewed them as dangerous (Whittemore, 1968). Others saw creativity as the antonym to accuracy, with creative work in English, particularly writing, assumed 'sloppy' (Summerfield, 1968: 22) or 'vague' (Whittemore, 1968: 45). Even more damningly, some critics explicitly blamed 'shoplifting, sexual misconduct, *etc...* on "creative work"' (Holbrook, 1968: 20). This scepticism, together with broader doubts as to the efficacy of the educational reforms of the 1960s (working-class children were still nine times less likely to go to university than those whose fathers were in professional occupations (Chitty, 1989; Gillard, 2018)), encouraged the Education Secretary of the newly elected 1970 Conservative government, Margaret Thatcher, and her 'preservationalist' (Knight, 1996: 62) allies to attempt to curb and discourage progressive pedagogy.

As an aside, it is worth exploring the personal growth image that Plowden popularised: she was among several educationalists of the 1960s who conceived the child as a growing plant nurtured by a gardener (a teacher). John Darling (1982) considers this horticultural metaphor in depth, suggesting that while used by philosophers such as Rousseau (1712–1778) to illustrate the care that children need to ripen to the 'fruit' of maturity, it has its limitations. Children (unlike plants) are not passive receptors but have their own agency; the criteria are inadequate (since people are more complex than plants, what does it mean to be fully grown?); the analogy breaks down because a seed cannot 'grow' into a gardener. From another perspective, however, the metaphor can be helpful, particularly in the light of two related notions. The first is that each growing plant – each child – is unique. It is not the business of education to try to make them identical, but to enable them to *grow alongside* (or understand) other plants and thereby create a more productive, beautiful garden. The second is that the soil – a child's home context and their pre-existing knowledge – is not necessarily a predictor of how the plant will grow: 'what emerges is more than the sum of its parts and therefore not predictable from the "ground" it emerges from' (Biesta and Osberg, 2008: 316). This speaks to the idea that education is not merely concerned with recycling already existing knowledge, 'planned enculturation' (*ibid*), but with growing new understandings and meanings *through the development* – the personal growth – of the individual. Perhaps for these reasons, the image proved enduring, and came to be particularly influential in English pedagogy (*e.g.* Dixon, 1967; Summerfield, 1968), as will be discussed in more depth in Part II.

1.3.2 The 1990s – flexible skills for twenty-first century employers

A second creative 'revolution' took place 30 years later, when an updated view of creativity became seen as 'centrally relevant to education as never before' (Craft, 2005: 3). Britain in the 1990s was different in many ways from the Britain of the 1960s. The concept of the family was more flexible; there were more women in the workplace; there had been dramatic increases in the use of technology. The country was transitioning swiftly from a manufacturing economy to a knowledge-based economy, so needed a workforce able to identify and solve problems. Culture (including popular culture) was actively promoted as a key UK industry and export (Hattenstone, 2008). It was therefore argued that education – which has a 'dynamic' (Craft, 2005: 6) relationship with shifting world of work – could be remodelled around creativity and so prepare children to work effectively in this evolving economy. This 'new' creativity retained personal growth as an important element, but now included notions of community and collaboration fuelled by the need to respond to the changing social, economic, technological and political context (Fryer, 1996; Burnard, 2006; Jeffrey, 2006); and such a view was recognised internationally too, for example in Canada, the US and Singapore (Craft *et al.*, 2008).

There was simultaneously a revival of interest in creativity for personal and social wellbeing as awareness grew of the co-participative, child-centred approach to early education in the Italian town of Reggio Emilia (Malaguzzi, 1996) and Jerome Bruner's work on discovery learning in America. For Bruner, a school is a culturally productive democracy, one that shares existing knowledge *and* negotiates new forms, and learning is dependent upon cultural context:

> [Y]ou cannot understand mental activity unless you take into account the cultural setting and resources, the very things that give mind its shape and scope. Learning, remembering, talking, imagining: all of them are made possible by participating in a culture.
>
> (Bruner, 1996: x)

He argues that learners should be encouraged to recognise their culture, yet also challenge it and change it where need be. To do so they need to think, talk, imagine: verbs particularly associated with creativity. In Britain, progressive educationalists such as John Elliott (1998) similarly advocated that if children learn to see themselves as 'creators of innovative experiments in living' (1998: 70) they thereby avoid losing future agency. This position, however, ran counter to the idea that high culture should be explicitly taught to working-class children who might otherwise lack 'cultural capital' and be disadvantaged in comparison to middle-class children (Whitty, 2010), and is less prominent in the contemporary literature. Furthermore, the pro-creativity movement clashed with restrictions imposed by the brand-new National Curriculum, a result of the Education Reform Act of 1988. The impact of the Curriculum in the field of secondary English in England will be explored more fully Chapter 4, but it is important to introduce it here because its advent – dubbed 'the worst of times' for creativity (Anning, 1996, n.p) – prompted specific debate about its impact on creativity in classrooms everywhere. Educationalists felt threatened and disempowered (Davison, 2009); there were warnings that teachers committed to creative practice were vulnerable to burn out (Anning, 1996). Project 1000, a survey of over 1,000 teachers across all subjects and phases undertaken soon after the Curriculum's introduction, found creativity to have been neglected as a direct result (Fryer, 1996).

Into this messy situation, in which creativity was being promoted as economically necessary on the one hand yet arguably stymied on the other, arrived the influential report *All our Futures: Creativity, Culture and Education* (NACCCE, 1999), its title making explicit the authors' view that creativity, culture and education are intrinsically connected. Like the Plowden Report, it appeared shortly after the election of a Labour government after years of Conservative rule – in this case, Tony Blair's New Labour, on his promise to prioritise 'Education, education, education' (1996, n.p.).

All Our Futures influenced policy without being a policy document *per se*. It positions creativity not only as a means of enriching learners' lives through developing their cultural understanding, but as 'essential' to 'unlock[ing] the potential of every young person' and, accordingly, 'Britain's economic prosperity' (1999: 5). Defining creativity as 'Imaginative activity fashioned so as to produce outcomes that are both original and of value' (1999: 30) – a phase which became the 'standard' (Runco and Jaeger, 2012: 92) definition although (as Runco and Jaeger point out) it relies heavily on Stein's (1953) work of 50 years previously – it argues that creative approaches are needed throughout the education system: in school management, in the design of the curriculum and in teaching methods. It recommends developing cross-curricularity to capitalise on 'overlaps' (NACCCE, 1999: 78) between subject areas, and further proposes that links are developed with outside agencies.

All Our Futures was not universally embraced, even by pro-creativity critics. Some noted that while it divides creative learning into four elements – Using Imagination, Pursuing Purposes, Being Original, Judging Value (1999: 31ff) – these are weighted differently in different subjects in the Curriculum, undermining the argument that creativity can be truly multi-disciplinary (Blamires and Peterson, 2014). The multiple examples of creative practice in STEM (Science, Technology, Engineering and Mathematics) subjects were seen by some (*e.g.* Craft, 2001) to discredit arts subjects, while others saw rather a tendency to *promote* a traditional, arts-based view of the curriculum through *All Our Future's* twin emphases on creativity and culture (Blamires and Peterson, 2014). And, while the report recommends a structured curriculum to support creativity (thereby preventing it from being dismissed as an attempt to reboot the child-centred learning of the 1960s), it does not make clear *how* it expects an understanding of culture to be promoted whilst simultaneously encouraging creative production (Banaji and Burn, 2010).

Ashley Compton (2011) underlines the difficulty of putting *All Our Future's* recommendations into practice. Taking its definition of creativity as a framework, she highlights how three documents that draw on the NACCCE research – each designed for a different stage – interpret creativity in different ways. *Birth to three matters* (Sure Start, 2003), concerned with pre-school education, prioritises making meaningful connections and developing a young child's imagination and resourcefulness, thereby associating creativity with being a competent learner. Yet *Curriculum guidance for the foundation stage*, while stating that 'creativity is fundamental to successful learning' (QCA, 2000:

116), appears to privilege the arts rather than the other areas of the curriculum, implying that creativity is mainly associated with the aesthetic. Thirdly, the primary National Curriculum (DFEE/QCA, 1999b) points to the importance of creativity as a 'universal' and 'essential' skill, yet includes creativity only rarely in subject-specific curriculum statements, thus inadvertently implying that it is *not* an integral part of the curriculum. Compton's view is that the Sure Start definition is the most useful for educators, given its emphasis on children taking responsibility for their own learning. Her work emphasises the challenge of establishing shared understandings about creativity, and she echoes calls for further research in the area (*e.g.* Sternberg, 1999; Jeffrey, 2006; Fryer, 2012).

There were, then, uncomfortable and paradoxical tensions between economic and education policies at the turn of the millennium. The government-championed revived interest in a social, collaborative notion of creativity as central to the economy butted against the embedding of a Curriculum seen to stifle creativity. These contradictions meant that there continued to be no consensus on the value or role of creativity in schools.

1.3.3 The 2000s – a chimera of creativity?

As the Labour government consolidated power, creativity continued to be actively promoted into the millennium. It led to 'creative thinking skills' being added to the National Curriculum (DfEE/QCA, 1999a: 22), a requirement that was retained and developed when the Curriculum was revised in both 2004 (DfES/QCA) and 2007 (DCSF/QCA). Numerous projects and publications made for an 'unprecedented resurgence' (Burnard, 2006: 313) in the field of creativity scholarship, including new research arguing that it is through creative dialogic teaching and learning that knowledge 'emerges' (*e.g.* Biesta, 2004; Biesta and Osberg, 2008: 313). Ken Jones' definition of creativity – 'a capacity for meaning-making' (2009: 8) – appears in his literature review for the centrally funded *Creativity, Culture and Education* series, the very existence of which indicates a combined academic and political interest in creativity and schooling. Yet, despite high-profile activity which promoted a collaborative, risk-taking, arts-based view of creativity, other forces were simultaneously suppressing it. This suppression contributed to the further squeeze on creativity enforced by the current Curriculum (DfE, 2014), as this section explains.

Some research was well received, including the curriculum models developed by the National Endowment for Science, Technology and the Arts (NESTA) and the Association of Teachers and Lecturers (ATL) (Whitty, 2010; Blamires and Peterson, 2014). Others were less so. For instance, the Qualifications and Curriculum Authority's guide for schools, *Creativity: find it, promote it* (QCA, 2005) was problematic because its definitions of creativity are muddled (Compton, 2007); while the *Opening Minds* project run by the Royal Society for the Arts, Manufactures and Commerce (RSA), whilst in tune with the economic debate, was critiqued as lacking clear definitions of competence and appropriate focus on the local context (Aynesley *et al.*, 2012).

The award-winning *Creative Partnerships* programme (which ran from 2002 until it was shelved by the Conservative/Liberal Democrat coalition government in 2011) offers another good example of the tensions at play. In an apparent 'cultural turn' (Hall and Thomson, 2013: 315) in policy, the programme sought to create opportunities for students through collaborations with outside artists, developers and scientists. Schools experiencing the limitations of the National Curriculum were enthusiastic to participate (Thomson *et al.*, 2012). It was recognised for expanding creativity in schools on a local level and, where a strong relationship between teachers and creative practitioners was forged, had a substantial impact (Pahl and Pool, 2019). However, teachers were often insufficiently involved (Wyse and Spendlove, 2007) and the programme is elsewhere criticised as lacking deep curriculum theorising (Thomson *et al.*, 2012). Its radical aspirations were therefore not fully achieved.

These projects – and, accordingly, much of the contemporaneous literature – focused on the economic benefits of creativity because of the associated political imperative. There was comparatively little attention paid to (and investment in) creativity for cultural, aesthetic and personal development (Barnard, 2006), with Mike Fleming a relatively lone voice in calling for creativity in the arts to provide the essential ethical nourishment for 'affirming and revealing humanity' (Fleming, 2010: 61) – although the importance of such 'nourishment' as a core ingredient of English education is discussed further below. Another reason for the limited impact of such projects is that insufficient research was conducted into which creative approaches work best across the curriculum (Craft, 2005). There was particular disagreement between the arts and STEM factions, and even within them: Benson (2004), for instance, argues that Design Technology is overlooked at the expense of the other STEM subjects.

A further problem was that the long-term, visionary aims of *All Our Futures* to promote creativity sat awkwardly with the political imperative to engineer immediate improvements in educational standards (Burnard, 2006; Joubert, 2010). In many cases, despite creativity being encouraged, ever-increasing pressure on schools to outscore their rivals in national tests (the results of which were published from 1991 onwards) resulted in a more limited curriculum. Primary schools reported compromising the breadth of the curriculum and creative opportunities to test preparation (NACCCE, 1999); a significant number felt it necessary to devote up to 50% of lesson time to literacy and numeracy alone (Benson, 2004). This generated issues down the line: it is difficult for students to show creativity at secondary level if they have not experienced it at primary school.

Secondary schools, increasingly steered by an accountability 'delivery chain' (Ball, Maguire and Braun, 2012: 73) of which they were perhaps unwilling links, also began to delimit their curriculum offer in an effort to maximise their GCSE and A level outcomes, at the expense of creative opportunities for students. This happened despite evidence that standardised curricula with set learning outcomes mitigate *against* helping students become flexible learners who can solve problems (Elliott, 1998; Craft, 2001). Criticism of assessment-centric practice came from a diverse range of commentators – from the National Primary Headteachers Association (Compton, 2007) to the children's author Michael Rosen (2015) to academics (*e.g.* Yandell, 2008) – all of whom argued that teaching to the test stifles creativity and prevents sustainable improvements to pedagogic practice.

Their views of these critics were, however, ignored by policy-makers; if anything, positions became more entrenched when Michael Gove, then shadow Secretary of State for Education (2007–2010) – afterwards Secretary of State (2010–2014) on the election of a Conservative-Liberal coalition government – publicly shared his enthusiasm for Michael Young's work on 'powerful knowledge' (*e.g.* 2009) and ED Hirsch's on cultural literacy (1988). Gove's drive culminated in the publication of a new knowledge-based National Curriculum (DfE, 2013/2014). Very soon, the examination boards themselves were bemoaning the 'false dichotomies between learning and assessment' (Burdett, 2015: 17), and stressing:

> A 'one hit and you're out' mentality does not reflect the way in which knowledge, skills and competence are built up over time. It is inconceivable that a crafts person would achieve competence on the first try.
>
> (Huddleston, 2015: 30)

Even the Office for Standards in Education (Ofsted), seen by many as in part responsible for the accountability culture, became concerned by evidence that schools assume examination specifications to *be* the curriculum and therefore delimit opportunities for learners (Ofsted and Spielman, 2017; Ofsted, 2022). However, with performance in the Programme for International Student Assessment (PISA) tests in Reading, Mathematics and Science increasingly governing the national curricula in many countries (Wyse *et al.*, 2014), the Department for Education's controversial decision to opt out of the new PISA creativity test (TES, 2019), and the introduction of the CCF and ECF (DfE, 2019a, 2019b) in England, the situation is unlikely to be relaxed any time soon.

On the creativity-accountability balance beam, then, schools are apparently obliged to see accountability as weightier. The disconnect between the political context, educational research and educational policy has had a marked impact on how creativity is seen and valued and, accordingly, on the presence or absence of creativity in classrooms. Although valued by educators, creativity is often seen in political discourse as subsidiary to measurable outcomes, with the *contribution* of creativity to successful outcomes generally unacknowledged. This is true of all subjects, but we now turn to focus specifically on secondary English.

1.4 Creativity and the English teacher

While the previous section focused on literature concerning policy, this section considers literature focusing on the classroom, examining in particular recent research on creativity and the English teacher, and what is known and thought about creativity in English pedagogy. Adopting the view that 'Teachers cannot develop the creative abilities of their pupils if their own creative abilities are suppressed' (NACCCE, 1999: 90), the section looks at the relationship between English education and creativity in general, but also its impact on English teachers' agency.

1.4.1 The perceived decline of creativity

It is generally recognised that many English lessons in England are currently explicitly driven by assessment preparation at both primary and secondary levels, even for classes years away from examination (*e.g.* McCallum, 2012; Hodgson and Wilkin, 2014; Yandell and Brady, 2016; Bomford, 2018). Commentators voice their dismay that, accordingly, the role of the English teacher has been eroded: rather than having the freedom to make professional decisions about lesson content and approach, what to teach and even how to teach it is often out of a teacher's hands. This encroachment on teachers' authority and agency dates from the inception of the National Curriculum (Stubbs, 1989) but grew steadily to the point that it is now 'a given' (Anderson, 2013: 113) in English circles that prescription and quantification seriously impacts what happens in the classroom. The emotive language of the title of John Yandell's article, *Thoughtless Language, or the Death of Child-Centred Education* (2003), published when the Curriculum was just over a decade old, demonstrates his fear both of the uncritical practice that is being promulgated by default and the danger in which he perceived English to be.

To be clear, critics are not arguing that assessment *per se* is conceptually flawed (although there is a parallel debate surrounding how creativity can be assessed (*e.g.* Craft, 2001; Blamires and Peterson, 2014)). Rather, they are concerned with the form of the assessment, how the results are used (or misused) for accountability purposes, and how this affects teachers and learners. Some schools, for instance, are accused of 'read-icide' (Gallagher, 2009: n.p.), the killing of reading for pleasure through over-testing; while artistry and creativity are in danger of being relegated from writing pedagogy (Cremin, 2016: 3).

Charting how both the content and style of lessons have changed since the introduction of the Curriculum, and harking back to a time when a creative, child-centred, personal growth pedagogy held sway and teachers were empowered to make their own decisions, the literature suggests that subject English is now reduced and delimited. Anderson (2013) highlights this by comparing how she used a resource called *The Island* in her own classroom in the 1980s (pupils wrote diary entries about surviving on a deserted island; drew and labelled maps; read challenging literary extracts about islands; imagined, told and wrote camp-fire stories; planned a documentary, *etc.*) and use of a similar resource in a lesson she observed 30 years later, when pupils merely identified parts of speech in an artificial piece of purple prose.

In terms of lesson style, this last example is typical of those using the four-part structure (starter, introduction, main activity, plenary) introduced through the National Literacy Strategy (DfEE, 1998) and more recently reinforced by a pedagogy informed by a particular version of cognitive science which recommends all lessons should follow a set structure, beginning with 'retrieval' of prior learning – despite evidence that such an approach is not necessarily appropriate for English (Rosenshine, 2012; EEF, 2021). Kate Bomford argues that English lessons have hence become 'over-determin[ed]… depersonalised closed systems' (2018, n.p) that deny the opportunity for the deviations where *real* learning (prompted by the unscripted questions of engaged students) often happens. There is no space for serendipity. Good practice may be turned on its head, with teachers typically requiring their classes to write *in preparation for tests*, rather than using tests to assess more substantive learning (Cremin and Myhill, 2019), while the dominance of the now near-ubiquitous PEE (point, evidence, explain) paragraph is decried and its successor, WHW (what, how, why) also challenged. Although structures to support thinking and writing can be helpful, it is ironic that the *purpose* of an English lesson might be to write a formulaic paragraph, rather than that paragraph be the vehicle to demonstrate broader understandings (Gibbons, 2019).

1.4.2 The diminishing role of the creative teacher

English teachers did not sign up to teach such lessons. They were inspired to teach because they want to contribute to society; they want to develop fine future citizens (Marshall, 2000; Goodwyn, 2016). They are well-qualified and have a passion for their subject which they want to share (Blake and Shortis, 2010). In a survey of over 1,000 teachers (alumni of one of the largest PGCE programmes in the UK), 35% agreed that 'to be creative' was a key driver to their entering the profession (Perryman and Calvert,

2020). English teachers (and Music teachers) are seen by students as those most likely to be creative (McCallum, 2012).

The literature suggests that there are two key characteristics of a creative English teacher: first, taking risks and being creative in one's own practice; second, encouraging and facilitating learners to explore meanings, question, find things out (Elliott, 1998). Although both positions could coexist in one practitioner, 'teaching creatively' is not a synonym for 'teaching for creativity' (NACCCE, 199: 102). A more useful distinction might be between 'teaching creatively' and 'creative learning' that involves a 'learner inclusive' approach (Jeffrey and Craft, 2004: 84) – particularly if one accepts that implicit in Biesta's description of the 'gap' (2004: 13) between teacher and learner through which education happens is the idea that the teacher benefits as much as the learner.

The suggestion that *teaching* creatively, in a way that ignites children's interests and so inspires them to *learn* creatively, builds on Dewey's contention (1916) that good teaching is built on interaction between a child's experience and the content being taught, and that the most effective lessons are those in which creative processes are set up carefully by the teacher (Friere, 1968; Ofsted, 2010; Anderson, 2013). Such lessons involve dialogic, active, questioning, challenging approaches, through which students are encouraged to envisage, explore and critically reflect. In the field of English, this is all bound up in themes of individuality, freedom and growth (Green and Cormack, 2008; Goodwyn, 2016).

Yet, to reiterate, the literature indicates that to teach English in the way here described is extremely difficult in the current climate. Although three decades of prescriptive curricula and oppressive testing have gradually de-professionalised teachers of *all* subjects (Biesta *et al.*, 2015), there is particular angst in the field of English when teachers and students are denied the opportunity to focus on what they believe really matters – 'the local, the particular' (Yandell and Brady, 2016: 46). If creativity and individuality lost to a punitive accountability system that sucks any remaining pleasure from the classroom experience, English teachers risk becoming unfulfilled and demotivated.

Some respond actively by capitalising on initiatives such as First Story (https://firststory.org.uk), Paper Nations (https://papernations.org/) and the National Writing Project (https://www.nationalwritingproject.uk), all of which provide platforms that encourage creativity in schools through writing, although arguably these currently have a relatively limited reach.[2] Elsewhere, there is encouragement for teachers to become 'disruptive professionals' (Thomas, 2019: n.p.) who act subversively to be the creative teachers they wish to be – and possibilities to do so within the boundaries set by the Curriculum are explored later in this book.

Other English teachers, however, are simply calling time. They leave not just because of the workload and other well-documented stresses of the role, but because 'they find themselves profoundly at odds with official prescriptions' (Goodwyn, 2016: 7), particularly the accountability agenda that 'stifles creativity' (Perryman and Calvert, 2020: 16). This haemorrhaging of English teachers is not just a problem in terms of supplying sufficient suitably qualified professionals for today's classrooms. Early career English teachers will lack experienced colleagues to turn to; awareness of how things might be done differently is being diluted or erased. Many newer English teachers, weaned in schools where accountability is all-dominant, have narrow conceptions of what counts as writing and low opinions of themselves as writers (Cremin and Oliver, 2017). Thus, as well as matters of lesson content and style being vulnerable, there are key questions about ethos, professional behaviours and sensibilities.

This leaves a situation, then, in which the problems are starkly defined. The pressures of the accountability agenda and the concomitant loss of creative practice are keenly felt, but the situation cannot easily be altered while the status quo is maintained (Dymoke, 2011; Smith, 2018a) and teachers feel mere cogs in the academic machine.

1.5 Summary: creativity as a 'journey of becoming'[3]

This chapter has shown that critics understand creativity to be a principal ingredient of a good English education, crucial in developing understanding and maintaining learner engagement; and as a foil to mechanistic exercises. Yet it is far more besides. It is funda-mental, *vital* in the life-giving sense of the word, essential to human life (Summerfield, 1968). The literature here surveyed (*e.g.* Craft, 2005, 2006; Cremin, 2009; Dymoke, 2011; Bomford, 2018) emphasises that creativity (and creativities) should be valued and promoted both for the self and for the collective – we can appreciate the Big C creativity of Milton, Matisse and Mahler, Angelou, Eminem and Rihanna at the same time as, and even as a means of, developing personal growth, 'little c' creativity in ourselves and our learners. Creativity celebrates the imagination; it encourages risk-taking, collabora-tion, agency. There can *be* no true education in English without creativity (McCallum, 2012): it is the essential 'force that through the green fuse drives the flower' (Thomas, 1934: n.p.).

More broadly, since creativity is reliant on communication, it has liberal and human-ist connotations (Craft, 2006; Chappell *et al*, 2019); it is associated with social justice and so has political agency (Craft *et al*., 2008; Amsler, 2015). Creativity offers opportunity, and so is especially significant to those who are unlikely to be offered opportunities elsewhere. Creativity runs counter to other powerful discourses that currently domi-nate education, including the importance of examination results as the measure of an individual's success – what has been termed 'the old, tired industrial model of education' (Moules *et al*., 2011: 2). Yet it is simultaneously a *victim* of this 'old, tired' model (*e.g.* McCallum, 2012; Anderson, 2013; Goodwyn, 2016; Thomas, 2019). This book is a bid to untangle and smooth these threads.

1.6 An overview of the book's structure

To contribute to and illuminate the debate about the impact of today's English cur-riculum policy in contemporary classrooms, Part II next provides a historical exegesis of English curriculum policy – the long view. It explores of the place of creativity in English policy over time: how it is defined, what is its status, how its presence or absence is justified; all of which enables consideration of the significance of the loss of the term 'creativity' from the current Curriculum. Chapter 2 explores English curriculum policy from 1905 to 1959, while Chapter 3 covers 1960–1988. Both demonstrate how English, informed by experienced subject experts, was grounded in humane, creative practice: English and creativity have always been intimately connected. Chapter 4 shows how, while this view was maintained by Cox (1989), successive National Curricula (1995–2014) – by now influenced more by the economic agenda – reshape English to the point at which creativity vanishes entirely, rendering the subject apparently foundationless.

However, all is not lost: Part III provides grounds for optimism, as subject experts with extensive professional understanding offer lived insights about how the Curriculum is interpreted *in practice* through the trope of a playscript that re-presents research interviews. Each of the three acts suggests that creativity continues to inspire and inform teachers' practice notwithstanding the policy. In Act 1, *Why English, and what does creativity have to do with it?* they discuss their thoughts on the relationship between English and creativity; in Act 2, they consider how they manage to be creative in spite of the Curriculum, and in Act 3, they make suggestions to ensure that creative English continues to flourish.

Part IV reflects on the lessons learnt. Chapter 5 considers how teachers might 'inhabit' the policy and make it their own, and recommends developing communities of practice of English teaching professionals to support them. I nonetheless call for further research into opportunities for the meaningful restoration of creativity to English curriculum policy to help rebalance the experience of all learners, and thereby equip them for the challenges of the future. Some ideas for creative practice based on the tradition of English teaching I advocate are finally offered in Chapter 6.

Notes

1 For present purposes, the term 'education' refers to compulsory schooling for children aged 4–16.
2 3,000 young people across 120 schools participated in First Story and Paper Nations combined in the 2016/17 and 2017/18 academic years (Millard *et al.*, 2019).
3 Chappell *et al.*, 2016:1.

Part II

Policy documents and official guidance: the English curriculum and creativity in context

Preface to Part II: A note on my approach: why policy documents and how are they used?

This section tells the story of creativity in English from the very start, by charting how creativity has been presented in English policy documents since the formal inception of the subject at secondary level in maintained schools. The focus on English policy documents (rather than the wider academic and professional literature) enables an understanding of officially recommended practice. Policy documents represent the national line: almost by definition, they might be assumed to have universal readership. School leaders, heads of department, all those training to become English teachers in this country should have encountered them. They could be said to be carriers of the culture of English teaching, representational images: important, widely publicised snapshots of what was advocated at any given time. Given that policy offers a framework for professional practice, this focus also provides the opportunity to appreciate the context in which English educators in England work, affording a view of how teachers themselves are valued.

An immediate challenge in determining the presence or absence of creativity in the early policy documents is that the term 'creativity' had not then been coined. The adjective 'creative' is first applied to English pedagogy in a written text in 1919 (Sharwood Smith, 1919: 29) in the proceedings of the English Association conference of 1918; this suggests that the term was already in common parlance (at least among the delegates). Forty years later, by the late 1960s, there is widespread use of the noun 'creativity' in English circles, as evidenced by publications from the Dartmouth Conference (*e.g.* Dixon, 1967; Summerfield, 1968), yet it is not until a few years later that 'creativity' first appears in a secondary English policy document (Bullock, 1975: 6). Its presence gains momentum through successive iterations of National Curriculum, so that by 2007 'creativity' is one of the so-called 'four Cs' around which the English NC orders are centred (DCSF/QCA, 2007), but it then disappears altogether (DfE, 2014). This presents a situation in which the term 'creativity' is absent from both the first (BoE, 1905/1912) and last (DfE, 2014) documents in this section, but for different reasons. It is absent from the first Blue Book because it did not yet exist, yet its prominence in the late twentieth

DOI: 10.4324/9781003243311-4

century and its status in the 2007 Curriculum suggest its absence from the 2014 version is deliberate.

Given that the earlier policy documents thus lack explicit reference to creativity, the focus is therefore on lexis associated with creativity (drawn from the literature discussed in Chapter 1) – terms such as *make, imagine, conceive, collaborate, discuss* – but I also looked beyond the surface for words, phrases and arguments that suggest the spirit of creativity, such as themes of personal growth, child-centred learning and enjoyment. For instance, the Newbolt Report (1921) describes children co-creating a play with the teacher acting as scribe, an activity recommended as preferable to 'premature essay writing' in the development of language skills and confidence because children 'like' to do drama and such an activity is 'fun'; developing and performing a play is 'in the fullest sense, practical English composition', and a class of playwrights is better equipped to study playwrights (1921: 311–312). I interpreted this as creative teaching, even though the term 'creative' is not used.

2 Rooted in creativity

The development of subject English

2.1 Introduction

The chapter opens by exploring how creative practice is present in and promoted by the work of Matthew Arnold, the Victorian poet and school inspector who had a strong influence on the development of English (Section 2.2). It goes on to present, in turn, a summary of early English curriculum policy. Section 2.3 focuses on the Board of Education's Blue Books (1905–1912); Section 2.4 examines the Newbolt Report (1921) and Section 2.5 looks at the Blue Books post-Newbolt (1924–1959). Each section explains how the respective documents view the relationship between English and creativity, which notions of creativity are in play, and the role creativity is seen to have in learning. The chapter concludes that English and creativity are positioned as interdependent, borne of a humane, child-centred view of education rooted in personal growth.

In both this and the following chapter, the discussion on each document (or group of documents) is prefaced with some brief biographical details of the respective authors, to provide context, followed by a summary of how each document positions subject English within the wider curriculum. They then go on to investigate the presence and role of creativity, considering in each case whether English and creativity are explicitly or implicitly connected, how creativity is valued and the role that creativity is seen to have on learning.

Adopting the structure of the majority of the policy documents themselves, speaking and listening, reading and writing are discussed within each section in that order. These categories reflect the three main components of school English, as laid out in the original Blue Book (1905/1912), reinforced by Newbolt (1921) and formalised by Cox as Attainment Targets in the first National Curriculum (1989; to borrow the words of one: '[s]peech, reading and writing… are interwoven in children's growth in language; but, as a matter of convenience, each of these aspects is separately treated' (DES, 1959: 135). However, this is not to suggest that the categories do not overlap, and there are of course other ways of conceptualising the subject (*e.g.* one model pairs speaking with writing as *producers* of language, while listening is paired with reading as *receivers* of language (Sampson, 1922; BoE, 1937; McCallum, 2012)).

2.1.1 Opening questions

Before you continue your reading of the chapter, pause to reflect and then look forward:

- Return to the range of definitions of creativity presented in Chapter 1, together with your own definition, then choose one or both of the following challenges:

DOI: 10.4324/9781003243311-5

- Imagine that the word 'creativity' does not exist. How might you explain 'creativity' in an English education context without using any word containing the 'creat-' root?
- Re-write your definition of creativity as an acrostic or haiku or rhyming couplet OR think of a metaphor that describes your conception of creativity in English. (When you have finished the chapter, return to your response and revise it if necessary in the light of your reading.)

- As you read on, which themes connecting subject English and creativity are most apparent? Note down *when* and *where* these key themes first emerge.

2.2 The legacy of Matthew Arnold

Before turning to the first policy documents, it is helpful to go even further back briefly to discuss the legacy of Matthew Arnold (1822–1888), the critically recognised poet and respected inspector of government schools. While Arnold's work is not a policy text *per se*, it provides crucial context for the policy texts that follow. In his belief that high-quality literature is a counterbalance to stultifying industrialisation lies the seeds of creative practice in school English. He believed in the transformative power of the imagination: for Arnold, 'the happy moments of humanity… are the flowering times' (1869: 69).

Arnold grew up in a household seeped in education and literature. His father was the Headmaster of Rugby School, with a mission to help the pupils become socially useful; his younger brother Tom became a literary professor and his youngest brother William was a novelist. The family were friends of Wordsworth (1770–1850), the Romantic poet whose verse highlighted the travails of the working class and who described the 'still, sad music of humanity' (1793). The twin influences on the young Arnold in terms of art and sensibility from a socially aware father and the future poet laureate would have been profound. (Arnold later quotes Wordsworth generously in his essay *The Study of Poetry* (1880)). Arnold won prizes for his poetry as a boy; he continued writing during his undergraduate days studying Classics at Oxford.

However, Arnold's literary output gradually decreased as his career as an elementary school inspector – taken to supplement his income on his marriage in 1851– took more of his energy. Although government grants for schools had been introduced in 1839 (Gillard, 2018), mass elementary education for the working class in both rural and newly industrialised areas was still at that time piecemeal, mostly organised by the Church of England and nonconformist churches and, where available, only offered to children up to the age of 10 or 11. The Revised Code of 1862 aimed to improve provision by awarding grants only to those schools in which children passed tests in reading, writing and arithmetic. However, in consequence of this well-meaning but clumsy 'payment-by-results' system, Arnolds's inspector's role changed from that of 'guide' to 'examiner in the 3Rs' (Dover Wilson, 1932: xiv). Having been impressed by practice in France and Germany when he travelled abroad as Foreign Assistant Commissioner in 1859 and 1865, Arnold spent much of the rest of his life lobbying for all children in England (particularly the working class) to be culturally educated.

It is in his series of essays *Culture and Anarchy* (1869), the product of a series of lectures he gave when elected Professor of Poetry at Oxford (breaking the mould in so doing by lecturing in English rather than Latin), that Arnold most clearly advocates an English education that promulgates a love of culture as the means of preventing discord (Logan, 2012). Arnold asserts himself to be a 'believer' in culture and sets out to demonstrate 'what good it can do' (1869: 4). He dismisses a traditional Classical education as a mere 'badge' (*ibid*) of culture, suggesting instead that culture is not something held by individuals but by a responsible society: culture should be 'a study of perfection' (1869: 47) inspired by the moral and social desire of doing good for all. For Arnold, culture should be 'of service' (*ibid*); it is concerned with *becoming* rather than *having*; it is about our collective striving for – and responsibility for sharing – beauty and human perfection. Thus,

> [i]t is in making endless additions to itself, in the endless expansions of its powers, in endless growth in wisdom and beauty, that the spirit of the human race finds its ideal. To reach this ideal, culture is an indispensable aid, and that is the true value of culture.
>
> (ibid)

Arnold's conception of 'culture' is the creative output of poets and writers. Learning to appreciate their creativity, Arnold suggests, enables children to access the 'wisdom and beauty' of English poetry and wider literature and so learn to *question* things; once inspired, they will be impelled to seek ever more 'wisdom and beauty' and continue after other intellectual pursuits – including challenging the status quo. The implication is that pursuing 'culture' together in this way would enable the industrial poor – victims of the factories that fed Britain's industrial dominance – to escape the 'anarchy' of lives in which they had 'lost [them]selves' (1896: 208) – and, perhaps, the wider political 'anarchy' that was sweeping through mainland Europe in the nineteenth century. He equates beauty with harmony, arguing that if culture, 'the true nurse of the pursing love' (1869: 108) were seen as important as economic success, people exposed to art and beauty would become alive to opportunities: everyone would be encouraged to nourish their best selves and realise the need to put common good above personal gain. Thus, appreciating culture is not an end in itself, but a means of 'growing and becoming' (1869: 94), as individuals *and* a society.

Arnold's view of the transformative nature of culture is idealistic and perhaps uncomfortable to modern sensibilities. At first glance, he seems to have a paternalistic view of the poor and an elitist view of culture. However, Arnold makes clear that education should not be 'Intellectual food prepared in a way that [politicians and religious influencers] think proper for the actual condition of [what they call] the masses', as that is 'indoctrination' (1869: 69/70)'; and unlike his fellow poets Coleridge (1817) and Eliot (1923), he does not see either the creation or appreciation of culture as the preserve of the few. Instead,

> culture works differently. It does not try to teach down to the level of inferior classes; it does not try to win them for this or that sect of its own, with ready-made judgements and watchwords. It seeks to do away with classes; to make the best that has been thought and known in the world current everywhere; to make all men live in an atmosphere of sweetness and light, *where they may use ideas, as it uses them itself,* freely, nourished and not bound by them.
>
> (ibid, my emphasis)

This quotation makes clear his egalitarian, humanist stance. He argues that such an education is the means of changing (to appropriate the words of one of his most famous poems) the 'darkling plain' of the present into 'a land of dreams' with 'joy... love... light... certitude... peace [and]... help for pain' (1851). In an inspector's report written over a decade after *Culture and Anarchy*, he cites Comenius to reiterate the point that learning is everyone's birth right: 'The aim [of education] is to train generally all who are born men to all which is human' (1880, n.p. *in* Newbolt, 1921: 48).

Such is Arnold's later influence that his metaphors of growth and nourishment are echoed in the literature on creative English pedagogy throughout the twentieth century and beyond (Holbrook, 1968; Summerfield, 1968; Stevens, 2011; McCallum, 2012). He is referred to explicitly by Newbolt[1] and, later, Plowden (1967: 216) and Bullock (1975: 135). However, while the Education Act of 1870 went some way to ensuring universal free schooling for every child aged 5–13, by no means all actually attended, and there was no official adoption of Arnold's recommendations on the teaching of literature and language in his lifetime. John Ruskin invited his readers to 'Commiserate [with] the hapless Board School child, shut out from dreamland and poetry, and prematurely hardened and vulgarised by the pressure of codes and formularies. He spends his years as a tale that is not told' (Lawson and Silver, 1973: 330). It was not until 1905, after Queen Victoria's long reign had come to an end and Arnold had been dead for 17 years, that the seeds he had sown properly began to germinate in policy.

2.3 Suggestions for the consideration of teachers and others concerned in the work of public elementary schools – the first Blue Books (BoE, 1905/1912; 1914)

2.3.1 Context: the establishment of subject English

By the start of the twentieth century – in no small measure due to Arnold's work – the new subject of English had become established to the extent that it was recognised by further education institutions: Oxford had opened a School of English in 1893; Cambridge was to follow suit in 1917 (Shayer, 1972; Medway *et al.*, 2014). Both offered courses that focused on English literature. A parallel developing interest in English language is reflected in *Pygmalion* (Shaw, 1913). The famous story of a young, uneducated flower seller, taught to adopt Received Pronunciation and thereby become a 'fair lady', is more than a rags-to-riches fairy tale: Shaw explores themes including education, art and humanity. The play is a critique of the attitudes and values of Edwardian society – ironically, a society which needed to be sufficiently educated to recognise the classical allusion in the title and thereby judge itself.

In schools, subject English provision varied according to the type of establishment (Medway *et al.*, 2014). Children from middle-class homes attending fee-paying grammar or independent schools were typically taught by university graduates with no formal teaching qualification who usually offered a watered-down version of their degree course (which is perhaps why Lucy Honeychurch in *A Room with a View* blames her predicament on 'the nonsense of school-girls' (Forster, 1908: n.p.). The vast majority of children – the offspring of the working class – were taught in the maintained public elementary schools.

The Education Act of 1902 improved and strengthened the 1870 Act by making schooling mandatory for all and raising the school-leaving age from 10 to 14 (Aldrich, 2005; Gillard, 2018), so creating a fully universal education system in England (although some children were still exempt from staying on past the age of 10 if their family's economic circumstances necessitated). Elementary school teachers consequently found themselves dealing with a suddenly increased and older pupil population. These teachers were usually generalists with a Teaching Certificate, rather than subject specialists. Thus, English might be taught by any member of staff with availability on their timetable; a single class might have three separate teachers for 'grammar', 'composition' and 'literature'. Unsurprisingly, English was 'in a somewhat sorry plight' (Shayer, 1972: 2).

The Board of Education (BoE), the forerunner of today's Department for Education, provided help in the form of a paperback volume entitled *Suggestions for the Consideration of Teachers and Others Concerned in the Work of Public Elementary Schools* (BoE, 1905). As the title suggests, it contains practical advice for teachers on subject content and pedagogical approach. The fact that it was printed and published by His Majesty's Stationery Office (HMSO) emphasises that it was government-sanctioned. For this reason, it appears to be the first policy document in the field and so becomes the first text explored in this book.

It must have been popular: the 1905 edition was reprinted in 1912 (with the English content identical to the first). Circular 753, *The Teaching of English in Secondary Schools* (BoE, 1910), echoed its key messages and then a second, slightly expanded *Suggestions* appeared in 1914, reprinted in 1918 and 1921. Over the next four decades, five further editions of *Suggestions* appeared (discussed below in Section 2.5), each containing a chapter on English. The final edition (1959) focuses on the primary phase only (ages 5–11), but the others cover the entire period of compulsory schooling, although I focus on secondary-specific content (age 11 and above) where possible. Bound at first in blue card and, later, blue hardback covers, the publications became known as the Blue Books. I adopt this snappier title from here on (Figure 2.1).

Coincidently or not, the year after the publication of the first Blue Book (BoE, 1905) saw the establishment of the English Association (EA) (1906) by a group of teachers and academics. Intended to serve teachers in grammar and independent schools – perhaps as a response to a perceived need for the professional and pedagogical guidance that the Blue Book provided their elementary school colleagues – it sought principally to offer practical, subject-related advice. The EA was clearly both popular and active, running regular conferences, and was relatively prolific, publishing around 50 pamphlets between 1907 and 1921 on topics pertinent to English teachers (English Association, 1907–1921).

While the EA pamphlets are not policy documents and are not explored further in this book, they provide important context. Their authors are known, while the entire Blue Book series is anonymous. However, the tone and content of the Blue Books and EA pamphlets are very similar. For example, the Blue Book recommends a child has 'liberty of expression' (1905/1912: 22) to ask questions of the teacher as well as respond to a teacher's verbal questions; while Miss Gill of the EA urges the same: 'What the children *want* to know is of much importance' (1909: 2, emphasis original). It is perfectly possible that they were written by the same individuals, or at least that they were in conversation with each other. This suggests that discussions about what represented good practice in English took place across the various settings: there was enthusiasm and energy to grow the nascent subject. On the other hand, the Blue Book writers are unlikely to be the same BoE inspectors as those who signed off 'stagnant' English departments without complaint (Medway *et al.*, 2014: 3) in the early decades of the

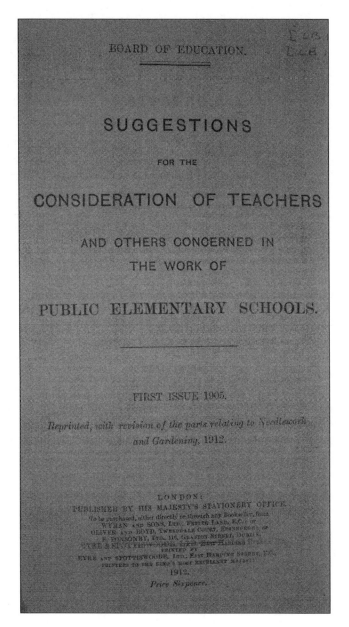

Figure 2.1 Frontispiece – Suggestions for the Consideration of Teachers and Others
Concerned in the Work of Public Elementary Schools (*photographed by author*)

century, indicating that, as now, not everyone involved in English education saw the
subject in the same way.

The following section explores what was advocated in the 1905 and 1914 editions.

2.3.2 Creativity for personal growth

The opening of the first Blue Book suggests that the intended readership was catholic: lecturers in colleges, experienced teachers, new teachers, inspectors, all working together, across all subjects, with the stated aim of furnishing guidance to the profession and 'to encourage careful reflection' (BoE, 1905: 3). It is stressed that teachers should respond thoughtfully to the challenges of the classroom. Yet the tone is tentative. A message that appears in the *Prefatory Memorandum* (and is reinforced in each subsequent edition – often in the same words) is that the book – as the title makes plain – contains *suggestions* only: teachers, as professionals, are free to practice in any way that they see fit. Teachers are recognised as creative practitioners, mindful of their responsibilities.

Throughout, a child-centred view is advocated. The general Introduction stipulates that education should be relevant to the child: 'enforced recollection of words and phrases which convey no meaning should be avoided' (BoE, 1905: 6). Instead, interest, understanding and 'formation of character' (*ibid*) are promoted; there is a need to appeal to a child's imagination through passages of 'best literature' (*ibid*), history and music; class discussion is encouraged as a way to share viewpoints; while testing – or 'put[ting] a pecuniary value on the success of a child in giving correct answers' – is a surefire way to 'to spoil teaching, to weaken or destroy the interest of the pupil, and to misdirect the whole purpose of school life' (1905: 10). Rather, a teacher's role is to promote 'active curiosity'; they 'must know the children and sympathise with them... and adjust his (*sic*) mind to theirs'; teaching should take account of the past experience of the child; each lesson must be 'a renewal and an increase of that connected store of experience which becomes knowledge' (1905: 11).

Chapter 4 of both editions is entitled *The teaching of English,* coming after generalist chapters on the curriculum (Chapter 2) and methods (Chapter 3). That it precedes all other curriculum subjects underlines the stated point that English is the most important. It begins by emphasising the centrality of language: without good English teaching to develop an understanding of language – 'the most perfect and accurate instrument mankind has for the expression of thoughts and ideas' – the child is but a 'slave... with a mind in which his passions and prejudices masquerade as thoughts' (BoE, 1905: 21). This analogy, emphasising how a child is disenfranchised without language (both to receive and convey), suggests the extent of Arnold's influence, the humane tenor of the document and the theme of personal growth.

2.3.2.1 Speaking and listening

The chapter goes on to discuss how 'practice in speaking English', whether 'incidental' or 'systematic' (BoE, 1905: 22), is the most important aspect of English: it is the foundation of an entire education; therefore, every lesson should include opportunity 'for developing the power of *connected* and *continuous* speech (BoE, 1914: 29; emphasis original). Good teaching of oracy provides 'not only [...] accurate *expression* for thought, but also [enrichment of] the child's vocabulary by giving him larger powers of expression and therewith a wider range of available thought' (1905: 21, emphasis original). Children should be granted the 'liberty of free expression,' as to fetter individual response is 'disastrous' (*ibid*), and it is emphasised that oracy should continue to be promoted among older learners (1914). Use of dialect is 'not… necessarily bad' (1905: 23) – there is explicit advice that, while children should be encouraged to pronounce words clearly (aided through the use of tongue-twisters and singing lessons), local variation in both pronunciation and terminology is natural and appropriate.

The use of rhymes, games and stories is also recommended to develop confidence in oracy, as well as the learning of some poetry by heart, according to the child's preference, so that (in words strikingly similar to Arnold's) their 'memory is enriched with a store of beautiful thoughts expressed in beautiful language' (BoE, 1905: 24) which will both enhance their expression and be a source of pleasure.

2.3.2.2 Reading

It is argued that confidence in oracy leads to confidence in reading. Teachers should encourage reading for pleasure, instilling a love of literature in a new generation and broadening children's perspectives. The first edition provides no list of recommended authors; rather, encouragement that reading material should be drawn from 'the national literature', a 'rich source' of sustenance that will lead to a life of 'wide sympathies, of noble ideals and of courageous endeavour' (BoE, 1905: 21), with the teacher trusted to select appropriate texts. The Circular (1910) later makes explicit that literature lessons should focus on the text itself (rather than literary history and the lives of the authors which had been the focus of 'literature' lessons in the past; something that has seen a recent resurgence in schools since the introduction of the GCSE Assessment Objective to show awareness of 'context'). The second edition (BoE, 1914) recommends novels that could spark the imagination of older learners, such as *The Water Babies* (Kingsley, 1863), *Robinson Crusoe* (Defoe, 1791) and *Tom Brown's School Days* (Hughes, 1857). While far from contemporary, the implication is that such texts are enjoyable, nourishing and life-enhancing. There is an explicit warning that creating 'distaste' (BoE, 1905: 21) in a child for literature will deny them opportunity; implicit is the suggestion that a child who does not read will lack sympathy, nobility and courage – perhaps, so soon after the end of the bruising second Boer War (1899–1902), these heroic ideals were particularly valued.

There is criticism of a previous (undated) Code which had recommended the reading of only two or three books a year – instead, as 'unlimited supply' (BoE, 1905: 28) as possible is recommended for personal consumption; silent reading for pleasure is explicitly encouraged in the next edition (1914). The importance of furnishing schools with book corners and ample libraries enabling children to choose their own reading matter from a range of good-quality literary material (fiction and non-fiction) is stressed, and the new National Home Reading Union, which involved parents in encouraging reading, is promoted (1905).

2.3.2.3 Writing

Both editions conclude the chapter on English with further emphasis on the importance of oracy, in stating that writing should be introduced only when oral expression is well-established: 'Good written English is only more careful spoken English' (BoE, 1905: 26). This point is backed up in the Circular, which states that 'oral composition' is the precursor to written composition (BoE, 1910). Initial lessons see the teacher writing on the blackboard 'at the children's dictation' (1905: 26), so it is their *own* words that are used as models for sentence construction. The first edition advocates that exercises in composition should develop in parallel with the individual child's abilities and interests, implying a link between creative practice and independent critical thought, although it does also recommend the reproduction of the stories of others. The next, more expansively, recommends that children are encouraged to experiment when writing, 'to compose independently and freely' (1914: 37) and 'develop[ ] the imaginative powers' (1914: 38). This 1914 edition is the first to refer to a claim attributed to Robert Louis Stevenson that his habit of writing descriptions of everyday life was the best preparation for his narrative writing, and offers topics to inspire writing, such as describing the same landscape in winter and summer, or retelling a story or historical incident from an onlooker's perspective.

The only real point of difference is that while the first edition presents Latinate grammar lessons as 'valueless' as they 'tend to obscure rather than reveal thought' (1905: 30), the Circular (1910) recommends the middle ground, suggesting that grammar is important but should not be 'abstract' or 'isolated from Composition and Literature' (1910: 4), a view echoed in the second edition (1914). Children were also to learn to correct their own work.

These early policy documents, then, establish a child-centred approach to learning to foster personal growth, stimulated by generous exposure to literature. Children are seen as individuals, encouraged to express their own views in their own voice and follow their own interests. A teacher's role is to be responsive to their needs and provide guidance.

2.4 *The Teaching of English in England*: **The Newbolt Report (1921)**

2.4.1 *Context: post-war reconstruction*

The next Education Act was passed in 1918, towards the end of the First World War (1914–1918). Britain was by then financially broken, with debts of 136% of its Gross National Product (www.nationalarchives.gov.uk), although it was the human cost of the conflict – 2 million British soldiers were killed and 1.5 million wounded (Herbert, 2018) – that weighed more heavily on the public consciousness. Unemployment was high and public spending was slashed, but a more democratic society was beginning to emerge: women over 30 were given the vote, the strict class hierarchy was dissolving (the power of the upper class declined markedly), and the working class began to be employed in white collar jobs (www.nationalarchives.gov.uk).

Designed to set the country back on track, the main proposal of the 1918 Act was that all children should remain in school until the age of 14 without exemption. It encouraged full-time education up to 16 (although it was not until 50 years later, in 1971, that universal education to age 16 was enforced) and recommended part-time education until 18.

It is perhaps significant for the story of subject English that in July 2018, just a month before the Act came into law, the English Association held a major conference at the University of Reading. It is here that is found the first reference to the term 'creative' being used in a recognisably modern sense in the field of English pedagogy when Sharwood Smith argues that an essential element to enable the growth of 'the true self of the child' is 'The encouragement of a creative spirit. Children could and should write for themselves.' (1919: 29–30). This suggests that he saw creative work as more than merely a means to develop a child's appreciation of literature: it contributes towards personal growth ('the true self') and, hence, human understanding. This chimes with an apparent theme of the conference, where English was positioned as 'a subject including the whole of English culture – in a word... Humanism' (Dover Wilson, 1919: 30).

It is very likely that Sir Henry John Newbolt (1862–1938), an active member of the EA (and, later, its president) was present at this conference. Newbolt was middle class, the son of a country vicar; he had been a day boy at the newly established, progressive Clifton College in Bristol, before gaining a scholarship to read Classics at Oxford. He was a lawyer, novelist and historian, but is most remembered today – like Arnold before him – as a poet. It was perhaps the fame of Newbolt's patriotic poems *Vitai Lampada* (1892) and *Drake's Drum* (1910), together with his role in the War Propaganda Bureau, that reassured the president of the Board of Education – who in May 1919 commissioned *The Teaching of English in England* (1921), the inaugural government-commissioned report on English – that Newbolt was the man for the job.

Newbolt's position in the EA makes it unsurprising that his committee of six women and eight men included EA members or those otherwise involved in debates about

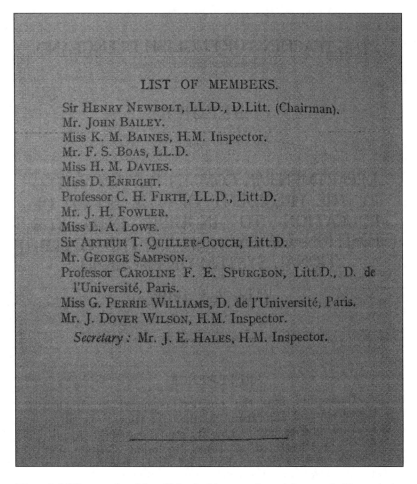

LIST OF MEMBERS.

Sir HENRY NEWBOLT, LL.D., D.Litt. (Chairman).
Mr. JOHN BAILEY.
Miss K. M. BAINES, H.M. Inspector.
Mr. F. S. BOAS, LL.D.
Miss H. M. DAVIES.
Miss D. ENRIGHT.
Professor C. H. FIRTH, LL.D., Litt.D.
Mr. J. H. FOWLER.
Miss L. A. LOWE.
Sir ARTHUR T. QUILLER-COUCH, Litt.D.
Mr. GEORGE SAMPSON.
Professor CAROLINE F. E. SPURGEON, Litt.D., D. de l'Université, Paris.
Miss G. PERRIE WILLIAMS, D. de l'Université, Paris.
Mr. J. DOVER WILSON, H.M. Inspector.

Secretary : Mr. J. E. HALES, H.M. Inspector.

Figure 2.2 The membership of Newbolt's committee (*photographed by author*)

English, both academic and pedagogic (Figure 2.2). I have written in depth about the committee membership elsewhere (Smith, 2021), but it is worth emphasising their expertise here. Among their number were Frederick Boas, a founder member of the EA and author of an EA pamphlet on Wordsworth (1914); John Fowler, author of EA pamphlets such as *The Teaching of English Composition* (1910) and *School Libraries* (1915); and the Shakespeare expert John Dover Wilson, author of EA pamphlet *Poetry and the Child* (1916). We know that Dover Wilson was also interested in Arnold's work – he went on to edit the 1932 reprint of *Culture and Anarchy*. He and another committee member, Miss KM Baines, both Board of Education school inspectors, would have known of the Blue Books, and possibly contributed to them. Included too were Newbolt's former schoolmate from Clifton College, Sir Arthur Quiller Couch, novelist, critic and editor of the popular *The Oxford Book of English Verse 1250–1900* (1912); and George Sampson, already widely published (*e.g. Cambridge Readings in Literature* (1918)), who went on to write further works in the Cambridge Literary series (1924, 1926, 1941) as well as *English for the English* (1922), the first full-length book on English teaching. In other words, Newbolt gathered around him the expert and erudite, men and women who were familiar with the work of elementary *and* grammar and independent schools; and who were presumably respected both by English teaching professionals of the day and, through their works, the wider public. The committee consulted widely, calling over 100 witnesses, including representatives of 13 bodies. Their Report draws explicitly on both EA and BoE publications, synthesising views on English teaching; it ultimately influenced English teaching for decades to come.

2.4.2 Creativity: the cornerstone

It could be argued that the humanist mood of the 1918 English Association conference set the tone *for The Teaching of English in England* (1921). The EA Chairman had told the conference:

> The moral of the war was, not that [the State] should develop trade, but that they should develop humanity. A chief burden in maintaining and keeping uppermost the spiritual element in man must rest... more upon the teaching of English and English literature than upon any other subject.
>
> (Childs, 1919: 3)

English teaching was none other than the vehicle through which peace might be preserved. Newbolt echoes this tentative optimism. In the Introduction to *The Teaching of English in England*, he states that the most important result of education is not knowledge, but 'experiences of human beings which are gained by contact with human beings' (1921: 8). In other words, he believed that the way to prevent further calamitous warfare is through the enriched human understanding that results from studying English.

Newbolt's remit was to consider 'the requirements of a liberal education, the needs of business, the professions, and public services, and the relation of English to other studies' (Newbolt, 1921: 4) in response to English education having been deemed 'unsatisfactory' (*ibid*). Even before the War, concern about English teaching had been expressed: a BoE report claimed boys have 'little skill or facility' (n.d. *in* Fowler, 1910: 1) to express themselves either orally or in writing, and a letter to *The Times* complained 'The English boy cannot write English' (*ibid*), suggesting that the reach and influence of the

Blue Books (and EA pamphlets) had not been what their authors had hoped. Newbolt himself reports that some children were leaving school functionally illiterate.

Yet Newbolt is emphatic that the poor state of English is not the teachers' fault. Rather, he suggests, it stemmed from the 'failure' of the whole education system 'due to a misunderstanding of the educational values to be found in the different regions of mental activity, and especially to an underestimate of the importance of the English language and literature' (1921: 4). As a new subject, Newbolt acknowledges that English had no 'definiteness of aim' (1921: 105), people were sceptic of its value and there was suspicion and distrust of adventurous (creative) methods. To persuade the public of the importance of English, Newbolt uses an architectural metaphor reminiscent of the Bible that would have undoubtedly resonated with the original audience English is described as the keystone rejected by the builders because 'the arch is too faulty to admit it' (1921: 5). (Christ is repeatedly referred to as the 'corner stone' in the New Testament, *e.g.* 1 Peter 2: 4–8; Acts 4: 10–12). The committee saw its task was to rebuild the arch of the educational system with the keystone of English in its central place and, as a result (and maximising the impact of the image) 'bridge social chasms which divide us' (1921:6), bringing 'national unity' (1921:14). This closely mirrors Arnold's philosophy – the Report even quotes Arnold directly, 'Culture unites classes' (1869 *in* Newbolt, 1921: 6), to underline their liberal, humanist viewpoint.

Accordingly, Newbolt oversteps his brief to discuss education in general as well as the place of English within it. He defines education as the development of the human spirit: 'The first thought of education must be fulness of life, not professional success' (1921:61). Yet, for Newbolt, it was not simply the case that every teacher is a teacher of English (as the Circular had argued (BoE, 1910)); in his Report, the terms 'English' and 'education' are tantamount to being synonymous. The point is oft re-stated: English is 'the true starting point and foundation from which all the rest must spring' (1921: 14); it is both 'the very stuff and process' and 'the principal method' (1921: 56).

The Report's definition of English is noteworthy. English is an 'art, a means of *creative expression*, a record of human experience' (1921:11, my emphasis) – with an explicit statement that it does not include grammar and philology (the study of the development of language and texts) as these are 'scientific studies' (*ibid*). The word 'creative' is emphasised through its reappearance on the following page: English in the 'highest' sense is

> ...the channel for formative culture of all English people, and the medium of creative art by which all English writers of distinction, whether poets, historians, philosophers or men of science, have secured for us the power of realising some part of their own experience of life.
>
> (1921: 12)

Here, the association of 'culture' and 'creative' is again reminiscent of Arnold: Big C culture is seen as potentially enriching for 'us', everyman; but the importance of children being writers too (as proto 'mini c' creatives) is also stressed.

The Report's main recommendations are that children should be 'train[ed]' in 'sounded speech'; standard English (both spoken and written); reading; and the 'use of literature' (1921:19). Yet while the tone might appear authoritarian, the noun 'use' rather prosaic, and the verb 'to train' perhaps severe, this may have been a deliberate attempt to assuage the traditionalists and reassure them that a creative curriculum will be suitably formal. Similarly, the Report praises the 'army' (1921: 25) of teachers:

perhaps, in the post-war context, the military semantic field is deliberately redolent of self-sacrifice and heroism. The recommendations are in fact underpinned by a liberal, life-enhancing stance.

2.4.2.1 Speaking and listening

This is emphasised when the Report reinforces a point made in the Blue Book (BoE, 1905/1912) that talk is the *foundation* of English, not least because good oral skills are the prerequisite of good writers. Drama, too, is 'very important' (Newbolt, 1921: 310): children should dramatise familiar ballads, stories or fairy tales, or famous historical incidents; schools in districts where a genuine dialect survives should make use of any traditional fragments of old folk plays. Children are encouraged to consider and take pride in the language of their community.

The emphasis on dialect is significant. Newbolt argues that teachers should encourage children's 'self expression' (*sic*) through a constant use of classroom talk to develop 'connected and continuous speech' (1921: 70). While some might argue that encouraging dialect is a covert means of restricting social mobility by keeping the working class in their place, this would appear contrary to Newbolt's ideal that children should become 'bi-lingual' (*sic*) by learning 'standard English' (*sic*) too (1921: 67). This is not to gain 'social superiority' (*ibid*), but because English had been voted the international language by the Northern Peace Union after the First World War and it was important that English children could speak a standard version to communicate with their European neighbours. This suggests an ambition that international travel (whether for commerce or tourism), or at least dialogue with international visitors, was something for which all children should be prepared, and demonstrates Newbolt's vision of a then undreamt-of future for working-class children.

2.4.2.2 Reading

Concerning reading, Newbolt argues that children should learn not merely the skill of reading (including reading aloud), but find in literature 'a possession and a source of delight… an equipment for the understanding of life' (1921: 19). He strongly recommends modern literature as well as the classics:

> [W]e think that the students are far more likely to perceive in literature not merely a school subject but the most direct communication of experience by man to men if they are encouraged to find out how the life of their own time has been interpreted by contemporary writers.
>
> (1921: 186)

This indicates that Newbolt recognises culture as something living, constantly remade and directly related to his humanist perspective. Furthermore, the Report criticises practice whereby literature is taught through 'linguistic, historic and comparative methods' (Newbolt, 1921: 118) as such methods, it argues, fail for want of emotion. Instead, it advises teaching literature alongside the visual arts, music and architecture, to enable focus on beauty and expression; once again, Arnold's presence is felt through this endorsement of culture as a means of both providing pleasure and stimulating thought.

2.4.2.3 Writing

Writing too is presented as a tool for thinking. Creative approaches are encouraged as a means of exploring the art of others – by writing a poem, a child can both better appreciate the writing of published poets and develop thought. Children should take stimuli from literature, their wider reading, their environment and their own experience, to create something of value for themselves. Exercises in 'descriptive and imaginative writing, as well as practice in verse composition, in letter writing, and in dialogue... with a view to encouraging self-expression' (Newbolt, 1921: 103) are recommended, although the Report is critical of some practice where 'imaginative subjects' are insufficiently challenging. 'Full use' should be made of any teacher who has a 'special aptitude' for teaching poetry or written composition (1921: 348).

In summary, the Report presents English as a fundamental tool for the 'full development of mind and character of English children' (Newbolt, 1921: 20) and simultaneously a fine art which should be taught as such. There is explicit reference to creative English in the Arnoldian sense of imbibing or *taking* culture to inform and inspire. However, the Report also goes beyond Arnold, promoting personal growth through emphasising the importance of discussion and through encouraging imaginative topics for writing, thus developing learners' creativity through *making*. Newbolt yokes these elements together in the Conclusion: 'a humanised industrial education is the chief means whereby the breach between culture and the common life of man may be healed' (1921: 352). He is perhaps attempting to reassure capitalist politicians that the Report's view of English is suitably 'industrial' (even though it contains relatively little emphasis on functional English) whilst being humane. The explicit reference to 'culture and common life' mirrors the title of *Culture and Anarchy*; that Newbolt recognises a breach between them acknowledges that Arnold's ideal is yet unrealised but still possible. The final phrase is pleasingly ambiguous – the 'healing' of an English education can be applied to the individual and the collective.

2.5 *The Blue Books* (BoE, 1923, 1924, 1927, 1937; DES, 1959)

2.5.1 Context: continuity across the mid-century decades

The interwar years saw universal suffrage, a further blurring of class boundaries as the working classes increasingly took on non-manual roles, the rise of the Labour Party and trade unions, and the expansion of the welfare state. The standard of living improved for the working class through the council house programme. However, the economy remained relatively stagnant, and the Great Depression of the 1930s led to high unemployment in many sectors. School milk to support children suffering from poor nutrition was introduced in 1934, while cultural nourishment was made possible through the burgeoning film industry, the vast expansion of public libraries (stock was tripled during the 1930s) and the launch of the Penguin paperback in 1935 (Morgan, 1984; Gillard, 2018).

At the end of the Second World War (1939–1945) – as after the First – there was seen a need to revitalise the education system in a bid to rebuild the nation, resulting in the Education Act of 1944, designed by the Conservative Rab Butler with cross-party consensus. The Act gave greater responsibility to local authorities, changed the elementary system to the tripartite system (primary, secondary, further education) and strengthened provision to increase the school leaving age to 16. However, it did not deal with the curriculum itself for party political reasons (Tomlinson, 1949 *in* Medway *et al.*, 2014), so policy concerning subject English remained unchanged.

The following year, in 1945, Clement Attlee's newly elected Labour government launched a radical agenda to rebuild a near-bankrupt country, investing vast sums on welfare, including the introduction of National Insurance and the National Health Service. The Festival of Britain of 1951, celebrating British industry, arts and science, attracted 8 million visitors, symbolising a new optimism (Morgan, 1984). However, this coincided with the beginnings of the Cold War, one of the factors that led to Winston Churchill's Conservatives being re-elected in 1951. The party remained in power for 13 years, pursuing policies that favoured business. There was increased prosperity and decreased unemployment, albeit at the expense of the welfare state (ibid). The government, however, showed little interest in education (Gillard, 2018). Throughout this period, therefore, the Newbolt Report and the Blue Books that followed it – and are the focus of this section – continued to represent recommended practice.

2.5.2 Continuing to cultivate

The Newbolt Report had galvanised educationalists and practitioners: according to the bibliography in *The Teaching of English in Schools 1900–70* (Shayer, 1972) there were 18 books on English method published over the next ten years (the highest number in any decade until the 1960s). Three new Blue Books appeared in quick succession. The 1923 version was written explicitly in response to Newbolt, whilst noting Newbolt's dependence on its predecessors: 'this Report emphasises anew many of the points to which the *Suggestions* direct attention…' (1923: 23). The next – an edition devoted entirely to English – comments on teachers' 'enthusiasm' for Newbolt (1924: 4), with further homage paid in the following edition (1927). And they grew in weight as well as number: while the 1905 edition is a pamphlet of approximately 130 pages, the 1937 version is a thick book of almost 600 pages set in a dense font. A Prefatory Note states that they should be 'part of the necessary equipment of every teacher' (BoE, 1927: 3), which makes clear the breadth of the intended readership.

The Blue Books series post-Newbolt (BoE, 1923, 1924, 1927, 1937; DES, 1959) are discussed here as a unity because of the overlaps between them. While some points are revised and extended from edition to edition, and examples of good practice increasingly provided, the key themes remain constant. Each edition echoes its predecessor, often word for word. English is both an art and a 'living language' (BoE, 1924: 4). A key point reiterated from the original 1905 edition is that the purpose of the Books is not to dictate 'any rigid or unthinking uniformity of method' (BoE, 1924: 3), but to offer ideas and stimulus. It is when the teacher approaches their role creatively and is responsive to learners' needs that learning happens.

2.5.2.1 Speaking and listening

Following their predecessors (BoE, 1905, 1914) and Newbolt (1921), the Blue Books state that developing a child's capacity for talk as crucial: it is made explicit that linguistic development is otherwise impossible. New experiences in a child's life are seen as vocabulary-enriching opportunities, speech being 'an effective instrument of understanding and thought, and hence, of communication' (DES, 1959: 135).

Extending Newbolt's acceptance of dialect for cultural and historic reasons, they emphasise the importance of the child's home language. The term 'bilingual' is used (BoE, 1927: 74; 1937: 378), echoing Newbolt, suggesting that dialect and Standard English are equal but separate. The advice is not to attempt to 'nullify' (BoE, 1923: 24) a child's home language but help them 'purify' (*ibid*) it for occasions when Standard English is required. Teachers are twice warned that they should guard against 'slovenliness' (BoE, 1927: 74; 1937: 377) – perhaps to assuage traditionalists for whom the use of Standard English is non-negotiable – yet the liberal and child-centred underlying message is clear: children should be able to use their own dialect 'freely and boldly' (BoE, 1937: 378) and teachers should 'seek to encourage [children's] power of vigorous and racy expression [since]... even slang has its place' and thus a child 'will have frequent occasion to remind himself that language is the creation of the many and not of the few' (BoE, 1937: 391). The final edition is sensitive that 'children associate their way of speaking with those they care about in their homes and neighbourhoods', arguing that 'it would be unproper and unwise for teachers to try to discredit [dialect] use' (DES, 1959: 146).

Further, good oral work results in good writing: a teacher's responsibility is to ensure their students have something worth saying, as one cannot 'make bricks without clay' (BoE, 1924: 23). Thus, 'every oral lesson is a lesson in composition' (1924: 25).

2.5.2.2 Reading

Again echoing previous editions, reading is seen as developing both children's intellectual and emotional understanding (BoE, 1927, 1935). The importance of good libraries is repeatedly stressed. The final edition cites Dr Johnson's remark that 'Babies do not want to hear about babies; they like to be told of giants and castles and of somewhat which can stretch and stimulate their little minds' (n.d *in* DES, 1959: 168). There is the warning that trying to teach Shakespeare to children at the elementary stage is folly: teachers should be allowed to judge when (and even if) to do so (BoE, 1923, 1927). Across the series, the reading of poetry is recommended, chosen according to children's interests. The approach should be not through formal analysis, but artistic and creative methods, enabling children to discover meanings themselves.

2.5.2.3 Writing

To 'feed' (DES, 1959: 164) children books to stimulate their writing is promoted, and writing should also emanate from their experiences – 'the sights and sounds, the thoughts and feelings of everyday life' (BoE, 1923: 39). A child-centred view is evident: teachers should strive to ensure that the child's pleasure at '"self-expression" in language' (BoE, 1924: 26) is not compromised. Later editions contain lists of possible classroom activities, including the active modelling of writing by the teacher (BoE, 1924; 1927).

Encouraging children to write poetry is also encouraged:

> Good teaching of poetry cannot fail to stimulate the creative impulse, and in literature, as in the other arts, creative work, even though of no particular merit in itself, is of great help in developing the power of critical appreciation.
>
> (BoE, 1927: 92)

Here, the children's compositions are seen to be of little worth, but such activities are promoted because engaging in them will help develop a 'sensitiveness to the poetic values' (BoE, 1927: 92). However, a later edition presents a different perspective. It describes the '*art* of expression' (BoE, 1937: 352, my emphasis) in children's writing – implying inherent merit – and so recalls Newbolt's point that imaginative writing *is* of value, albeit if only to the child themself.

Despite the above allusion, the term 'creative writing' is not used once across the series, yet it is stated that children should be allowed to write 'independently and freely' (BoE, 1923: 31), with the topic 'factual or… imaginative according to a child's own gifts and interests' (DES, 1959: 162). Such writing enables children to 'put themselves in other people's places, to realise that there are more sides than one to every question, and by so doing he can help to lay the foundations of sympathy, toleration, justice, and other essentially social forces' (BoE, 1923: 40); the teacher's role is as discussant and audience (DES, 1959). This, again, is a child-centred view, in which the teacher promotes creative work to develop the child's social and empathetic skills; it is also humane, in striving for the common good, redolent of Arnold.

The value of children's writing is emphasised through discussion of assessment. Compositions should be marked carefully by a teacher who has an 'enlightened idea' (1927: 102) of the improvements needed. A child should not feel too anxious about technical accuracy or presentation as that 'clogs… thought' (BoE, 1923: 31). Instead,

> The chief criterion by which the pupils' compositions will be judged will be their truthfulness in the widest sense – the truthfulness with which they record their experiences and impressions; the accuracy with which they describe things or scenes; and the honesty that they show in stating, when called upon to do so, what they really think or feel, and not what they imagine they are called upon to think or feel.
>
> (BoE, 1937: 396)

The writing should be genuine, a means of expressing what is important to the writer; the ideas and content are more important than a polished product. This is an example of creative practice that recognises personal growth.

There are strong themes connecting the Blue Books. They are child-centred; they foreground the importance of oracy and accepting dialect; they promote the exploration of language; they hold that the purpose of learning to read is to love and learn from literature; grammar is presented as subservient to the writing, grammar teaching arising naturally from writing being undertaken. They promote a broadminded, forward-looking approach – they welcome the use of new technologies such as the wireless and, later, television. The centrality of the teacher is crucial. The Conclusion to the English chapter of the 1937 edition is worth quoting in full:

> It is evident that the task of the English teacher is no light one. It requires an interest in children, an interest in words, and in interest in the larger world. Specialised knowledge is of less importance than such interests as these, for they can easily flower into the relevant kind of knowledge, whereas knowledge without these interests can only succeed in imprisoning the child's vital and curious mind within a mesh of facts. With such interests and aims the English teacher in the Senior School should succeed in the essentials of his (sic) task: the training of a young

citizen who can speak clearly and sensibly, who can write with order and expressiveness, who can find what he (sic) wants in books, who is alive to the fullness of words, and who confronts his environment with enjoyment, with self-reliance, and with an openness to new ideas and new experiences.

(BoE, 1937: 400)

The imagery is striking. Such a teacher celebrates the freedoms that creativity provides, rejecting external structures of a fixed, uncreative curriculum that might 'imprison' a child's mind: the implication is that the teacher can create learning experiences that they judge appropriate. References to vigorous life ('flower', 'vital', 'alive') reinforce the message that such an approach allows for personal growth; hence, the child is free to develop, alert to the fulness of life.

2.6 Conclusion and summary

So far, then, the policy documents collectively reveal that creativity was valued and promoted in English from its inception as a school subject. Creative English, inspired by Arnold, was established through the Blue Book series and embraced and developed by Newbolt (1921) – decades before the so-called revolutionary creative movements of the 1950s and ahead of what is claimed to be the 'first wave' (Craft, 2005: 11) of creativity in the 1960s.

An important theme is the interdependence of creativity and culture. While 'culture' is a concept perhaps as contested and slippery as 'creativity' (Green and Cormack, 2008), various notions of culture happily coexist in the policy documents. 'Big C' or high culture is recognised as a core element. The canon of English Literature is revered in the Arnoldian sense – rather than reserving the 'best' that has been thought and said for an elite minority (as TS Eliot might have it), literature is a treasure to be shared, democratically, for the nourishment, pleasure and delight of all (BoE, 1905/1912; Newbolt, 1921). Equally, these same policy documents also stress the importance and value of lived, everyday culture. The policy documents recognise that culture is iterative, constantly being made – thus, dialect is promoted as having socio-cultural importance (*e.g.* Newbolt, 1921; BoE, 1957); *contemporary* literature is encouraged alongside the canon.

The semantic field of culture is helpful in considering another theme featured in the literature, that of personal growth. To reiterate, culture is associated with growth; personal growth is about enculturing – or creating – oneself (Darling, 1982); that individual is then able to contribute to society. Once again, English policy documents appear ahead of their time – as shown in Chapter 1, personal growth does not feature in the broader literature until the 1960s (Jack, 1962 *in* Darling, 1982; Lytton, 1971).

In summary:

- Even before the term 'creativity' was coined, the relationship between creativity and subject English is presented with remarkable consistency in the policy documents over the five decades surveyed in this chapter.
- The policy documents suggest that creativity is nurtured by being exposed to high culture and practised through everyday culture.
- Creativity is predominantly concerned with personal growth and the associated forging of human connections.

Note

1 Newbolt cites Arnold 18 times, often quoting him directly and approvingly. Other Victorians we now might associate with creative thinking are also cited (Ruskin, six times; Carlyle, five times; Morris, twice), but these references are simply to provide examples of 'good' writing than explore their ideas.

3   The flowering of creative English

3.1 Introduction

This chapter picks up where the last one left off, focusing on English policy from the 1960s to the advent of the National Curriculum. Section 3.2 covers the gap between the final Blue Book and Bullock Report (1975), taking in the Dartmouth Conference of 1966 and the Plowden Report (1967). Section 3.3 explores the Bullock Report, while 3.4 moves on to the Kingman Report (1988). Each sub-section is prefaced with brief historical context.

The creative themes of the policy documents explored in Chapter 2 are, broadly, developed further in this phase. Bullock, building on the work of those official publications, presents English as a creative subject concerned with nurturing children's interest in language, developing their enjoyment and confidence in expressing themselves through the spoken and written word, and encouraging a love of literature (both canonical and contemporary); and implies that such a view of English depends upon what we now term 'creativity', even before the term was coined. However, the Kingman Report, with a more limited conceptualisation of both English and creativity, is a harbinger of what is to come in the National Curriculum.

3.1.1 Opening questions

As you read this chapter, consider whether the themes discussed in the previous chapter remain significant in this:

- Is the close connection that was established between creativity and English retained in the period covered by this chapter?
- If so, is creativity still presented as being associated with personal growth and the development of human relationships, or do other notions of creativity come into play?
- How is creativity seen to be best nurtured and developed?

3.2 From the Blue Books to the Bullock Report: creativity comes in from the cold

3.2.1 The educational and political context

To recap (given that the final Blue Book (DES, 1959) focused on primary practice), there had been no official guidance relating to secondary English since the Blue Book of 1937, and no policy update since Newbolt (1921). Yet it is interesting that the humane,

DOI: 10.4324/9781003243311-6

creative, child-centred practice that these documents advocated was apparently not commonly enacted. An His Majesty's Inspectorate (HMI) report from 1951 found 'English in both grammar and modern schools to be competent but dull' (Medway *et al.*, 2014: 38). Practice was seen as 'largely stagnant' (*ibid*: 3), with formulaic text-books, uncontextualised grammar exercises and stale literary appreciation dominating; a personal growth approach was then a rarity (Dixon, 1967). One student of the 1950s remembers getting the slipper if he got more than three spellings wrong (BBC, 2007).

One of the factors preventing many English teachers from following the official steer provided by the Blue Books was the pressure of accountability. At primary level, English was one of the two subjects (with Mathematics) tested in the 11-plus exami-nation, 'the task-master' (Plowden, 1967: 2) for teachers. The prize for the lucky 25% of state-funded learners was a potentially life-changing grammar school place. The second big test came at secondary level, when 16-year-olds from grammar and inde-pendent schools were entered for Ordinary (O) levels. The exam papers of the 1960s were almost indistinguishable from those of the 1920s (Shayer, 1972; Bullock, 1975), consisting of 'naming of parts'-style tasks with little thought to relevance or interest for the candidates (Hall and Hewings, 2001: 89). Teaching was often spent in turgid preparation. However, the majority of secondary students, destined for employment that did not require academic qualifications, did not sit school-leaving examinations at all (Newsom, 1963; Medway *et al.*, 2014). Accordingly, there was little impetus on their teachers to inspire or the students to achieve: English practice was often drear, 'sterile' (Dixon, 1967: 10).

Curriculum reform appeared long overdue, but there was no political impetus to change things. Nonetheless, despite (or because of) a lack of official line in the years after the Second World War, practice in some areas developed markedly: a creative, child-centred personal growth model began to be increasingly accepted. For example, the post-war period saw the founding of the grass-roots London Association for the Teaching of English (LATE) in 1947 (Gibbons, 2013), a coming together of teachers of English in the maintained sector in the capital. LATE teachers *did* have impetus: they taught modern as well as classic novels (something seen as daring, despite the recommendation originally having come from Newbolt), and began to publish stu-dent-friendly textbooks to replace formal grammar books (Medway *et al.*, 2014). LATE inspired the foundation of the National Association for the Teaching of English (NATE) in 1963, providing a new opportunity for teachers across the country to work together along similar lines (Gibbons, 2017). NATE became the equivalent body to the English Association for the maintained sector.

Harold Wilson's Labour government was elected in 1964 on a reform ticket, ousting Churchill's Conservatives. Capturing the freshness of the Swinging Sixties, the new government liberalised divorce and abortion laws and legalised male homosexuality. Their educational reforms included abolishing selective education, freeing primary teachers from the pressure of preparing pupils for the 11+, and at secondary level had particular impact on the examination system. Inspired by the Newsom Report (1963), *Half Our Future*, the government introduced the Certificate of Secondary Education (CSE) to enhance the prospects of those 13–16-year-olds (typically average and low-er-attaining learners) not entered for O levels. The CSE included teacher-assessed com-ponents and shorter, more accessible questions, and so were less pressurised than O levels (Medway *et al.*, 2014). For teachers, there was a fresh interest in inspiring CSE students and promoting their sense of self (Shayer, 1972).

3.2.2 The influence of Plowden and the Dartmouth Conference

To inform future policy and practice, the government commissioned *Children and their Primary Schools* (Plowden, 1967). Although this book's focus is secondary English, it is important to consider Plowden here, both because of her Report's impact on policy and because it is reflective of secondary practice and thinking of the time.

As outlined in Chapter 1, Plowden advocated a child-centred, creative approach. Although only 35 paragraphs of the 1,252 that make up her Report are explicitly on English, Plowden echoes the Blue Books' recommendations for oracy, reading and writing. Her Report emphasises the importance of providing opportunities for rich classroom talk to give children confidence in speaking; she recommends that teachers should be more relaxed about 'correctness' and 'accent' than 'fluency, vigour or clarity of meaning' (1967: 211). Borrowing the nutrition imagery that is a recurring trope of the Blue Books (*op cit*) – and seen elsewhere by those championing a humane approach (*e.g.* Arnold, 1869; Boas, 1919) – children are presented as 'literary cormorants, *swallowing* all that comes within their reach' (Plowden, 1967: 218); reading is said to 'awake new interests as well as *nourishing* existing ones' (1967: 215) and children need '*nourishing...* with great poetry' (1967: 217, my emphasis in each). Literature is as vital as food. That diet should be administered by enthusiasts – 'a teacher can only share with children what he (*sic*) understands and likes' (1967: 217). And, as in the Blue Books, where they are said to 'blunt' children's sensitivity to language (BoE, 1937: 163), textbooks are to be deprecated – '[children] learn to write by writing and not by exercises in filling in missing words' (Plowden, 1967: 222). Instead, Plowden enthuses on practice she had observed in some schools, where children undertake:

> free, fluent and copious writing on a great variety of subject matter... Sometimes it is called 'creative writing', a rather grand name for it. Its essence is that much of it is personal and that the writers are communicating something that has really engaged their minds and their imaginations... It is nearly always natural and real and sometimes has qualities which make it most moving to read.
>
> (1967: 219)

This first reference to the term 'creative writing' in a policy document – albeit a rather patronising one – suggests that the term is commonly understood. Plowden argues that such writing supports personal growth.

In parallel, the creative, child-centred approach popularised through the work of LATE and NATE gained traction at secondary level (Perry, 1974) within the newly liberalised context, drawing the attention of American academics concerned at the state of subject English in the United States. Accordingly, a contingent from Britain was invited to join them for the *Anglo-American Seminar on the Teaching of English* at Dartmouth College, New Hampshire, in 1966. It became known as the Dartmouth Conference and was an important influence in English education over the next decade on both sides of the Atlantic. Publications arising from the conference, such as *Growth Through English* (Dixon, 1967) and *Creativity in English* (Summerfield, 1968) became seminal texts for English teachers. The titles – Dixon's borrowing imagery used by Arnold (1869: n.p.) when he talks of our 'growing and... becoming' – make explicit the personal growth and creative themes of the conference. Although not policy texts, they are important in understanding subsequent official documents.

Like Plowden, Dixon (1967) suggests that creative approaches building on learners' own language and life experiences strengthen what is innate within them. Equally, just as Plowden argues that the writing of poetry enables children to write from 'deeply-felt experience' (1967: 220), Summerfield emphasises the importance of creativity for personal development: 'without the exercise of imagination we not only fail to know others but also fail to know ourselves' (1968: 37). He argues that 'creative English' helps to form 'more articulate, more effectively human people' (1968: 40). His vision combines teaching creatively and creative learning:

> "Creative English" is not for me a matter of simply eliciting verse or worse, but rather of establishing a relationship and an ethos which will promote experiment, talk, enquiry, amusement, vivacity, bouts of intense concentration, seriousness, collaboration, and a clearer and more adequate self-knowledge. This will involve us in talk about our selves (sic), our language, our behaviour, our attitudes and beliefs, and, when appropriate, in recording such things in writing. And the teacher's sense of his (sic) role is crucial. If he is prescriptive – knowing what he wants, knowing all the answers beforehand – he will be less effective than if he is prepared to allow the pupils' awareness of criteria to grow for itself in the business of making, modifying, and so on.
>
> (Summerfield, 1968: 44)

This view is of creativity celebrating the personal through the expressive. It is about developing human relationships and the right 'ethos', the conditions in which learning best occurs. The repeated use of 'our' stresses the connection between the individual and the collective, and how language is central to the development of both. Plowden had concluded her Report with a similar point: 'We cannot afford to slacken in advancing the power of language which is the "instrument of society" and a principal means to personal maturity' (1967: 223). Summerfield's teacher is not one who knows all the (examination) answers, but who encourages questions; one who privileges child-led approaches in which the process is as valuable as the product.

3.3 *A Language for Life*: The Bullock Report (1975)

3.3.1 Context: the 1970s – a climate of creativity?

Notwithstanding this groundswell of interest at both primary and secondary levels, creative practice was still not universally accepted. Tussles for English continued to be rehearsed across teaching communities and beyond. Five years after Dartmouth, the educational philosopher John Wilson rhetorically invites consideration of what education in English should include and who has the authority to judge:

> Does "being educated in English"… imply knowledge of grammar and syntax? Competence at 'literary criticism' (and what is this anyway?)? Ability to produce 'creative writing' (another obscurity)? Knowledge of the dates of authors and the dimensions of the Shakespearean stage? And so on.
>
> (1972: 9)

He does not proffer answers, and questions remained about English subject content. The political establishment especially was suspicious of child-centred practice. For example, John McGregor – briefly the Conservative Secretary of State for Education (hereafter Education Secretary) – claimed in an interview that a perceived fall in educational standards was a direct result of notions of child–centred learning popular from the late 1950s to 1960s (Ribbins and Sherratt, 1997), although he presented no evidence to support this opinion.

Figure 3.1 Front cover – *A Language for Life (photographed by author)*

Such scepticism was one factor that led the then Conservative Education Secretary, Margaret Thatcher, to commissioning the first report on English teaching since Newbolt (1921). In the event, *A Language for Life* (Bullock, 1975) was published two years later, during Wilson's second term as Labour Prime Minister. Perhaps contrary to Thatcher's intention, the Report criticises an anti-creativity position.

Alan Bullock (1914–2004) in some ways had a similar educational background to Thatcher. She was a grocer's daughter who went to grammar school and thence to Oxford; he was the son of a gardener and a maid, went to grammar school and thence to Oxford. Yet there the parallels end. She read Chemistry; he read Classics and Modern History. She became Prime Minister; Bullock became an accomplished writer and champion of the arts: as an eminent historian, his publications include biographies of Hitler (1952) and Ernest Bevin (1960). He was the first Master of St Catherine's, Oxford, a college that was pioneering in promoting the arts and sciences as equals, and was made the University's Vice Chancellor. He completed his term in 1973, the same year in which he became Chair of the Tate Gallery, and began work on *A Language for Life*.

Bullock set about the task in a strikingly similar way to Newbolt. His committee was not as balanced in terms of gender as Newbolt's, consisting of 16 men and 6 women, but it did include teachers, teacher educators and academics (among them, James Britton and Professor Brian Cox, of whom more later). Together they consulted some 1,400 primary schools, 400 secondary schools, 56 organisations (including NATE, The Arts Council, the Secondary Schools Examinations Council, The Nuffield Foundation) and 66 individuals, as well as Her Majesty's Inspectorate (Bullock, 1975). This involvement of so many in the field of English education suggests that Bullock, like Newbolt, wanted to do a thorough job.

3.3.2 *A Language for Life*: a defence of creativity

The stated aim of *A Language for Life* (Figure 3.1) is to be valuable to a wide target audience (everyone 'from parents to publishers' (Bullock, 1975: xxxii)) and – as a priority – support the teaching profession. Ostensibly responding to anxieties about reading standards in schools, primary and secondary, the Report goes far beyond. Bullock's tone is confident and knowing: the introduction, citing Newbolt, reminds critics that it is common to hark back to a golden past when standards were supposedly better, but suggests that the issue is whether education is equipping children with what they need *now* and for their futures.

He engages specifically in the creativity versus formality debate, stating – possibly to the dismay of the Conservatives – that there was no evidence that school English was declining, as some critics were suggesting, 'in a climate of unchecked creativity' (Bullock, 1975: 6). The negativity of the phrase 'unchecked creativity' encapsulates the difficulties faced by those who wished to promote creativity. The alliteration suggests that detractors assumed creativity is always 'unchecked' (and thereby somehow leads to a curriculum that is itself unconstrained, unbridled, uncontrolled – with the unspoken dangers of social upheaval that such abandon might lead to); there is no hint that the critics had considered a 'checked' or controlled climate of creativity, such as might be developed in a classroom context – the very approach to creativity that Bullock's Report goes on to support. Bullock does however accept that in some schools the personal growth view had become so all-pervasive that children were falling back on cliché rather than expressing genuine feeling.

Bullock promotes the centrality of language within and beyond school. Talk and listening, reading and writing are presented as a 'unity' (1975: xxxv) – the importance of the 'wholeness' of language is several times repeated (*e.g.* 1975: 242, 340). Language is described as developing incrementally and organically 'through an interaction of writing, talk, reading, and experience' (1975: 8); the teacher's role is to 'intervene' (1975: 8) to develop children's confidence and fluency. Like Newbolt, Bullock states that the job of teaching English is too important for non-specialists and calls for properly-qualified teachers. It is made clear that 'Literacy is a corporate responsibility' requiring a 'community of endeavour' (1975: 26), restating the message of the Blue Books and Newbolt that every teacher is a teacher of English. He calls for all teachers to be trained appropriately.

Language (in any mode) is shown to be the key to learning. In a striking metaphor, the Report suggests language functions as a 'filing pin' (Bullock, 1975: 48) that can store an infinite number of pieces of information collected one by one, enabling children to link the new to the familiar, classifying experiences so they can be applied to other situations. Language development and learning are presented as heuristic, both dependent on 'discovery' (1975: 50); children should use language to find out for *themselves*. A key recommendation is that every school should develop a policy of language across the curriculum.

3.2.2.1 Speaking and listening

Bullock reinforces this point through his discussion of oral work. Talk is defined as the 'instrument for learning and for thinking' (1975: 154), which highlights the central role of talk in society. It is recognised that our use of language should be appropriate to each of the speech communities to which we belong: like the Blue Books and Newbolt, the Report states that a child's home language should be valued alongside Standard English.

Drama is seen as particularly important too because it provides opportunities for improvisation of language not afforded elsewhere:

> In drama an element of invention lies round every corner, and dialogue has a way of surprising itself so that nothing is predictable [while] [a]ll writing, even when at its most creative, tends in school work to be a patterning of words within which thoughts and feelings have to be contained and ordered.
>
> (Bullock, 1975: 158)

This emphasis that teachers should create opportunities for practising talk through drama reminds schools that drama 'warrant[s] serious study' (1975: 160) and so deserves curriculum time. The quotation not only illustrates Bullock's awareness that everyday language use is innovative, but draws attention to his suggestion that 'creative' writing has limitations: the very act of writing something down imposes a shape which constrains it. Creative writing is here set in opposition to drama, thus intriguingly as offering *less* potential for personal growth than extemporised verbal language.

3.2.2.2 Reading

In terms of reading, the Report moves swiftly beyond the necessity of decoding to a consideration of content, describing reading for meaning in hermeneutic terms:

> … reading is more than **a reconstruction of the author's meanings**. It is the perception of those meanings within **the total context of the relevant experiences**

of the reader – a much more active and demanding process. Here the reader is required to engage in critical and creative thinking in order to relate what he reads to what he already knows; to evaluate the new knowledge in terms of the old and the old in terms of the new.

(1975: 79, emphasis original)

This passage suggests that new understanding is formed through the merging of the text and all that the reader brings to it. The fact that 'critical' and 'creative' are combined demonstrates Bullock's recognition that reading competence *depends* upon imaginative or original thought.

Discussing the reading of literature in particular, Bullock refers directly to Dartmouth's re-emphasising of the long tradition that literature supports personal or moral growth: teaching literature 'provides imaginative insight into what another person is feeling; it allows the contemplation of possible human experiences which the reader himself has not met' (Bullock, 1975: 125); indeed, 'To read intelligently is to read responsively; it is to ask questions of the text and use one's own framework of experience in interpreting it' (1975: 129). This commitment to developing empathy recalls earlier policy and guidance (*e.g.* Newbolt, 1921; BoE, 1927, 1935). A good reader, then, is recognised as one who uses language skilfully and imaginatively to relate what they read to their own experiences, and thereby create new and significant understandings. A good teacher of reading, Bullock notes, does not waste time on plot summaries and cataloguing characters; they are creative, encouraging prediction, anticipation, speculation. The Report, too, is mindful that canonical literature is not altogether popular with students, so – again, like Newbolt, and now perhaps capitalising on the work on LATE and NATE – recommends the study of modern 'fresh' (Bullock, 1975: 135) work to encourage enjoyment.

3.2.2.3 Writing

The discussion on writing opens by acknowledging the high prestige writing holds in education: it is the means of demonstrating what has been learnt. The Report notes approvingly that the scope of writing activities in junior schools had increased since the demise of the 11+, with teachers no longer feeling the need to teach to the test. Bullock then tackles head-on the thorny topic of 'personal' (as opposed to 'impersonal' or transactional (1975: 163)) writing:

> The form that has attracted most attention is that which has become known as 'creative writing', a term which has acquired emotive associations and has sometimes polarised attitudes… The truth is, of course, that 'creative writing' has come to mean many things. At its best it is an attempt to use language to recreate experience faithfully and with sincerity. It draws upon all the resources of language inventively yet in a form which is organic with the feelings or experience from which it grew. From this point there is a sliding scale of interpretations. Some teachers encourage children to strive for effect, to produce the purple patch, the stock response. Others have merely adopted the label and apply it to any kind of writing.

(1975: 163/4)

It is made explicit in this report that the term 'creative writing' is confusing for many and is controversial, but the reference to 'faithfulness and … sincerity' calls to mind the 'truthfulness in its widest sense' of the last Blue Book (BoE, 1937). The metaphor of growth reappears, linked to 'feelings' and 'experience', indicating Bullock's belief that learning is a result of living – language is for life.

Bullock resists providing a definition of creative writing, but does say what it is not: it is not 'spontaneous' writing, nor writing using 'colourful or fanciful language… divorced from real feeling' (1975: 163/4). Instead, effective writing arises from 'corporate enterprises of the classroom' (*ibid*): it is the product of effective talk. The 'solution' (*ibid*) is for the teacher to encourage a child to articulate their intentions, then help them to achieve by providing guidance on appropriate techniques. This is an explicit endorsement of child-led teaching.

The Report proposes adopting categories developed by the Schools Council Writing Research Unit (Britton, 1975), which divided language users into two modes, *participant* and *observer*. In each mode, writing might be Transactional-Expressive or Expressive-Poetic, where 'expressive' sits in the overlapping circles of a Venn Diagram. All writing is thereby seen as 'expressive.' For Bullock, an 'expressive' writer is one who offers feelings and beliefs to their audience, a trusted teacher, and enjoys 'the sheer satisfaction of making, of bringing into existence a pleasing verbal object' (1975: 164). While the term 'creative' is not used, the physicality involved in expressive writing is shown as joyous, life-enhancing, and thereby promoting personal growth.

Bullock discourages the decontextualised teaching of spelling and prescriptive grammar, instead encouraging risk-taking, experimental approaches to develop students' self-confidence. He suggests that successful teachers use imagination and inventiveness, pedagogy described as 'creative' elsewhere. Finally, citing Newbolt (1921) in asserting that the teaching of writing should be far more than preparation for limited, rigid examination syllabi, the Report calls for a broader approach to assessment, including school-based assessment with external moderation.

It is for all these reasons that I suggest Bullock deliberately, playfully and creatively gave his report an ambiguous title – *A Language for Life* – encouraging his reader to capitalise on the array of meanings that are offered and see perhaps unexpected meanings. 'Life' may be interpreted in several senses, all of which are pertinent. 'Life' is our everyday existence, the humdrum, the quotidian: we need language to get through the day. 'Life' is the span of our existence, from birth to death: we need language to survive our tenure on earth. 'Life' is also vital – the adjective is 'lively' – and so suggests energy: we need language to bring us joy. The preposition 'for' has various connotations that further enrich these interpretations. 'For' can be purposeful and suggest intent (language *promotes* life); it also can mean to acquire or gain (language *gives* life); it can equally suggest a sensitivity to (language *appreciates* life).

A Language for Life endorses much of the philosophy and creative practice that came to the fore during the 1960s. Bullock promotes dialogic teaching by emphasising the interdependence of oral language and learning. He describes a good reader as one who is in dialogue with a text – asking questions, anticipating, speculating – and shows that personal growth is enhanced through writing. All of this is made possible through a teacher who provides the right creative opportunities.

3.4 *The Teaching of English Language*: **The Kingman Report (1988)**

3.4.1 *Context: towards the National Curriculum*

Education policy under Margaret Thatcher's premiership confirms that she was unconvinced by the Bullock Report. Replacing Edward Heath in 1975 as the leader of the Conservative Party, Thatcher became Prime Minister after the general election of 1979, promising to deal with the Northern Irish 'Troubles', high unemployment and high inflation. She presided over Britain joining the European Economic Community (EEC) in 1973, a decision confirmed by a referendum in 1975 when 67% of the population voted in favour (Morgan, 1984). She was ambitious to improve the economy: at the time, Britain's Gross Domestic Product (GDP) lagged behind the USA, Japan and Germany and was on a par with France.

Thatcher bid to improve Britain's place in the free market through introducing a free market economy into education: according to neo-liberal orthodoxy, student performance indicators should determine which schools should thrive and which should fail. At the same time, traditionalists in the Conservative party were voicing a desire for state control of curriculum content (Gillard, 2018). A National Curriculum with national performance indicators was proposed, to satisfy both needs (although it could be argued that the 'National' Curriculum was a misnomer from the start, since it applied only to England and Wales – not Scotland or Northern Ireland – and only to maintained schools).

The Education Reform Act of 1988 accordingly paved the way for the National Curriculum. It gave sweeping powers to the new Education Secretary,[1] Kenneth Baker. Baker commissioned John Kingman to advise on how English language is best monitored and assessed, and on teacher training – at the time, 28% of those teaching English in secondary schools (responsible for 15% of English teaching nationwide) had no formal qualification beyond O level (Kingman, 1988).

In some respects, parallels may be drawn between Kingman (1939) and the writers of the previous Reports. He too progressed from a working-class background via grammar school to Oxford. However, while Newbolt and Bullock were prominent in the Arts, were at the peak of their professional achievements when commissioned (both were in their 60s) and were successful writers (as had been Arnold), Kingman was different. A statistician and former Professor of Mathematics at Oxford, he was in his early 40s and newly installed as the Vice Chancellor of the University of Bristol (a post he held from 1985 to 2001) when commissioned. Kingman's background does not suggest expertise in English or education, and his career was arguably still in the ascendency: perhaps he felt that he had something to prove. (Whilst at Bristol, Kingman gained notoriety for having the third-highest Vice Chancellor's salary in Britain, his pay doubling in his final year in office.)

His committee consisted of 13 men and 6 women; they included novelists, broadcasters, businesspeople and academics; but there were only two teachers, both from independent girls' schools in London; one Professor of Education, based in London; and one Local Education Authority adviser from Berkshire (Kingman, 1988). It is not obvious that there was anyone to represent English teachers in maintained schools around the country. (He did, however, like Bullock, include Professor Brian Cox, whose influence on subject English is discussed in Chapter 4.)

Schools' contributions to Kingman's inquiry were more limited than those of Newbolt, Plowden and Bullock, with just 14 primaries and 16 secondaries involved (although 240 individuals and organisations were canvassed), perhaps due to tight dead-lines. However, the committee chose their own way in spite of advice received. For instance, the Report admits that although 'almost all' (Kingman, 1988: 57) evidence submitted argued *against* testing – particularly of seven-year-olds – for both practi-cal and pedagogical reasons, Kingman recommended testing anyway. His paymaster, Baker, who spoke disparagingly of educationalists' 'smug complacency' in rejecting testing (Independent, 1987 *in* Simon, 1991: 540) would have been pleased. Kingman's was the first Report in which advice from the field of English educators was ignored.

3.4.2 Creativity criticised

The remit of *The Teaching of the English Language* was to present a 'model' of spoken and written English (Kingman, 1988: 4), and it thus did not have the full scope of its predecessors; perhaps as a result, it differs markedly from all the policy documents that predate it in both tone and structure. It discusses spoken and written language inter-changeably, 'touching on' (1988: 3) literature and drama only insofar as they illustrate the model proposed. Talk, writing and reading are discussed below in the sequence in which they appear in the Report as a means of highlighting some of the contrasts.

The Report's only explicit reference to 'creativity' is at the start, where Kingman explicitly echoes Newbolt's concerns about the state of English education; yet he goes on to claim that teachers – while not 'indifferent', and 'anxious' to support children's language development (Kingman, 1988: 1) – labour under a misguided belief that 'con-scious knowledge of the structure and working of the language... damages creativity' (1988: 1). There is no evidence to substantiate this claim about teachers' attitudes and beliefs, and no further specific discussion of creativity.

Rather, Kingman is critical of practice reported in schools. In a contradictory par-agraph, he notes the 'debt' that his committee owes to the Bullock Report, citing its 'great influence on the teaching and learning of English in British schools' (Kingman, 1988: 2), but then points to 'deficiencies' in pupils' language use as reported by some school inspectors, a 'narrow diet' of writing and reading taught separately, and a lack of consensus regarding what English should consist of and how it should be taught (1988: 2). However, he notes that not all of Bullock's recommendations had been imple-mented, particularly regarding the needs of training teachers.

The semantic field in Kingman's Report is strikingly authoritarian. In tune with the prevailing political mood, it states that 'accurate use of the rules and conventions' are impor-tant 'to increase the freedom of the individual' and promote 'personal liberty' (1988: 3). The notion of power is conspicuous – language enabling humans to 'name [what] we have power over' and 'defend their rights and... fulfil their obligations' (1988: 7). Whilst it is acknowledged that 'pupils should develop as human beings as well as com-municators' (1988: 10), there appears to be more weight put on developing children's language skills to meet their adult needs. Critical intellectual development comes before 'social, personal and aesthetic development' (1988: 7). Themes that can be traced through previous reports are conspicuously absent: the noun 'growth' appears five times, but always concerning linguistic and intellectual growth, never 'personal growth'.

3.4.2.1 Speaking and listening and writing

The idea promulgated in the previous Reports that talk inspires good writing is here turned on its head: Kingman declares that command of written structures ensures that they are 'available for use in speech if the occasion demands, thereby increasing the power and flexibility of the oral repertoire' (1988: 10). This is followed by the claim that

> Children who read Tolkien and then write their own fairy stories are engaged in a total process of language development which, among other advantages, may one day contribute to the writing of clear, persuasive reports about commerce or science.
>
> (1988: 11)

It is not clear whether Kingman is suggesting that following Tolkien's lead and becoming an acclaimed author is as valuable an aspiration as the ability to write an authoritative piece on industry. There is passing reference to the notion that experimenting with various modes of writing should be encouraged for 'humanistic reasons' (1988: 10) – these perhaps are some of the unnamed 'advantages' – and a note that 'English teachers have an important part to play in nourishing both the intellect and the imagination' (1988: 11); but the overriding implication is that a key aim of developing the language of the individual is primarily to serve economic ends.

3.4.2.2 Reading

An interesting attitude towards literature may also be detected. Several previous reports paraphrase Arnold in describing English Literature as regarded as the best that has been thought and said; Kingman too describes literature as 'powerful and splendid' and praises its 'aesthetic properties' (1988: 11), but it seems implicit that literature's role is more to develop learners' vocabulary and English cultural knowledge than to enrich their personal lives. The 'literature of the past' (*ibid*) is presented as primarily valuable in understanding how it informs the language of today, with examples of 'our' (*ibid*) writers. Shakespeare, Blake and Edward Lear are among the list of exclusively dead, white male authors recommended in a passage that might have been taken from a report from a century ago, when post-war patriotism could be more easily rationalised, than a purportedly forward-thinking Report written in the latter part of the twentieth century when Britain had its first female prime minister and a growing black and minority ethnic population. (Newbolt (1921: 220) did at least recommend Jane Austen.) In mitigation, Kingman does later acknowledge that '[ethnic] groups settling in Britain have enriched English' (1988: 30), recommending that instances in which the grammar of Afro-Caribbean creole languages differ from Standard English could be explored to understand how language changes.

The Report is dismissive of classroom debates on moral and social issues prompted by literature that, it claims, characterised English lessons of the 1960s and 70s, since 'largely thematic discussions' on 'the relations between language, literature, politics and social conditions… offered little analysis of rhetoric, choice of language, metaphor, vocabulary and other persuasive and argumentative devices' (Kingman, 1988: 12). It thereby implies that the prime purpose of reading literature is to learn about language use. It maintains that the greater the child's knowledge about language, the greater their 'pleasure' (1988: 39) in literature. On the idea that reading literature might also provide solace, or enrich lives through enabling children to place themselves in another's shoes, it is silent. A teacher's role is to 'match' (1988: 11) a book to the child, which Kingman acknowledges requires 'fine judgement and sensitivity' (*ibid*) but presents a very different teacher–pupil relationship than previous policy documents (*e.g.* BoE, 1905/1912; 1935) that called for class libraries so that learners could make choices for themselves.

The Report's 'model' for language learning consists of (i) forms of the English language, (ii) communication and comprehension, (iii) acquisition and development and (iv) historical and geographical variation. It claims that a systematic understanding of formal language terminology is necessary to enable children to develop their use language across all modes. This message is repeated at the end of the Report: '"Knowledge about language" is not a separate component of... curriculum. It should not be "bolted on", but should inform children's talking, writing, reading and listening in the classroom' (Kingman, 1988: 48). Each element of the model is offered with examples of classroom approaches (*e.g.* investigating words containing the root 'self' and its antonyms to consider form and vocabulary; peer assessment of a formal debate concerning whether No Smoking areas contravene individual rights to consider persuasive talk; comparing passages from different versions of the Bible to examine language change over time) with some pointers to help teachers support less confident learners.

The importance of English across the curriculum is stressed, illustrated with exemplars and commentary. For instance, the work of a secondary-aged history student is cited, a narrative account of life in a poor household 300 years ago: 'And once they asked what is for dinner and the reply is potatoes they start to moan.' (Kingman, 1988: 34). Apparently without irony, the commentary is critical of the non-standard linguistic features and ambiguous use of 'moan'; there is no acknowledgement that the writing provides evidence that the learner has engaged with the topic (they have understood the monotony of a diet of potatoes), far less the notion that they could *deliberately* be using a limited, non-standard language palette better to put themselves in the persona of an unschooled child. The critique states that it is up to the teacher to decide how they might use the meta-language to help the learner develop their writing, indicating that the teacher's professional judgement is important; however, the tone suggests that the use of Standard English is seen as a more valuable educational outcome than nurturing imaginative engagement with the past.

To sum up, the dominant theme of the Report is that explicit knowledge about language develops wider knowledge and intellect, which are associated with freedom, power and economic success. Kingman does not disregard the development of the individual self, but this is subsumed within the broader theme. This emphasis is illustrated through the rigidity of the first 4 of the 14 Attainment targets the Report recommends for 16-year-olds:

1   *Speak in Standard English...* (regional accents are acceptable, but not dialect);
2   *Read aloud with appropriate stress, intonation and pause;*
3   *Use punctuation according to the conventions of Standard English;*
4   *Spell correctly*

(Kingman, 1988: 52)

Not until target 10, 'Express feelings and intentions as well as facts, ideas and arguments lucidly' (*ibid*), is any sense of the personal offered.

Kingman's Report, therefore, represents a departure from policy documents that preceded it. To reiterate, Kingman lacked expertise in the field, and was, perhaps, over-keen to please Baker; his committee may have been well-intentioned, but they too had very limited experience of English teaching, especially in the maintained sector. The Report is not necessarily entirely uncreative or anti-creative in terms of pedagogy – the examples provided of the four-part model in action include discussion, the use of first-person narrative and writing poetry – but is perhaps in spirit. It warns against a return to rote-learning but does not explicitly favour child-centred approaches either. Canonical literature is promoted as informing cultural knowledge rather than aesthetic or personal development. 'Knowledge' comes to the fore. The teacher is presented as an expert who should teach language explicitly (although 'sensitively' (Kingman, 1988: 13)) using formal terminology. The document itself lacks the nuances of language and metaphor of those that came before: it is a blunter report with a blunter message.

3.5 Conclusion and summary

It is clear that Kingman (1988) is the exception. The other policy documents discussed in this chapter, like those in Chapter 2, include notions of creativity at the heart of secondary English teaching. Written by experts in the field, and after wide consultation, they cumulatively prove that creativity in subject English is not a glue-and-glitter reward, a fanciful appendage to be included if time allows after the 'real' work of the classroom has gone on, but the very foundation of learning. Indeed, they emphasise that creativity depends upon yet also fosters hard work and resilience, a point echoed in the wider literature (*e.g.* Lytton, 1971).

Together, they have informed what emerged as hallmarks of good English practice as defined in the literature today (*e.g.* Fleming and Stevens, 2010; McCallum, 2012; Hodgson and Wilkin, 2014; Bleiman, 2020). Indeed, the subject functions best through maintaining a rich blend of the different notions of creativity presented in Chapter 1. Holding this multiplicity of senses of the term is not to confuse or dilute; indeed, acknowledging 'creativities' (McCallum, 2012: 25) is to celebrate the scope, breadth and depth of English. Further, the policy documents demonstrate that creativity works hand in hand with both big C and little c culture, culture being the means through which language is shared and developed, which in turn emphasises the importance of English in nurturing personal growth. Although personal growth is not named as such in the policies until Bullock (1975: 4), the idea is prominent in the earlier documents (*e.g.* Newbolt, 1921; BoE, 1927, 1937), reinforced by Plowden (1967) and the publications from the Dartmouth Conference, positioned throughout as crucial in promoting independent thought and developing the individual.

Taking the policy documents examined in Chapter 2 and the present chapter together, there are of course variations in the themes. In the earliest documents, creativity in *taking* and appreciating high culture is dominant; later, the pedagogy favours creativity in *making* everyday culture; often the two are blurred, melding the notions of Big C and little c creativities (Craft, 2001); the balance shifts in places. For example, the value of children writing poetry is presented sometimes as means of enabling them better to engage with published poetry (BoE, 1927), sometimes as means of developing their personal growth (Bullock, 1975).

Given this wealth of policy and guidance recommending creative English, therefore, and the associated arguments that such practice develops the confident, inquiring, thoughtful, sensitive, broad-minded individuals that are the requisites of a humane society, the question that emerges is why the more recent Reports (*e.g.* Bullock, 1975; Kingman, 1988) successively comment on the unsatisfactory nature of English in schools, even after the changes wrought by the Wilson government in the 1960s. Descriptions of English lessons as dry, unstimulating, dominated by grammar, suggest that the creative practice promoted was not widely practiced. Ironically, some of the poor classroom practice described by Kingman, including a 'narrow diet' (1988: 2) where reading and writing are taught separately, are not a result of the creative English of 1960s he so disparages, nor Bullock's influence (1975), but a textbook-based approach to English teaching. This suggestion reinforces the idea that many schools were not set up to be creative places (Lytton, 1971; Benson, 2004; Hodgson and Wilkin, 2014), and thus official endorsement of creative English practice did not have the impact intended.

However, as the very existence of the Kingman Report (1988) suggests, the ruling government 20 years after Wilson's was less desirous of a child-centred, humane, culture-rich view of English. It began to develop an accountability structure that would see children less as individuals to be nurtured, more as units to be compared one to another. Although the Kingman Report is an anomaly amongst the policy documents explored in this chapter about the flowering of creative English, Chapter 4 now explores how some of the ideas Kingman introduces gradually come to the fore through the various iterations of the National Curriculum, when policy documents become statutory, and the plant begins to wither.

In summary:

- The policy documents explored in Chapter 2, together with Plowden (1967) and Bullock (1975), demonstrate a remarkable convergence in describing and justifying what creative English *is* and what it can *do:* English is presented as a humane, unitary subject concerned with nurturing a child's personal (and thus social) growth through cultivating their interest in language, developing their enjoyment and confidence in expressing themselves through the spoken and written word; and encouraging a love of literature.
- Such a view of English *depends upon* creativity – even before the term 'creativity' was enregistered as a term relevant to education.
- Kingman (1988) signals the launch of the National Curriculum and the beginnings of a move towards prescription governed by assessment.

Note

1 With great prescience, the former Chief Education Officer of the Inner London Education Authority (which had been disbanded by Thatcher's government) warned that the Education Secretary's new powers were excessive:

> [W]hat if one day this country were to find itself with a Secretary of State possessed of a narrow vision of what education in a democracy should aspire to be, coupled with a degree of self-regard and intolerance of the opinions of others that caused him or her to seek to impose that vision on others?
>
> (Newsom, 1987 *in* Gillard, 2018, n.p).

4 Creativity 'cabined, cribbed, confined'[1]

English in the National Curriculum

4.1 Introduction

This chapter investigates how creativity has appeared in English policy over the last 30 years – the era of the National Curriculum. In contrast to the consensus traced through the policy documents explored in Chapters 2 and 3, the chapter demonstrates that the six iterations of the Curriculum (1989, 1995, 1999, 2004, 2007, 2014) have limited agreement on the purpose of English within the secondary phase and differing views on creativity. It reveals tension between whether the purpose of education is the development of humane individuals able to foster the wellbeing of themselves and others, or the development of adults who will contribute to the economy. It charts the increasing commodification of creativity as the latter view takes hold, showing how the Programmes of Study are often so structured as to *prevent* creative work – even when 'creativity' is apparently in political favour.

This chapter follows on directly from Chapter 3 in presenting how creativity appears in the English policy documents since 1989: the era of the National Curriculum. The final document covered in the last chapter, the Kingman Report (1988), is the precursor to *English for Ages 5–16* – more commonly referred to as the Cox Report (1989) – the first document discussed in this. The contrasting nature of the two reports is indicative of how creativity is variously understood and valued.

It is important at this stage to reiterate the significance of the National Curriculum (the Curriculum) on schools in England. While the policy documents presented in Chapters 2 and 3 were government-sanctioned, they did not have legal status. The introduction of the Education Act of 1988, however, meant that every maintained school became subject to a statutory Curriculum. While the influence of that Curriculum has been eroded over the past two decades by subsequent policy changes enabling academies and free schools to set their own curricula – currently only around 30% of state pupils attend schools still technically bound by the Curriculum (Blake, 2019) – the fact that GCSE examinations reflect the Curriculum's content for Key Stage 4 means that secondary English is effectively universally governed by the Curriculum orders.[2] The Curriculum therefore has a greater bearing on classroom practice than the pre-Curriculum policy documents.

A statutory Curriculum means not only that the government can hold schools to account (and so have a direct influence on what happens in classrooms), but that government is simultaneously held to account by the electorate (who need ocular proof that the government is succeeding in driving improvement). This may be one reason why the relative brevity of the 25-year period discussed in this chapter (1989–2014) is not reflected in the number of documents produced: there have been six published versions of the Curriculum, with another unpublished (DfE/WO, 1993). The effort and cost expended are also considerable – the Cox Report alone consists of around 80,000 words. The very number and length of the publications suggest how complex has been the Curriculum's history. This was perhaps always understood: Cox makes clear that his version for English is not definitive, although it is not until the fourth version that what had become accepted practice is actually stated: 'The National Curriculum is regularly reviewed,' ostensibly to 'meet the changing needs of pupils and society' (DfES/QCA, 2004: 3). However, as established in Chapter 1, the correlation between changes of government and iterations of the Curriculum indicates that those perceived changing needs vary according to political hue, with English in particular subject to battles within and between groups of educationalists and politicians (Davison, 2009).

Accordingly, this chapter is structured to tell the story of the Curriculum within its political context. The first half provides a socio-political overview of the three governments who have directed Curriculum policy, offering background information on the authors of the Curriculum documents where known, followed by an overview of how each Curriculum positions the role and purpose of English. Section 4.2 looks at the Conservatives (1989–1997) and the first two Curriculum documents (Cox, 1989; DfE, 1995); Section 4.3 covers New Labour and Labour (1997–2010) and the 1999 (DfEE/QCA), 2004 (DfES/QCA) and 2007 (DCSF/QCA) Curricula; while 4.4 brings us up to date with the Coalition and Conservative governments (2010-) and the current Curriculum (DfE, 2014).

The second half (Section 4.5) then looks at the details of the English Programmes of Study. Speaking and listening (4.5.1), reading (4.5.2) and writing (4.5.3) are covered in turn. Through tracing the decline in child-centred oracy, reading for pleasure and expressive writing (established in Chapters 2 and 3 to be the interdependent components of a humane English curriculum) through the different iterations, it demonstrates how successive Curricula became increasingly antithetic to creative work, even in times when 'creativity' is officially promoted.

It is worth pointing out that, since the term 'creativity' is by now firmly enregistered as a term relevant to education, its incidence can be plotted through the Curriculum. Its presence or absence is deliberate: to include or ignore creativity is a calculated decision. The challenge here is that creativity is not always *labelled* as such, even post enregisterment. Paradoxically, one document that might claim to be 'creative' is not necessarily so, while another that does not explicitly include the term might be brim-full of creativity. We need to read between the lines.

4.1.1 Opening questions

Language changes; definitions change. As you read this chapter, think about the following:

- How does the concept of creativity in English change through the various iterations of the National Curriculum? Are there ever different 'creativities' apparent simultaneously?
- If creativity is evident in the respective Curriculum documents, how is it regarded or valued?

4.2 Disunited factions: the conservatives, English and creativity 1989–1997

4.2.1 *Context: romantics and pragmatists, traditionalists and modernisers*

As outlined at the end of Chapter 3, the Conservative Party under Margaret Thatcher pressed ahead with the introduction of a National Curriculum as part of their strategy to revitalise Britain's economy. The socio-economic context for *English for Ages 5–16* (Cox, 1989) was, therefore, almost identical to that of *The Teaching of English Language* (Kingman, 1988).

1989 was the year in which Tim Berners-Lee invented the World Wide Web. It also coincided with Thatcher's tenth year as Prime Minister. Although she had marked her arrival in Downing Street with St Francis of Assisi's prayer for peace and harmony, the decade is arguably better remembered for violence: the Falklands War, the bitter year-long Miners' Strike, IRA bombings. Yet her policies of low taxation and increasing home ownership – and a disorganised opposition – meant that Thatcher was twice re-elected, although the unpopularity of the poll-tax forced her from office in 1990. She was replaced by John Major.

In macro-economic terms, Britain's GDP continued to lag. By 1989 Britain had dropped to seventh place in the world rankings, one lower than it had been on Thatcher's election (www.nationmaster.com). Britain was then preparing for the transition of the European Economic Community to the European Union and the arrival of the single market in 1993. The imperative for economic success in international terms was keenly felt.

Regarding education policy, the Conservatives remained divided between romantics who believed education was concerned with accruing cultural knowledge and modernisers mindful of the needs of industry in the global marketplace (Aldrich, 2005). A safe pair of hands was therefore needed to chair the committee to draw up the first Curriculum for English. The Education Secretary, Kenneth Baker, chose Professor Charles Brian Cox (1928–2008), known as Brian Cox. As co-editor of the anti-progressive *The Fight for Education* (Cox and Dyson, 1969b) and *The Crisis in Education* (Cox and Dyson, 1969a), the first of the so-called Black Papers that criticised comprehensivisation, and a member of both Bullock's and Kingman's committees, he was regarded as appropriate and onside.

However, as Cox himself implies (1991), Baker had not done his homework. Like *A Language for Life* (Bullock, 1975), *English for Ages 5–16* (Cox, 1989) was more child-centred and liberal than the Government might have hoped (Cox, 1995; Gibbons, 2017), perhaps due in part to the striking parallels between elements of Cox's background and those of Arnold, Newbolt and Bullock, which gave him a view of the transformative power of education. Cox too was born into a working-class home (in Grimsby); he too won a scholarship to Oxbridge. After graduating from Cambridge, he was briefly a supply teacher, then a lecturer in English Literature at Hull; he was next a professor at Manchester, becoming pro-Vice Chancellor in 1987. His whole career had been in education. Like Arnold and Newbolt, he was a gifted poet; like Bullock, he was a writer – he appreciated the Arts, and was to go on to chair the Arvon Foundation (a charity promoting creative writing). It is unsurprising that Cox's National Curriculum echoed the work of Newbolt and Bullock more closely than that of Kingman.

Cox was in his 60s and at the top of his field when invited to chair the committee. Its members (7 men and 3 women) were chosen by Baker, but Cox said he found in them a progressive momentum (Cox, 1991; Cox 1995; Gibbons, 2017). They included representatives from maintained and independent schools, local authorities and universities. They consulted widely: their Report credits around 100 organisations, including local authorities, broadcasters, subject associations and universities; there are an additional 68 individuals mentioned, including John Dixon, the language expert Dr Ron Carter and sociolinguist Professor Peter Trudgill, who offered a range of expertise across English Language and Literature and from infant to higher education. The resulting Report (1989) and Cox's later reflections (1991, 1995) suggest that these experts were heeded.

4.2.2 *English for ages 5–16* (Cox, 1989): a defence of creative English

Cox was acutely conscious of the tensions concerning creative English, making explicit in the Introduction to *English for ages 5–16* his awareness of the political and educational debate: 'no position is neutral' (1989: 57). Rather than come to a 'timid compromise' (1989: 58) about what English is and means, his ambition was to build bridges between polarities separating 'individual and social aims, … or language and literature' or (perhaps pointedly) 'craft and creativity' (1989: 57). He uses as the epigraph to the introductory chapter Raymond Williams' argument that formal education is 'a particular set of emphases and omissions' (1965 *in* Cox, 1989: 57), then goes on to demonstrate his child-centred perspective through quoting Plowden: 'at the heart of the educational process lies the child' (1967 *in* 1989: 61). Through this pairing, Cox emphasises first his understanding that education policy is partial and yet that young lives are at its centre and, second, signals his debt to the creative thinkers of the 1960s.

Cox goes on to state that the 'overriding aim' of the English curriculum is 'to enable all pupils to develop to the full their ability to use and understand English' (1989: 58), with the two core purposes:

> First, **English contributes to the personal development of the individual child because of the cognitive functions of both spoken and written language in exploratory learning and in organising and making sense of experiences**… Secondly, **English contributes to preparation for the adult world.**
>
> (1989: 59; emphasis original)

While he stresses that they are interlinked, it is noteworthy that the *personal development* of individuals is foremost, with language presented as a means of *making sense of experiences* before the 'complementary' (*ibid*) purpose of readying the child for adulthood. Further, Cox suggests that English should take learners beyond the core Attainment Targets of Speaking and Listening, Reading and Writing: it should enable them to explore their own and others' linguistic and cultural identities; they should use language for organisational purposes, or 'create and keep artistic artefacts – poems, plays, stories' (*ibid*). The range of language uses given reinforces the notion that education in English allows learners to deploy language *as they choose* to have power over their own lives.

Cox identifies five 'views' that, together, summarise the role of English as a school subject: personal growth, cross-curricular, adult needs, cultural heritage and cultural analysis (1989: 60), popularly known now as Cox's models. The product of extensive research by Cox and his committee, these are the views of *teachers* – not politicians, not theorists, but classroom practitioners – demonstrating that Cox sought, trusted and valued professional testimony. It is striking that Cox chose not to present the views in alphabetical order: 'personal growth' heads the list, which echoes the first core purpose quoted above, 'English contributes to the *personal development* of the individual child' (*op cit*, my emphasis). This implies that Cox sees personal growth as the most important. He defines it as:

> a view [that] focuses on the child: it emphasises the relationship between language and learning in the individual child, and the role of literature in developing children's imaginative and aesthetic lives.
>
> (1989: 59)

This emphasis on the relationship between *language* and *learning* emphasises that it is through language that children understand the world; while the emphasis on the *imaginative and aesthetic* reminds us that art is a carrier of experience, something to which Cox draws attention in explaining how 'cultural heritage' and 'cultural understanding' are concerned with 'passing on the culture from one generation to the next, and with critically understanding what that culture consists of' (1989: 60), a notion echoing Gadamer's (1975/2004) ideas on the genesis and purpose of culture discussed in Chapter 1.[3]

Second in Cox's sequence comes cross–curricular, and third is adult needs (including the importance of English 'in a European context' (1989: 58), both for commercial reasons and inter-cultural relations). This implies a continuum from knowing oneself to learning at school to becoming an adult. Cox explains that the views look both 'inwards' (to the self) and 'outwards' (to the world) (1989: 60), but the suggestion is that the 'outward' is *dependent* on the 'inward': if the child is not whole in herself, the 'inward', they will not be equipped to go beyond and interact with others 'outwards', whether in the curriculum, the workplace or, in a broader sense, through the connections that language provides us to other places and other times. Cox is thus emphasising the importance of personal growth as the foundation in preparing a learner for life, all of which indicates how far Cox's vision for the English Curriculum appears inspired by policy documents discussed in Chapters 2 and 3. His view of English is undeniably creative, even if the term is hardly used. Perhaps this is a calculated omission, given the contentiousness of the debate.

Significantly, Cox's name is the last that can be associated specifically with any one iteration of the Curriculum. The authors and committee members of the five subsequent versions are absent. There is no suggestion that they requested anonymity; rather, the lack of named author is symptomatic of a 'seismic shift' (Bleiman, 2020: 24) towards an increasingly centralised approach to English education policy from the 1990s onwards.

4.2.3 The second National Curriculum (DfE/WO, 1995): creative English curtailed

English for ages 5–16 was 'generally welcomed' (Marshall, 2000: 6) by the profession on publication, despite its volume making it difficult to translate into classroom practice. Yet Baker was unhappy. Cox later acknowledged he had failed in his aim to 'overcome dogmatism' (Cox, 1991: 18) and unite factions within the Tory party (Knight, 1996; Gibbons, 2017). For romantics, Cox's Curriculum did not sufficiently celebrate the canon of English literature. (Cox had resisted calls to include lists of prescribed texts.) For modernisers, it was insufficiently rigorous, and this proved decisive in the light of Britain's relative economic decline in the new more globalised market economy (Morgan, 2014).

Such were the tensions surrounding the new Curriculum that David Pascall, a manager at BP and chair of the National Curriculum Council, was called to review it almost immediately. Pascall's draft replacement, similar in tone to the Kingman Report (1988), states the prime purpose of English education is to enable children to 'master the basic skills' (DfE/WO, 1993: 71) to serve the needs of industry. It focuses on 'correct' (*ibid*) uses of English at the expense of personal growth. Recognised as too controversial amongst educationalists, it was shelved (Marshall, 2000; Gibbons, 2017).

The second National Curriculum (DfE/WO, 1995) was in response to Ron Dearing's *The National Curriculum and its Assessment: Final Report* (1994), known as the Dearing Review. Dearing had come from humble origins to become a career civil servant, Chancellor of the University of Nottingham and Chair of the School Curriculum and Assessment Authority. An economist, he has no obvious interest in English or expertise in education. While designed to placate educationalists – this revised Curriculum appears more 'humane' than Pascall (Gibbons, 2017: 69) – it is rather a watering-down of Pascall (even using identical wording in places) than a slimming down of Cox. Consultations with English teachers and subject bodies were summarily ignored, with the imposition of a list of authors from the English literary heritage (discussed further below) causing particular concern. The government was so keen to put its stamp on the Curriculum that it was prepared to antagonise the profession.

4.3 New Labour and Labour, 'raising standards', and creativity brought to the fore 1997–2010

4.3.1 Context: from All Our Futures to PISA and PIRLS

Tony Blair's New Labour party swept into government in 1997. It was a time of optimism: Blair was Britain's youngest Prime Minister for decades; the popularity of Cool Britannia made social and cultural waves; and the dot.com boom, on the back of the rise of the internet, was generating jobs and investment. New Labour aimed to create a 'learning society', realising the need in a post-manufacturing economy to move from a low-skill, low trust education system to a high-skills, high trust system (Morgan, 2014: 16). The theory was that social change could be promoted by ensuring more students met national standards and so be well-equipped for dynamic twenty-first-century employment.

At the same time, the increasing economic internationalisation of the 1990s saw education becoming increasingly globalised too, although there was no consensus about what education was for. While high-profile publications like *Education For All* (UNESCO, 1990) and the Delors Report (1996) promoted a humanist education relevant to the priorities of society, two new international league tables – the Programme for International Student Assessment (PISA) and Progress in International Reading Literacy Study (PIRLS) – altered the landscape by effectively marketising education, positioning countries as competitors in a global field rather than united in a global collaborative endeavour. Now, not only were Britain's schools compared with each other (which was pressure enough for teachers), but with international rivals, raising the stakes even higher.

The New Labour government invested handsomely in education (annual spending rose by an average of 5.4% across Blair's premiership (Gillard, 2018)), but some policy decisions sat in uneasy tension with each other. They considered radical reforms. One idea was to make a clean break from traditional subject-based education in favour of an alternative model such as recognition theory, which sees knowledge as having many forms and questions *which* knowledges are most worthy (Facer and Thomas, 2012). Another was to look at revising the curriculum and assessment structure for 14–19-year-olds: the resulting Tomlinson Report (2004) recommended wholesale changes and was endorsed by schools and universities (McKendrick, 2004). However, in both cases (and others), the government concluded that such change would have been too great a leap and risked being unpopular with Labour traditionalists and the (small c) conservative electorate (Aldrich, 2005; Baker, 2005). The systemic status quo thus remained unchallenged.

Another tension during this period was the active encouragement for – yet simultaneous constraint of – a revised brand of creativity in education. On one hand, *All Our Futures: Creativity, Culture and Education* (NACCCE, 1999), commissioned by Education Secretary, David Blunkett, strongly promoted a problem-solving, collaborative view of creativity, as described in Chapter 1. Its publication both reflected the growing understanding of the importance of developing a creative workforce and triggered a revived interest in creative teaching and creative learning (Burnard, 2006; Dymoke, 2011), although it was contested in some quarters; the *Creative Partnerships* programme (also described in Chapter 1) is another example of an ambitious but flawed initiative.

On the other hand, while creativity was ostensibly encouraged for learners, the climate for teachers became *less* creative. The new Curriculum (DfEE/QCA, 1999a) – the first under New Labour – far from enabling teachers to return to professional autonomy, was accompanied by the controversial National Strategies (DfEE, 1998), with prescriptive content that laid down not only what should be taught but *how*. Cox was among the many critics of the prescriptivism of the Strategies, suggesting that teachers would be repelled by having to teach 'mechanistic skills' rather than what they came into the profession to do: develop students' 'creative imagination and an open mind resistant to propaganda' (1998 *in* Gillard, 2018, n.p.). Thus, despite promising creativity, the government was less than creative in its own practice, becoming instead increasingly controlling.

4.3.2 The third National Curriculum (DfEE/QCA, 1999a): creativity becomes official

This third Curriculum, published two years after New Labour's election and in the same year as *All Our Futures*, focuses on developing skills needed for the workplace to drive Britain's economy. The very first line of the general Foreword (applying to all subjects, not just English) promises that the Curriculum will 'raise standards' (DfEE/QCA, 1999a: 3). Interestingly, although 'raising standards' appears first in Pascall's proposals (DfE/WO, 1993: iii) it was not included in the subsequent Curriculum (DfE/WO, 1995); yet here a phrase from an ultra-Conservative source becomes official Labour policy, an indication of the complex nature of the shifting in the debate about the purpose of education, beyond party lines. The idea of raising standards is not necessarily contentious (Ken Robinson jokes, 'after all, who would want to lower them?' (2008, n.p.)), but it is a decisive moving away from 'the personal development of the individual child' (Cox, 1989: 59), and indicates how education had become aligned with national economic well-being. The implication was that if 'standards' are raised, so would 'prosperity' (NACCCE, 1999: 5).

The Foreword continues by laying out the Curriculum's aims:

> [T]o ensure that pupils develop from an early age the essential [...] skills they need to learn; to provide them with a guaranteed, full and rounded entitlement to learning; to foster their creativity; and to give teachers discretion to find the best ways to inspire in their pupils a joy and commitment to learning that will last a lifetime.
>
> (DfEE/QCA, 1999a: 3)

Here the term 'creativity' is brought to the fore explicitly for the first time in a National Curriculum. This is the notion of creativity as expressed in *All Our Futures*: 'imaginative activity fashioned so as to produce outcomes that are both original and of value' (NACCCE, 1999: 30) – an outcomes-oriented notion of creativity is associated with raising standards. This is not to say that personal growth is entirely forgotten: there is the wish for students to find 'joy' and, a few pages later, English is said to contribute to learners' spiritual development by enabling them to 'explore and reflect on their own and others' inner life' (DfEE/QCA, 1999a: 8), perhaps an element of personal growth by another name. Yet it is perhaps 'joy' tethered to 'commitment to learning' that is the goal here, less joy in learning for learning's sake, more practising the virtue of working hard, given the emphasis on 'essential skills' assessment, attainment and employment opportunities in the surrounding text.

The fourth Curriculum (DfES/QCA, 2004) is a re-publication of the 1999 version, identical in subject content but with a greater emphasis on developing skills through cross-curricularity. Since there are no changes to English Orders, it does not constitute a separate document for the purposes of this book.

4.3.3 The fifth National Curriculum (DCSF/QCA, 2007): creativity as key concept

The publication of the next Curriculum (DSCF/QCA, 2007) coincided with Gordon Brown taking over from Blair as Labour Prime Minister (he dropped the 'New'). Drawing even more explicitly on the arguments for creative teaching and learning outlined in *All Our Futures*, it was promised that this Curriculum would ensure that all learners were 'actively and imaginatively engaged in their learning' (Jewell, 2007). Creativity is made prominent across subjects.

In English, 'Creativity' is given status as one of the four Key Concepts, alongside 'Competence', 'Cultural understanding' and 'Critical understanding' (DCSF/QCA, 2007: 62).[4] To spell out exactly how it was to be understood, a definition is provided, accompanied by an 'Explanatory note' in the margin. According to *this* Curriculum, creativity is concerned with:

a   *Making fresh connections between ideas, experiences, texts and words, drawing on a rich experience of language and literature.*
b   *Using inventive approaches to making meaning, taking risks, playing with language and using it to create new effects.*

c   *Using imagination to convey themes, ideas and arguments, solve problems, and create settings, moods and characters.*

d   *Using creative approaches to answering questions, solving problems and developing ideas.*

> <u>Explanatory note</u>: Pupils show creativity when they make unexpected connections, use striking and original phrases or images, approach tasks from a variety of starting points, or change forms to surprise and engage the reader. Creativity can be encouraged by providing purposeful opportunities for pupils to experiment, build on ideas or follow their own interests. Creativity in English extends beyond narrative and poetry to other forms and uses of language. It is essential in allowing pupils to progress to higher levels of understanding and become independent.
>
> (2007: 62)

The adjectives stand out: 'fresh', 'rich', 'inventive', 'new', 'unexpected', 'striking', 'original' – a semantic field conveying value in novelty, risk-taking and discovery. The verbs suggest energy, fun and an appetite for change: 'make', 'play', 'engage', 'surprise'. Enjoyment is clearly allied to achievement and fulfilment, as it is in *All Our Futures*. The serious justification for creativity in the Curriculum is nailed home in the final sentence of the Explanatory note: creativity is 'essential' for students to make progress.

However, as we will see, analysis of the Programmes of Study suggests that despite this apparent emphasis, the English orders allow for little creativity. This inherent contradiction is discussed in depth below, but is hinted at in the definition above: the Explanatory note refers to how creativity is shown when learners 'surprise and engage *the reader*' (my emphasis), as if creative work is manifested only through writing.

4.4 Coalition and the conservatives: the revival of knowledge and skills 2010–

4.4.1 Context: changing gear: Michael Gove

Despite the public investment under (New) Labour, classroom time expended, and the consistent increase in the number of students getting high GCSE grades, Britain's PISA scores remained relatively static (White, 2012) and Britain's relative GDP continued to trail behind those of USA and Germany (Conway, 2015). Thus, when Conservative Michael Gove became Education Secretary on the election of the Coalition government in 2010, he could point to these statistics as evidence that the problem-solving, collaborative, practical skills view of creativity that had been writ large in education discourse had failed, at least by these markers, and claim that Labour's approach was not working.

Energetic and driven, Gove launched a wholescale programme of educational change. Although he retained – and even strengthened – some Labour policies (including academisation and performance measures), he was ambitious to change the National Curriculum as quickly as possible. Gove positioned himself as the champion of a knowledge-rich curriculum based on EH Hirsch's arguments for cultural literacy and Michael Young's concept of 'powerful knowledge' (Abrams, 2012; Morgan, 2014). Rather than being concerned with personal development, or fitting a child with the creative, flexible skills to forge unique human relationships as advocated by Biesta (2006), Gove's mission was to increase learners' access to employment through providing them with specifically sanctioned 'powerful' sets of knowledge and ideas that would, in theory, level the playing field for those lacking 'cultural capital'.

Gove's reading of Young is perhaps a mis-reading. For example, Gove advocates teaching a *permanent* body of knowledge, seemingly ignorant of Young's recognition that powerful knowledge is flexible according to need (Burns, 2018) and far from recognising that culture and knowledge are continually remade (Gadamer, 1975/2004; Biesta and Osberg, 2008). An indication of how Hirsch and Young's ideas were over-simplified is the apparent contradiction within the terms of reference provided to the expert panel commissioned to develop the sixth Curriculum: schools were to be given 'greater freedom over the curriculum' yet also ensure children 'acquire a core of knowledge in the key subject disciplines' (DfE, 2012: n.p.): the aim seems to have been simultaneously to liberate schools from the constraints of a prescriptive curriculum yet *also* require learners to acquire a body of fixed 'knowledge', the success of which was to be measured by newly revised GCSEs that were more prescriptive than ever.

Indicators of Gove's determination to push his faith in powerful knowledge is the privileging of STEM subjects over the arts and humanities, despite the creative industries being one of Britain's strongest exports (British Council, 2010; Last, 2017); and the controversial withdrawing of the popular A Level in Creative Writing, deemed insufficiently rigorous (Taylor, 2015). His zeal also led to a nationalist focus, perhaps influenced by a growing disillusionment towards the European Union within some quarters of the Conservative party. For example, he stipulated that the powerful knowledge required in the History curriculum should be Britain's 'island story', to the disquiet of History teachers (Bowen *et al.*, 2012).

Gove brushed aside criticism from educationists, writers, subject bodies and other influential voices, including three of the four members of his own expert advisory panel who urged him to take the middle ground (Mansell, 2012); he ignored the advice of the business community who called for creativity and the so-called soft skills of speaking and listening to be prioritised (Wintour, 2012). The authors of the new National Curriculum were carefully chosen to fit their text to Gove's vision. Their names were kept secret, a very different approach to the careful gathering of experts and consultation that had led to the development of previous key English policy documents.

4.4.2 *The sixth national curriculum (DfE, 2013/2014): creativity expurgated*

Given this context, the published aims from the introduction (applicable to all subjects) of the resulting sixth Curriculum (DfE, 2014) raise interesting questions:

> The national curriculum (sic) provides pupils with an introduction to the essential knowledge that they need to be educated citizens. It introduces pupils to the best that has been thought and said; and helps engender an appreciation of human creativity and achievement.
>
> (DfE, 2014: 5)

We are taken from the prosaic 'essential knowledge' of the first sentence to the grandiose 'the best that has been thought and said' of the second. The direct quotation from *Culture and Anarchy* (Arnold, 1869) is unacknowledged. Whose view of 'best' is assumed? The syntax makes ambiguous whether it is to be understood that 'essential knowledge' *is* 'the best that has been thought and said', or additional to it. The final phrase, separated from the main clause by a clumsy semi-colon, is unclear: pupils are to *appreciate* 'human creativity', not *be* creative (and why the redundant 'human', especially when there is no other allusion to humanity or the humane?). Is 'achievement' a result of 'creativity' or independent of it? Is a connection assumed between 'knowledge' and 'creativity and achievement', implying that creativity is somehow subsumed within 'knowledge', or not? This is significant because, in a curriculum that goes on to promote 'knowledge' extensively (the term appears a further 78 times in its 100 pages, with 20 references within the English orders), 'creativity' is absent entirely from the English orders[5] (Smith, 2019: 262).

This is followed by two short paragraphs promoting the importance of numeracy across the curriculum. Mathematics is positioned as a precondition of 'success' (DfE, 2014: 9), while the very next page then positions Language and Literacy as the means of 'access' to the curriculum (2014: 10). This juxtaposition of two words with the suffix '-cess' is striking. Coupled with the emphasis on STEM subjects and the demotion of the humanities, the implicit message is that English is the service subject, providing *access*, while mathematics, necessary for *success*, takes one higher. It is a long way from Cox's suggestion that while English provides access to the wider curriculum, leaners' understanding of English is therein symbiotically reinforced: 'There is much in the structured thinking, the imagination and the symbolism in mathematics and science and in other subjects that can extend the pupil's capability in English' (Cox, 1989: 54).

The Curriculum next attempts to justify the paradoxically crucial yet subordinate position of Language and Literacy: 'older pupils should be taught the meaning of instruction verbs that they may meet in examination questions' (DfE, 2014: 11). None of the previous Curricula refers to this banal truism. It implies that learners be taught to read and write *in order that* their reading and writing can be tested, thus obliquely suggesting that the purpose of education is to meet economic rather than humane aims.

The suggestion from these references to Language and Literacy that English is primarily a service subject is strengthened in the opening sentence of the Purpose of Study for English: 'English has a pre-eminent place *in education* and in society' (DfE, 2013: 2, my emphasis).[6] It continues:

> A high-quality education in English will teach pupils to speak and write fluently so that they can communicate their ideas and emotions to others and through their reading and listening, others can communicate with them. Through reading in particular, pupils have a chance to develop culturally, emotionally, intellectually, socially and spiritually. Literature, especially, plays a key role in such development. Reading also enables pupils both to acquire knowledge and to build on what they already know. All the skills of language are essential to participating fully as a member of society; pupils, therefore, who do not learn to speak, read and write fluently and confidently are effectively disenfranchised.
>
> (DfE, 2013: 2)

There is the shadow of negativity in this statement that is absent from its predecessors. The phrase 'high-quality' is used when it is surely self-evident. (Perhaps this is a veiled criticism of previous curriculum documents, or of teachers.) Literature is a tool to develop a range of intelligences (listed here in alphabetical order, presumably to avoid privileging one over the others) rather than a source of pleasure; reading is reduced to a means of acquiring knowledge. While the message that those who cannot communicate well are 'effectively disenfranchised' is ultimately similar to that of the previous Curriculum (DCSF/QCA, 2007) in emphasising the necessity of equipping students with English in order to participate in society, the deficit tone of the 2013 version is cold in comparison, reminiscent of Kingman (1988), although perhaps that is the point.

4.5 Towards the dismantling of unitary English

Sections 4.3–4.5 combine to indicate that, as successive governments took an increasingly active role in education policy, secondary English over the life of the National Curriculum suffered pressure as never before. Thirty years ago, the inner workings of the Department for Education were said to be a secret garden,[7] managed by experienced civil servants, into which no senior politician would dare enter (Donoghue, 2008). It has since become familiar territory to them, whatever their level of educational expertise.[8] This level of party-political interest, combined with a changing employment environment, local and international economic factors, and a newly competitive international educational field, created a complex context in which creativity is a pawn. While 'creativity' became recognised by some as valuable, different constituencies tried to harness specific elements to serve short-termist ends, and failed to do so. Gove, perhaps thereby suspicious of creativity, dismissed it, although it is ironic that he saw creative products of the past – cultural capital – as so important.

The second half of this chapter now examines the impact this context has had on how creativity is (and is not) manifested in the English Programmes of Study of the various National Curriculum orders. It explores how Speaking and Listening, Reading and Writing are each positioned, with particular focus on how creativity is presented and valued in each case. It explores how far the child-centred, personal-growth view of creativity that is the hallmark of the earlier documents is maintained in each of the three areas. To recap, the respective foci are the recognition of spoken non-Standard as well as spoken Standard English; reading for pleasure, with the learner choosing their own reading matter, and acknowledgement of the association between reading for pleasure and creative outputs; and opportunities for imaginative and expressive writing as a means through which children can explore their own and broader ideas.

4.5.1 The death of dialect and rise of spoken standard English

All the Curriculum documents agree and emphasise that an ability to use spoken Standard English fluently, accurately and with confidence is essential (as did the documents covered in Chapters 2 and 3). What is of interest here is whether and how the documents *also* recognise, celebrate and encourage the use of dialect, since this is an important indicator of the value each Curriculum puts on personal identity and, accordingly, the personal growth view of creativity.

Table 4.1 summarises the history. It shows that while Cox (1989) recognises the importance of a child's dialect being seen as valid as Standard English (both may be used in the classroom, with the child taught to use either *as appropriate*), reference to dialect is markedly reduced in next version (DfE/WO, 1995); by 1999 (DfEE/QCA), dialect is effectively outlawed and Standard (or 'formal') English expected. Dialect never returns, even in the 2007 Curriculum (DCSF/QCA) which heavily promotes 'creativity'. This suggests a change of direction, a different understanding of creativity.

Table 4.1 The death of dialect and the rise of standard spoken English

Number and Date	Key Ideas & Themes	Content/References
1. Cox, 1989	Identifies Speaking and Listening as the first Attainment Target; acknowledges the importance of Standard English (SE) in certain contexts. Importance of dialect in one's personal identity; the relation between this and personal growth. Active teaching/ celebration of dialect. SE not expected/ required by young learners.	• 'The development of pupils' ability to understand written and spoken Standard English and to produce written Standard English is unquestionably a responsibility of the English curriculum.' (1989: 67, emphasis original) • Presents SE as (merely) a 'dialect' and marker of class (1989: 11). • States non-standard dialect is not 'sub-standard'; warns of danger to 'self-esteem and motivation... by indiscriminate "correction" of dialect forms' (1989: 11). • Recommends teachers actively discuss when SE might and might not be used; children should be actively encouraged to use SE when 'necessary and helpful' (1989: 11), noting that SE is 'particularly likely to be required in public, formal settings' (1989: 18). • States (in bold) SE is included in levels of speaking and listening attainment 'wherever appropriate' (1989: 13) from level 7 upwards (i.e. expected attainment of average 15-year old). • States oral assessment should not be subject to social or cultural bias; is emphatic it is not the school's place to enforce Received Pronunciation (RP).
2. DfE/WO, 1995	SE positioned as superior and preferred.	• Removes designation of SE as a 'dialect', implying superiority of SE. • Requires formal language is given a more prominent position, albeit with 'appropriate sensitivity' (1995: 5). • Use of SE at younger age: pupils should 'begin to be aware of Standard English' to achieve level 3 (expected attainment of eight-year-old).
3 & 4. DfEE/QCA, 1999a (and 2004)	Speech for public life takes precedence over the private and personal. Emphasis on formality and conforming.	• Prime aim of the Speaking and Listening at KS3: to 'develop confidence in speaking... for *public and formal purposes*' (1999: 31, my emphasis). • Students should 'use the vocabulary, structures and grammar of spoken standard English fluently and accurately in informal and formal situations' (1999: 32).
5. DCSF/QCA, 2007	Apparent return to acceptance of non-standard forms... ... yet 'formal' talk trumps informal; emphasis on collaborative rather than personal talk.	• '[P]upils should be taught to 'vary vocabulary, structures and grammar to convey meaning, *including* speaking standard English fluently' (2007: 64, my emphasis). • Range and Content: 'prepared, formal presentations and debates...; informal group or pair discussions; individual and group improvisation and performance; devising, wscripting and performing plays' (2007: 69).

(continued)

Table 4.1 The death of dialect and the rise of standard spoken English *(continued)*

Number and Date	Key Ideas & Themes	Content/References
6. DfE, 2014	Attainment target renamed 'Spoken Language' and demoted below Reading and Writing; renewed emphasis on formal language. Sole allusion to dialect is regarding grammatical awareness.	• 'Listening' disappears. • Pupils should be taught 'using Standard English confidently in a range of formal and informal contexts…'; 'giving short speeches and presentations…'; 'participating in formal debates and structured discussions'); 'improvising, rehearsing and performing play scripts and poetry' (2014: 17). • Knowledge of grammar and vocabulary can be consolidated through 'analysing differences… between Standard English and *other varieties* of English' (2014: 19, my emphasis).

Cox (1989) begins by stressing that Standard English is non-negotiable, using bold type to emphasise the point. However, implicitly recalling Newbolt's argument that children should be 'bi-lingual' (1921: 67), he goes on to stress that Standard English is itself merely a dialect form, as valuable as the child's own dialect, and *both* dialects are subject to change. He recognises personal dialect as part of child's identity; he admonishes those tempted to 'correct' dialect forms, aware that a child's growth *in* school is dependent on the language they bring *to* school. Further, he suggests that alertness to the differences between dialects enables children to become proficient and critical users of language. Perhaps to win over those who value the traditional literary canon and might otherwise baulk at the promotion of dialect forms, he reminds us that dialects are found in 'folk songs, poetry, dialogue in novels or plays' (Cox, 1989: 18). In other words, both Standard English and dialect have a place in the classroom – it is the teacher's responsibility to help the child recognise which to use when.

Yet these arguments do not convince his successors: the second Curriculum (DfE/ WO, 1995) does not ignore dialect but, by removing the designation of Standard English as a dialect form, strongly implies its superiority; also, learners are required to use Standard English from a younger age. The third Curriculum tries to sidestep the issue by changing the labels: 'formal' (DfEE/QCA, 1999a: 31) language replaces 'Standard English'. Interestingly, 'formal' language should be used even in 'informal' (DfEE/QCA, 1999a: 32) situations. The term 'dialect' disappears for good. Alongside this, Drama, previously positioned as a means of developing self-expression (Cox, 1989) is given a skills-centred makeover as a means of exploring ideas and issues (DfEE/ QCA 1999a: 32). Thus, despite *All Our Futures* (NACCCE, 1999) actively promoting creative, collaborative, risk-taking oracy for economic ends, this Curriculum focuses on developing workplace skills and promoting conformity, in tune with its objective of raising standards and elevating the socially disenfranchised: in theory, if everybody speaks Standard English, there is no divide.

The 2007 Curriculum (DCSF/QCA, 2007), with 'Creativity' as one of its four pillars, is slightly less rigid, with fewer references to 'formal', and a range of opportunities given for collaborative talk, including Drama, which arguably accords with the risk-taking, experimental theme of *All Our Futures*. However, dialect is not resurfaced, and the scope for creative speaking and listening seems somewhat limited. The suggested activities appear designed to hone workplace-style skills: 'formal presentations and debates' (DCSF/QCA, 2007: 69) top the list, demonstrating a continued sense of economic imperative; and there is little to foster personal growth.

The 2014 Curriculum (DfE, 2014) is starker. Standard English only is required. Dialect is recognised only in the requirement to analyse the grammatical differences between Standard English and 'other varieties', with no suggestion of these 'other varieties'' intimate association with a place or the personal, and despite new evidence that proves groundless any fears that non-Standard speech translates to non-Standard written English (Snell and Cushing, 2022). The examples of language for classroom practice are almost all in formal contexts: there appears little room for experimentation or personal talk. In the same vein, 'Drama' is restricted to studying the work of dramatists at KS3 (DfE, 2013) and not mentioned at KS4 (DfE, 2014). 'Listening' is also omitted from this Curriculum, raising questions about whether English is still perceived as a subject that fosters humane relationships. This all suggests different understandings of educational rigour and of how to promote social justice; and an increasing need by the government to control the Curriculum.

In other words, while Cox (1989) encouraged child-centred, personal talk, the 1995 and 1999 Curricula offer successively fewer opportunities, which has serious ramifications for the promotion of creativity. It is striking that even the 2007 version that expressly includes creativity includes relatively little encouragement of creative talk. The current Curriculum (DfE, 2014) distances itself from active, creative classroom talk, concentrating instead entirely on the development of formal spoken English.

4.5.2 *Reading for pleasure becomes reading for learning*

This gradual privileging of formal language use is equally discernible across Reading and Writing. All the Curriculum documents agree that learning to read fluently is crucial for success in education and life beyond. Each also asserts the importance of reading canonical English literature – all six explicitly name Shakespeare, Dickens and Wordsworth, for instance. The question is whether such literature is *recommended* or *required* in each Curriculum, whether there are opportunities for the inclusion of modern and diverse literature, and how far reading for pleasure is encouraged simultaneously. The policy documents explored in Chapters 2 and 3 are unanimous in emphasising that creative personal growth is bound up with reading pleasure and freedom of choice – ideas echoed and endorsed by Cox (1989) – but some subsequent Curricula suggest a more ambiguous attitude to reading for pleasure. Their focus on reading skills for learning and defined lists of English texts arguably limit range and choice.

Table 4.2 summarises the story.

For Cox, reading is all about enjoyment. He coins the term the 'pleasure principle' (1989: 20): reading is its own reward. Yet he makes clear that pleasure from reading is not trivial or light-weight: it is the pleasure that comes from immersing oneself in a range of cultures, traditions and histories; from experiencing emotions vicariously and coming to sympathetic understanding; from expanding oneself 'emotionally, aesthetically and

Table 4.2 Reading for pleasure becomes reading for learning

	Key Ideas & Themes	Content/References
1. Cox (1989)	Reading as pleasure, nourishing personal growth; child-centred. Non-prescriptive. Forward-looking.	• Coins term 'pleasure principle' (1989: 20); states reading gives 'fundamental satisfaction' (1989: 20). • Books develop child 'emotionally, aesthetically and intellectually' (*ibid*); importance of 'personal response' (1989: 30); 'children construct the world through story' (1989: 94). • 'Creative' (1989: 95) approaches to class novel are *'central means* of enriching the curriculum' (*ibid*, my emphasis); 'Too much concentration on set texts for assessment purposes can turn pupils against reading' (1989: 20). • Declines to provide list of texts – 'wrong' (1989: 96). • Need for broad range/choice in class/school libraries (including media and IT texts).
2. DfE/WO, 1995	List of texts introduced, but continues to value personal response.	• Follows Pascal (DfE/WO, 1993) in providing list of texts 'from the English literary heritage in previous centuries' that pupils 'should' (1995: 20) read (with a note that Welsh schools can offer works by Welsh authors writing in English), as well as 'major writers' of unspecified nationality writing before and after 1900. Named male writers (52) outnumber female (10) by 5:1; all are white. • Encouraging reading for pleasure is of prime importance. • Pupils to 'respond imaginatively and intellectually' (1995: 19).
3 & 4. DfEE/QCA, 1999a, 2004	Increased formality; reading is for study. Workaday tone. Broader lists of texts	• Reading should be for 'understanding and appreciation' (1999: 34). • Use of verbs (in sequence, 'extract meaning', 'analyse', 'discuss', 'identify') suggest development of cross-curricular skills is priority; only a marginal comment states that pupils should read 'for pleasure and study' (*ibid*). • Texts should be drawn from the 'English literary heritage', including two novels and two poets published before 1914 taken from prescribed lists (including Oscar Wilde); plus major writers post-1914 including 'recent and contemporary', literature written 'by major writers from different cultures and traditions' (1999: 36), and non-fiction and non-literary texts, with examples offered. Combining the pre- and post-1914 lists, named male writers (120) outnumber women (36) roughly 4:1.

Table 4.2 Reading for pleasure becomes reading for learning *(continued)*

	Key Ideas & Themes	Content/References
5. DCSF/QCA, 2007	Reading for pleasure promoted in opening statement, but Orders imply emphasis on skills and understanding rather than pleasure. KS3- and KS4- 'appropriate' lists presented separately. Explicit reference to culture and identity. Improved gender balance.	• Opening statement: 'Pupils learn to become enthusiastic and critical readers of stories, poetry and drama as well as non-fiction and media texts, gaining access to the pleasure and world of knowledge that reading offers' (2007: 61). • Verbs in sequence: 'extract and interpret', 'infer and deduce', 'understand', 'select and compare', 'assess', 'recognise and discuss' (2007: 65). • Texts should be 'high quality' and 'have influenced culture and thinking' (2007: 70); references 'appeal and importance' of English literary heritage, as well as 'qualities and distinctiveness' of texts from other cultures/traditions (2007: 71); specifies that texts should 'be informed by the cultural context of the school' and 'help pupils explore their sense of identity' (ibid); stresses need for countries & cultures to be presented in texts 'sensitively and with understanding' (2007: 95). • Combining all KS3 and KS4 lists, named male writers (142) outnumber women (59), but by less than 3:1.
6. DfE, 2014	Endorses love of reading while strongly promoting English literary heritage. Names of specific authors (except Shakespeare) are removed	• Aims include developing pupils' 'love' of literature 'through widespread reading for enjoyment'; ensure they 'read easily, fluently and with good understanding... for both pleasure and information' (2013: 2). • At KS3, 'wide range of fiction and non-fiction', including 'high-quality works', two plays by Shakespeare and 'seminal world literature' (2013: 4) • At KS4, 'Pupils should be taught to: read and appreciate the depth and power of the English literary heritage... understand and critically evaluate texts... [and] make an informed personal response' (2014: 5). • Requires 'high-quality, challenging, classic literature and extended literary non-fiction' (2014: 5), focusing on English C19th-C21st texts and poetry since 1789.

intellectually' (1989: 20). It is through such experience that the 'inward' and 'outward' (1989: 60) child can truly grow. Like the Blue Books (BoE, 1905–1959), Newbolt (1921) and Bullock (1975), he recommends children should be free to choose their own reading matter from a broad choice, with a teacher guiding them to increasingly challenging material if necessary. He explains clearly why prescribed texts are to be avoided in the classroom, arguing that there is 'no consensus on which works should be chosen from the vast riches of written English' and that understandings of what be considered 'great works' might 'change radically during the course of time' (1989: 96); instead, he trusts teachers to choose the texts studied. He provides an Appendix of detailed list of active, creative, collaborative approaches to a class novel, since reading together in turn encourages further independent reading that enables learners to flourish across the curriculum and in areas associated with creativity – personal growth, humane understandings.

Whilst encouraging reading for pleasure, the second Curriculum takes Pascall's cue (DfE/WO, 1993) and introduces mandatory lists of 'major works of literature from the English literary heritage' (DfE/WO, 1995: 20) from which teachers should select, ostensibly to support learners be discriminating. It is a limited offering: male writers substantially outnumber women; all are white British (or Irish), ignoring international writers in English or in translation. Potentially controversial figures such as Oscar Wilde are excluded, presumably to avoid contravening Section 28, the infamous clause in a 1988 Local Government Act that banned the promotion of homosexuality in schools. It is difficult to argue that such an offer is humane if a significant body of humanity is missing. Although this Curriculum recommends activities that 'emphasise the interest and pleasure of reading' (1995: 20) rather than line-by-line study, the introduction of the lists reduces both choice for the child and agency of the teacher, curtailing creative opportunities.

The lists remain in the 1999 version, although with greater range and arguably offering increased scope: there is a greater proportion of women, global majority writers in English ('different cultures and traditions') are included and Oscar Wilde is permitted. However, the focus is now on reading *skills* rather than reading pleasure, indicating a change in tone. Rather than encouraging children to delight in the written word, reading becomes a tool for study. Ironically, the Preface of the glossy 1999 publication (DfEE/QCA, 1999a) presents quotations from prominent and diverse writers on 'The importance of English' (see Figure 4.1). Collectively they promote a personal growth view: these authors would baulk at the notion that readers were merely to 'extract meaning' (1999: 34) from their work.

The story is more nuanced in the fifth (2007) Curriculum. It appears liberal in its list of recommended authors – the widest, richest, most gender-balanced and diverse to date – and states that learners should become 'enthusiastic' readers for pleasure (2007: 61), recommending 'film resources and drama activities' (2007: 71) to engage them. However, the foregrounded verbs such as 'extract' and 'interpret' (while of course not antipathetic to pleasure, and important to literary study) could indicate that an atomistic, skills-based approach to reading is promoted.

The current Curriculum too aims to promote a 'love' (DfE, 2013: 2) of literature, celebrate the English literary heritage's 'depth and power' (*ibid*) – adjectives with perhaps triumphalist and nationalist connotations – and enable students to practice the skills necessary to access the wider curriculum. By dispensing with lists of recommended authors, choice appears much greater at KS3: the only requirement is to study two complete Shakespeare texts. Yet the challenging requirements of KS4 that include the study for examination of at least one Victorian novel, a play by Shakespeare and Romantic poetry effectively often results in schools treating KS3 as a proto-KS4 (Smith, 2020b); literature other than Shakespeare experienced by many secondary leaners all postdates 1789; and while 'seminal world literature' (2013: 3) is required at KS3, the exclusive English literary heritage diet at KS4 does little to include students who come from backgrounds adversely impacted by British colonialism. The 2019 PISA data

Without English, nothing. And without good English,

nothing very well.

Anne Fine, Author

English is the language of the future, the language of the

computer. English is the most important tool you'll ever

need, no matter what career you choose. You have the right

to English. Make it your right!

Benjamin Zephaniah, Poet, Writer, Actor, TV & Radio Presenter

A good book, studied with a good English teacher, takes you

on a journey in search of answers to the crucial questions in

life you didn't even know you wanted (or needed) to ask.

Professor Lisa Jardine, Queen Mary & Westfield College, University of London

Studying English literature at school was my first, and

probably my biggest, step towards mental freedom and

independence. It was like falling in love with life.

Ian McEwan, Novelist

Figure 4.1 The importance of English (DfEE/QCA, 1999a: 15)

(Videbaek, 2020) confirms that reading for pleasure has declined markedly amongst secondary students over the life of this Curriculum.

In short, whereas Cox explicitly counsels against prescription and over-concentration on set texts, subsequent Curricula gradually cement prescription to the extent that students today have little opportunity in school to read anything *but* complex required reading – even those Curricula that state that reading for pleasure should be encouraged. The result of this 'planned enculturation' (Biesta and Osberg, 2008: 316) is that the culture they are exposed to is narrow and creativity is stymied. Learners who are not free to grow their own reading are limited in the extent to which they can grow their own thinking and writing too.

4.5.3 The 'genrification' of creative writing

All the Curricula require learners to experience a range of writing opportunities. They agree that it is through writing that learning across the curriculum is made manifest – writing 'stores information' (Cox, 1989: 33) – and being able to write clearly and

Table 4.3 The gradual 'genrification' of creative writing

	Key Ideas & Themes	Content/References
1. Cox, 1989	Value is in the writing process as much as than polished product; positions writing as facilitator of learning and thinking.	• Writing positioned as both private, having 'cognitive function' in clarifying thought, and public/for an audience, 'storing both information and literary works' (1989: 33). • Divides writing into 'composition' and 'secretarial skills'; composing is 'obviously by far the more important' (1989: 36); agrees with Kingman that 'old-fashioned grammar teaching' is ineffective – grammar should not be at expense of 'subjective, creative, personal and expressive' (1989: 66). • 'Well-structured and interesting' (albeit inaccurate) preferable to 'badly structured and boring' but accurate (1989: 33). Suggests 80/20 composition/accuracy split for purposes of assessment. • 'The best writing is vigorous, committed, honest and interesting'… which are 'vital qualities' of writing (1989: 37). • Language is central to the self: writing should be based on pupils' existing competences (1989: 84).
2. DfE/WO, 1995	Advocates enabling, supportive atmosphere.	• Encourages broad range of writing opportunities, including children's 'own distinctive and original styles, recognising the importance of commitment and vitality in what they write' (1995: 23). • Opportunities for 'aesthetic and imaginative' (*ibid*) writing top the list of writing styles. • Writing should be 'neat and legible', pupils should be 'helped' to increase their spelling and 'encouraged' to use the 'grammatical, lexical and orthographic' features of SE (1995: 23/4). • Terms including 'appropriate', 'imaginative', 'thoughtful' and 'developed' far more frequent than 'accurate', 'correct', *etc.*
3 & 4. DfEE/ QCA, 1999	Introduces writing triplets: expressive writing takes precedence. Hierarchy indicates composition is valued over secretarial skills. Suggests the personal is recognised.	• Knowledge, Skills & Understanding • 1) 'Composition' is: 　"Writing to imagine, explore, entertain 　Writing to inform, explain, describe 　Writing to persuade, argue, advise 　Writing to analyse, review, comment" 　*followed by*: 2) Planning and Drafting; 3) Punctuation, 4) Spelling, 5) Handwriting and Presentation, 6) Standard English (DfEE/ QCA 1999a: 37–38). • Breadth of Study: 'The range of purposes for writing should… focus […] on creative, aesthetic and literary uses of language. The forms for such writing should be drawn from different kinds of stories, poems, playscripts, autobiographies, screenplays, diaries' (*ibid*: 39). • Audience for writing should include 'specific, known readers, a large, unknown readership *and the pupils themselves*' (1999: 39, my emphasis).

Table 4.3 The gradual 'genrification' of creative writing *(continued)*

	Key Ideas & Themes	Content/References
5. DCSF/QCA, 2007	Promotes Creativity through composition above the Competence of secretarial skills.	• Includes 23 'composition' processes, including (at KS3) requirement to: • a) write clearly and coherently, including an appropriate level of detail; • b) write imaginatively, creatively and thoughtfully, producing texts that interest and engage the reader; • c) generate and harness new ideas and develop them in their writing; … • f) use imaginative vocabulary and varied linguistic and literary techniques to achieve particular effects (DCSF/QCA, 2007: 67; itemisation original). • Not until items (t) to (w), under a sub-heading of *Technical Accuracy*, are Standard English, grammar and spelling found. • Range and Content: Learners should: 'a) develop ideas, themes, imagery, settings and/or characters when writing to imagine, explore and entertain' (*ibid*: 72); 'stories, poems, playscripts' (*ibid*) are listed first of the 23 genres.
6. DfE, 2014	Foregrounds examination-specific writing skills; grammatical knowledge and accuracy now top priority. Formal genres take precedence over imaginative, expressive genres	• Pupils 'should be taught to write formal and academic essays *as well as* writing imaginatively' (2014: 14, my emphasis). • 'It is important that pupils learn the correct grammatical terms in English' (*ibid*). • Pupils should be taught to 'write accurately, fluently, effectively and at length' (2014: 16). • List of suggested genres starts with the 'formal expository' essays; 'Stories, scripts, poetry and other imaginative writing' are at the bottom (*ibid*). • Repeated references to Standard English. • Separate section on Grammar and Vocabulary (approximately 150 words) is almost as long as the Writing orders themselves (approximately 190 words); accompanied by dense 18-page glossary defining the knowledge deemed necessary.

accurately is essential for adulthood. But how is functional and formal writing positioned in relation to independent, expressive, exploratory writing – sometimes known as 'creative writing' – and what bearing does this have on creativity?

Given Cox's position on Speaking and Listening and Reading, it is not surprising that his Curriculum promotes such writing as a tool of personal growth. However, given that they moved *away* from Cox's recommendations on Speaking and Listening and Reading, it *is* perhaps surprising that the 1995, 1999 and 2007 Curricula notably *follow* Cox in promoting the practice of creative writing, as shown in Table 4.3. In contrast, the 2014 version deliberately changes direction by foregrounding transactional writing, particularly writing required for examinations, and 'Creative Writing' is entirely absent.

Cox is alone in making explicit the duality of writing. It is both a 'process' and a 'product' (1989: 35), having both a public and private function, the latter fostering personal growth through enabling thought and reflection. It is striking that this is the only Curriculum to draw attention to writing's function in 'storing... literary works' (1989: 33): writing is a reservoir of culture. Given his perspective on the importance of reading for pleasure, Cox is here implicitly connecting writing as product – a created text – with personal growth; he is also positioning learners as future authors. This intimate association between writing and growth is emphasised – 'lively', 'vigorous', 'vital' (1989: 37) – and encapsulates ideas expressed by Newbolt (1921), Plowden (1967) and Bullock (1975) concerning life, culture, creative development and genuine self-expression.

Cox does not use the term 'creative writing' (perhaps because *all* original writing is newly created?) but his perspective celebrates writing as a creative enterprise that can encapsulate the personal, the humane and the expressive. Grammar is at the service of writing, not an isolated goal. He is concerned with the production of precise, accurate writing, but recommends secretarial aspects be taught *alongside* composition: a slightly flawed medium should not denigrate the strength of the message.

The next three Curricula (DfE/WO, 1995 to DCSF/QCA, 2007) follow Cox by placing imaginative, descriptive and expressive writing at or near the top of their respective lists of required skills, while narrative or fictional writing is placed at or near the top of the list of required genres. The similarities in this patterning are striking and, I suggest, not coincidental. Even though the term 'creative' is not always used, creativity is given status through the pre-eminent positioning of words in the creative semantic field: 'aesthetic', 'imagine', 'explore'. This suggests an awareness of the prominent place of creativity in political and popular discourse in the 1990s and 2000s – creative writing is a visible product that speaks to popular understanding of what English is about – and a sense that promoting creative writing in this manner highlights the creative credentials of these Curricula. And, like Cox, the requirements for accurate grammar and spelling are near the bottom of these lists, indicating that while these technical elements are necessary, they are subservient to content.

However, while these Curricula apparently champion creative practice, changes to the GCSE specifications muddy the message. The approach to the GCSE assessment of writing changed markedly over this period: as anxieties about fairness and accountability increased (Beadle, 2014), so opportunities for 'vigorous, committed, honest and interesting' (Cox, 1989: 37) writing diminished. When the first National Curriculum was introduced in 1989 the assessment of creative writing at GCSE was very flexible – popular examination boards initially offered assessment entirely by teachers, internally and externally moderated. This allowed much creative freedom for both teachers and learners, but resulted in diverse products that were, arguably, difficult to compare and quantify with a grade, and became plagued with issues of plagiarism (Demopoulos, 2005; Beadle, 2014). Over the years reforms were made; creative writing was examined through classroom-based Controlled Assessment, but this too was prone to accusations of irregularity (Beadle, 2014). For my own children, completing GCSEs aligned with the 2007 Curriculum, 'creative writing' meant composing a draft, having it edited by their teacher, then memorising an 'improved' version to regurgitate in examination conditions. The 'Creativity' that is optimistically foregrounded in the 2007 Curriculum was perhaps more honoured in the breach than the observance.

The current Curriculum (DfE, 2014) foregrounds writing as a pragmatic skill necessary to service examinations across the curriculum. Reversing the balance between composition and secretarial skills, the focus is on accuracy and formality. It is interesting, then, given that 'creative writing' is not mentioned once by name and is barely alluded to in the Curriculum ('imaginative writing' is at the very bottom of the list of genres, the list being headed by 'formal expository essays'), that the GCSE English Language examination specifies a creative writing task. However, marks are allocated such that content and organisation of the 'creative' writing piece are worth less than overall 'technical accuracy' (AQA, 2018). Accordingly, as described in Chapter 1, some teachers err on the safe side, promoting accuracy over flair and imagination. Despite the examination boards counselling against 'over-preparing students with formulaic methods', preferring 'an honest response where the student's voice can be heard, rather than an artificial, contrived construction' (AQA, 2018: 8), 'creative writing' is for many a limited, prescriptive genre: 500 words of prose, written in exam conditions, shoehorning in as many tropes as possible.

In conclusion, over the life of the National Curriculum, only Cox (1989) recognised the unitary nature of English speaking and listening, reading and writing that had grown with the subject. He knew creative writing to be the *product* of rich and varied classroom talk, and wide, independent reading. In contrast, through their well-intentioned but mangled attempts to promote the oracy and reading skills they believed would benefit industry and the economy, subsequent Curricula brought in by both the Conservative and Labour governments – even those ostensibly promoting creativity – separated writing from the other elements of unitary, creative English. They thereby starved imaginative, expressive writing of what sustains it. Today, as a mere component of a high-stakes examination and paradoxically absent from the Curriculum, 'creative writing' in policy is reduced to a tokenistic sub-genre where SPaG – spelling, punctuation and grammar – is rewarded more highly than originality and artistry.

4.6 Conclusion and summary: creativity quashed

In contrast to the main thrust of policy documents covered in Chapters 2 and 3, where there is consensus about the role of English in education and of creativity within it, this chapter indicates that the six National Curricula have only limited agreement on the purpose of English within the secondary phase and varying definitions of and perspectives on creativity. Cox built upon the work of the English Association, Newbolt, Bullock *et al.* in positioning English and creativity as intertwined, but the documents from 1995 onwards present a more limited view of creativity in English, and thus a different view *of* English. There is unanimity that English should develop students' literacy, enabling them to be confident speakers, readers and writers, access the wider curriculum, and prepare them for adulthood, but the underpinning principles differ. The tension lies in whether the purpose of education is the development of humane individuals able to foster the wellbeing of themselves and others and become custodians of the world, or the development of adults ready for the workplace.

Although Cox's vision of creativity is central to his child-centred, personal-growth-oriented conception of English (even though he does not use the word), we see an increasing commodification of creativity as the latter view takes hold from the second Curriculum onwards. The term 'Creativity' is included explicitly in the Curricula published between 1999 and 2007, but the notion of creativity presented is one focused predominantly on developing the problem-solving and collaborative skills deemed necessary to benefit Britain's changing economy. These documents increasingly forgo opportunities for language to be explored and celebrated, and for children to be encouraged to think, question and imagine; instead, formal language is foregrounded, Standard English becomes mandatory, and reading is reduced to a skill needed to access the curriculum.

That is not to say that problem-solving and collaboration were not aspects of Cox's vision too: he positions Drama as

> one of the key ways in which children can gain an understanding of themselves and of others, can gain confidence in themselves as decision-makers and problem-solvers, can learn to function collaboratively, and can explore – within a supportive framework – not only a range of human feelings, but also a whole spectrum of social situations and/or moral dilemmas.
>
> (Cox, 1989: 99)

However, problem-solving and collaboration for Cox are elements of a greater whole, one that involves the personal and the social; they are not an end in themselves. As a result, while Fleming (2010) suggests that creativity for ethical nourishment was ignored from the 1990s onwards in favour of creativity for economic ends across *all* subjects, the skills-centric nature of the Programmes of Study for Speaking and Listening and Reading imply that, in English, creativity was in danger of being ignored altogether. In this sense, the loss of 'creativity' from the current version (DfE, 2014) is not as sudden a departure as might first appear. A further irony is that personal wellbeing is also ignored in English policy: even while the general introduction to fourth National Curriculum of 2004 demands greater focus on personal, social and health education and purportedly aims to encourage pupils to develop 'personal response[s]' (DfES/QCA, 2004: 10) because the English Curriculum retains the Orders of its 1999 predecessor word for word, opportunities for a new emphasis on personal response are lost. This underlines that political and economic imperatives are key drivers of Curriculum content.

There are also tensions between the Reading and Writing orders in today's Curriculum (DfE, 2014), but for opposite reasons. It seeks to inculcate a 'love' of reading, at least in part to ensure students imbibe the texts representing cultural capital, yet simultaneously diminishes the means of developing the cultural capital of the future. Students are required to be passive consumers of a curated culture and have very little latitude to create culture that represents themselves through either speech or writing; they are receivers of a preordained canon, with few opportunities to make it anew. Even Kingman, whose *Teaching of English Language* is nearest in tone to the current Curriculum and positions English Literature as knowledge more necessary for nationalistic reasons than aesthetic, recognised that culture 'has to be revitalised by each generation' (1988: 11).

So, while Cox understood that English grew through an interdependent balance of oracy, reading and writing, it appears that the authors of the Curricula spanning 1995–2014 lacked deep understanding of the subject's dependence on creativity – or perhaps they actively rejected creativity, suspicious of its associations with freedom and choice (Whittemore, 1968; Sternberg, 1999). That recent policy writers remain anonymous means that this is open to conjecture, but the documents they produced lack a holistic underpinning, so are confused and self-contradictory in places. Perhaps, as Smit (2005) suggests, their data-driven worlds are now so separate from the relationship-based worlds of the classroom that it is difficult to make meaningful connections. Yet the result is that the English Curriculum is like a three-legged stool that wobbles with legs of uneven length.

In summary:

- Cox's notion of creative English followed in the tradition of the Blue Books, Newbolt and Bullock. He saw a humanist, child-centred, personal growth view of creativity that prioritised personal and cultural development as fundamental to English – and to life itself. However, his Curriculum was soon replaced because it could not meet everyone's interests.
- The 1995, 1999 and 2007 Curriculum documents use a revised view of creativity that focuses on collaboration, problem-solving and risk-taking, seen as important in preparing students for success in the post-millennium economy, alongside skills for employability.
- Creativity is then further reduced in today's Curriculum. Not only does the term disappear, but also its spirit. Implicit is a sense that creativity is an expendable extra to a knowledge-rich curriculum.

Notes

1 Shakespeare (1606) *Macbeth* Act 3, sc 4.
2 The Curriculum covers KS1 to KS4. This chapter focuses on Key Stages (KS) 3 and 4, being those covered at secondary level. KS3 typically spans school years 7–9 (for students aged 11–14), while KS4 covers the time spent preparing for public examinations (GCSE) in years 10–11 (for students aged 15–16). Independent schools have never been bound by the Curriculum. They are permitted to teach the less prescriptive International GCSEs ('iGCSEs') which include a coursework element; they are thereby even less constrained by the Curriculum than academies and free schools.
3 See also Smith, 2020a: 113.
4 There are a total of 33 references to 'creative', 'creatively' or 'creativity' in the KS3 and KS4 English orders, with another 82 references elsewhere, including Art & Design, Mathematics and Modern Languages.
5 Although missing from the English orders, 'Creativity' appears 11 times elsewhere in this Curriculum across Art, Design and Technology, Computing and Music.
6 Although the KS3 and KS4 English orders were published separately, in 2013 and 2014 respectively, the Purpose of Study statements are identical. For this reason, this chapter references the 2013 version.
7 The secret garden analogy is also one Gove favoured. He argued to the National College conference that 'there can be no going back to the secret garden when public and professionals were in ignorance about where success had taken root and where investment had fallen on stony ground' (Gove, 2010) and he justified the use of systematic synthetic phonics for beginning readers by arguing that 'Unless children have learned to read, the rest of the curriculum is a secret garden to which they will never enjoy access' (DfE, 2010: 43).
8 Of the 22 Ministers who have presided as Education Secretary between 1989 and 2022 (up to and including Gillian Keegan, appointed October 2022), only one, Estelle Morris (2001–2002), has been a teacher.

Part III

Conversations in creativity

Preface to Part III

As shown in Part II, the policy documents from the very inception of the subject (BoE, 1905/1912) to the introduction of the National Curriculum (Cox, 1989) forged the tradition of creative English. It is their notion of subject English that is promoted as 'best practice' by the research literature today, with a focus on how '*creativity and English* link to learning' rather than how '*creativity and learning* link to English' (McCallum, 2012: 32, emphasis original). It is this thread, combining humanism, personal growth and the exploration and celebration of language, that runs through a recent textbook for new English teachers (Watson and Newman, 2022); it holds that learning happens best when we are creative – and, consequently, creativity helps students achieve better grades. However, to reiterate, this relatively stable view of creative English that can be traced through over 80 years of official policy and guidance was followed by a period of *in*stability as Curriculum policy was repeatedly reinvented post Cox. Creativity was sidelined, and the view of what English *is* and what it is *for* became confused. That there are gaps between policy and practice in the wider educational context is well recognised (Smit, 2005; Ball, Maguire and Braun, 2012; Heilbronn, 2013; Biesta and Osberg, 2014; Bleiman, 2020), but it is interesting that, for secondary English, the gap is between the legacy of *former* policy and *current* policy. The 'planned enculturation' (Biesta and Osberg, 2014: 316) that today's Curriculum mandates (DfE, 2014) is, ironically, *counter* to the culture of creative English that had been developed through the policies of the past.

But what of those whose work is shaped by the policies and guidance, English teachers in schools today and those who work with and for them? For them, the topic is already in play – as co-readers of the policies, they will each have developed their own perspective through their lived professional lives. So how might their daily practice have shaped their responses to the Curriculum? What are *their* impressions on the presence of creativity in policy past and present, and why? Is it possible for creative practice to be celebrated in English classrooms notwithstanding the prevailing anti-creative orthodoxy?

To answer these questions, I followed the approach taken by the authors of some of the policies themselves. As Newbolt (1921), Bullock (1975) and Cox (1989) make explicit in their respective Reports, they and their committees consulted widely, each conferring with hundreds of relevant people. The names and roles of those who contributed, listed in the Appendices of their respective Reports, indicate that they were experts in their field, and included those in positions of leadership, representatives from relevant bodies, experienced and new teachers. I wanted to reach those who might have been consulted had the (unknown) authors of the current Curriculum undergone a

DOI: 10.4324/9781003243311-8

process of consultation as transparent as that of Newbolt, Bullock and Cox. I therefore set out to gather 'oral evidence' (Newbolt, 1921: 3; Bullock, 1975: 561) from a similar range of English teaching professionals (albeit at a smaller scale). In Part III, I use a playscript format to show how the policy documents are interpreted by those bound to deliver them.

The creation of the script

Selected to create as representative cross-section of the field as possible and to mirror the contributors to the seminal Reports noted above, the English teaching professionals I spoke with include current and former classroom teachers (from experienced Heads of Department to new teachers), a Headteacher, academics, teacher educators, and examiners; they come from different settings all over England; they represent diverse groups; almost all have a position of leadership or are otherwise influential, locally or nationally. As far as I am aware, this project is the first time that such a range of voices has been collated so that their perspectives can be shared and compared. While the participants were aware of my interest in English and creativity, it is important to stress that I did not know anyone's explicit views on creativity beforehand.

Our individual conversations – or 'colloquies'[1] – were loosely based upon eight quotations drawn from the policy documents and associated contextual literature, broadly grouped into four themes (On the purpose of education, On creativity, On creative English, On the components of the English curriculum) with two extracts per theme – one English education policy text and one secondary text. Together, the eight extracts represent publications across seven different decades; four extracts are taken from texts published prior to the first National Curriculum (Cox, 1989) and four subsequent. I invited the colloquists to respond to any of the quotations, in any order, in any way: they might agree or disagree; they might offer anecdote or opinion. (The quotations are placed at the start of each chapter in this section, and readers are invited to consider their own responses before continuing.)

It was then a creative leap to weave together the resulting transcripts into a playscript. The trope of a script underlines my interest in the humane: a script involves the *coming together* of people, a sharing of understandings, that I hold to be at the heart of English. Further, it is appropriate that a book about English teaching and creativity experiments with form, and underlines arguments made in Part II that rich oracy stimulates original, sophisticated writing.

The setting is a theatre space within the British Library, chosen because with its 200 million+ items, it is a world-class archive; it is the repository of every new book published in the UK; it is a major research library, with items in many formats (from ancient manuscripts to modern sound recordings); it is a modern, Grade 1-listed building that is widely accessible, with an inclusive ethos (www.bl.uk/about-us). It thereby represents the old and the new, high culture and everyday culture, historic and 'living' creative English.

I invite readers of this book to read the playscript aloud – even perform it – with their colleagues or interested others where possible. It is suitable for both new and experienced teachers taking part in professional development activities, departmental meetings and online English forums. It is designed to be accessible and manageable in a busy professional context: while each act follows immediately on from its predecessor, they are designed to be read separately if necessary (Act 1 takes just over 15 minutes to read aloud, with Act 2 around 10 minutes and Act 3 around 12 minutes.). Together, they are intended to promote discussion and debate around the subject of English and its relationship with creativity, the place of English within the statutory frameworks, and how English teachers might respond to challenges they perceive. The trope of a script in performance serves to emphasise the multiple layers of meaning and interpretation.

In Act 1, we are introduced to the cast as they discuss their own conceptions of creativity and different models of creativity. They affirm that they all view creativity (in a broad sense) as integral to English. In Act 2, they deplore the restrictive nature of successive iterations of the National Curriculum, particularly the instrumental measures adopted by some schools as expedient for exam success; yet simultaneously note the importance of the individual teacher as a foil to such practice. In Act 3, they consider the conditions necessary for enabling creative English to thrive, discussing the role of both school leaders and individual teachers in creating an environment that allows for agentive practice including experiment and judicious risk-taking in order that students flourish academically and personally.

Cast (in alphabetical order)[2]

AKOS: English PGCE tutor at a Russell Group university; former teacher of English with responsibility for gifted and talented students.

ALEX: Novelist, creative writing tutor and researcher; former teacher of English with responsibility for oracy and Key Stage 3.

ANNE: Teacher of English running a PGCE part-time with a School-Centred Initial Teacher Training (SCITT) consortium; in charge of recently- and newly-qualified teachers in her school.

DOUG: Head of English in independent school, having spent the early years of his career in a state-maintained school; award-winning poet.

GARY: Headteacher of a successful rural comprehensive school (Ofsted: 'Good'; Arts Council Platinum Artsmark Award). Regularly publishes opinion pieces on education policy in the national press and national education press.

GILL: Senior Lecturer in Education; English PGCE programme lead at a Russell Group university; former Head of English.

ISLA: Researcher; convenor of discussion

JACK: Active emeritus member of International Centre for Historical Research in Education, Institute of Education; founder member of London English Research Group.

JUDY: Senior Lecturer in Education; English PGCE programme lead at a post-1992 university, with experience in the Graduate Teacher Training Programme (GTTP), SCITT and School Direct PGCE programmes; former Head of English in inner-city school.

LEON: Visiting Lecturer and Research Associate at a Russell Group university; former Head of English and Deputy Head in a London school.

PAUL: Teaching and Learning Coordinator of Literacy Across the Curriculum in a South West school; former Head of English; active member of a Teachers as Writers group.

PHIL: Principal Examiner and Assistant Principal Moderator for popular examination board; formerly Lecturer in Education in a red-brick university, Advisory Teacher and teacher of English.

RUTH: Recently-qualified teacher of English in an 11–18 rural maintained comprehensive, judged Outstanding by Ofsted and awarded Gold Artsmark Award.

SARA: Raising Standards Lead in English in a city academy, judged Good by Ofsted, having begun her career in a neighbouring city academy; active member of a Teachers as Writers group.

TONY: Former Teacher of English in Zambia, Singapore and England; published poet; previously involved in Creative Partnerships.

Notes

1 I chose this term as, although admittedly archaic, a colloquy is a 'talking together; a conversation, dialogue. Also, a written dialogue' (www.oed.com). As 'interview' can have connotations of hierarchy (one might think of a police interview or a politician being grilled by a journalist), 'colloquy' better reflects the balanced, non-hierarchical nature of the conversations I tried to facilitate. The two participants (researcher and participant) accordingly are 'colloquists'.

2 In accordance with ethical protocols, the colloquists each agreed their pseudonym and pen portrait. I imagined a researcher-convenor figure (Isla) to represent me, thus separating my role as author of this book from a character in a playscript.

Act 1

Why English, and what does creativity have to do with it?

I.1 Introduction and opening questions

Before reading Act 1, consider your response to these statements about English, creativity and the purpose of education taken from the literature and policies discussed in Chapters 1–4. They are presented here in chronological order.

To what extent do you agree or disagree with each one? Do any of these quotations chime with the definition you wrote or the metaphor you devised at the opening to Chapter 2? What opposing perspectives might be offered? What questions might you have for the author of each statement? If possible, share your thoughts with your colleagues.

- *"Creative English" is not for me a matter of simply eliciting verse or worse, but rather of establishing a relationship and an ethos which will promote experiment, talk, enquiry, amusement, vivacity, bouts of intense concentration, seriousness, collaboration, and a clearer and more adequate self-knowledge. This will involve us in talk about our selves (sic), our language, our behaviour, our attitudes and beliefs, and, when appropriate, in recording such things in writing. And the teacher's sense of his (sic) role is crucial. If he is prescriptive – knowing what he wants, knowing all the answers beforehand – he will be less effective than if he is prepared to allow the pupils' awareness of criteria to grow for itself in the business of making, modifying, and so on. (Summerfield, 1968: 44)*
- *Does "being educated in English"… imply knowledge of grammar and syntax? Competence at 'literary criticism' (and what is this anyway?)? Ability to produce 'creative writing' (another obscurity)? Knowledge of the dates of authors and the dimensions of the Shakespearean stage? (Wilson, 1972: 9)*
- *[Creativity is] imaginative activity fashioned so as to produce outcomes that are both original and of value. (NACCCE, 1999: 30)*
- *Education is the engine of our economy… most important of all, we must ensure that more people have the knowledge and skills they need to succeed in a demanding economy. (Gibb, 2015, n.p.)*

I.2 Being 'educated' in English

The cast is seated comfortably in a loose semi-circle around three coffee tables on which the selected quotations are scattered. Behind them is a large screen which displays the quotation under discussion, when relevant and other images as stated in the script. Cafetieres and coffee cups, water carafes and glasses are also dotted around. The group appear earnest, engaged and absorbed.

DOI: 10.4324/9781003243311-9

We join the discussion as they consider what it means to be 'educated' in English, building on the questions Wilson (1972) poses, and whether this has a bearing on how they understand the relationship between English and creativity.

ANNE: I suppose the problem is that being educated in English means different things to different people. If you are David, who's just joined my Year 9 class from Hungary, being educated in English is being able to have conversations with peers. He doesn't understand most of what's going on in class, but he can tell me the witches in *Macbeth* are *deus ex machina* because we've been over and over it, so in that sense he is quite educated in English. But being educated in English doesn't stop on the 16th of August or whatever day it is that the results come out. I have a degree in English. Does that mean I'm educated in English? Yes and no. (*She shrugs*)

AKOS: Exactly – you don't just *have* English education, it's a *having*. It's an active thing!

GILL: And it's multi-layered, multi-disciplinary. I think being educated in English is about seeing *connections* between those different aspects of the subject.

JACK: (*Chiming in, animated*) Those connections might come from that expressive talk …

DOUG: (*Also enthusiastic, he picks up immediately*) … or through reading a shared bit of text…

JUDY: Or through the making of a text!

ALEX: English is a little bit of everything, essentially.

JACK: Exactly. Reading, writing and talking are all aspects of the same process. What we need is a unitary view of English that doesn't make an artificial division between Literature and Language.

ANNE: That's fine, don't have a problem with that. But in terms of creative writing (*gesturing to the quotation on the display and making air quotes*), well, some really good students are great at analysis but can't write creatively at all, and that doesn't mean they are not educated in English.

TONY: Perhaps. But creativity in English is not just about 'creative' writing. It's not just 'wow' words writ large. It's the whole range of writing, from poetry through to TV scripts to journalism, whatever. It's making things. So it might be a notice that's going out to parents, which is as dismal as you can get, but you're involved in something that's got to be made by somebody, it's got to be created.

GILL: Yes – *all* writing ought to be seen as creative writing.

(*Pause*)

In some ways I guess the word 'creativity' is slightly problematic. Would it be difficult to teach English creatively if you didn't at some level reflect on *why* it was creative, whatever your definition of creative might be?

ISLA: The difficulty in defining the term 'creativity' comes up a lot in the literature, of course.

JACK: Well, I could simply open my OED and find 'creativity', but the key question is, what do people mean by it? What's their investment? What's their agenda?

He pauses to allow the questions to sink in.

What's being contested here? What are the armies that are being assembled? In whose interests?

Lights dim momentarily and come back up

I.3 From skills to personal growth: the living of English

JUDY: I'm not sure that I like your military tenor, but those questions are interesting. Yet creativity's also to do with crea*ting*, which I think people lose sight of when they think of the word crea*tive*. What needs to be given time and space in this way of thinking is that you are actually in the process of *moulding* something; you are in the process of *building*; you are in the process of taking on new ways of looking.

LEON: For me, creativity is more about cognition. It's to do with *flexibility* and having an *imaginative response* to what one's provided with culturally and educationally. One doesn't sit down and think, 'I'll learn this for the exam.' That's useless. It's the *response* to it: 'What sense do *I* make of it? How do I relate it to my own life?'

AKOS: (*interjecting*) Yeah – oftentimes people want to learn more about themselves.

LEON: (*nodding, continuing his point*) But it's also, 'How do I relate it to the lives of those around me? How as I develop in age and maturity do I relate it to society around me?' All those are elements of creativity.

DOUG: And it does involve a degree of wilfulness and even a degree of intellectual stamina.

SARA: Totally! I think that when we talk about creativity in schools, people often think in terms of the arts and (*in a sing-song voice*) sitting down and doing a nice piece of creative writing – but actually creativity is *thinking*[1]...

(*the speakers almost overlap each other in their enthusiasm*)

LEON: ... and using inference, deduction, comparison

AKOS: ... and being open to interpretations

PAUL: ... and making decisions

GARY: ... and solving problems.

ANNE: It's about *discovery*. (*Short pause.*) But also understanding that you can't always make sense of everything.

They smile in recognition of a shared understanding.

ISLA: It's interesting to consider whether all those mental activities are *prerequisites* of creativity, or are developed *through* creativity or, indeed, whether there is a virtuous circle where creative practice reinforces what was already there.

LEON: I'd say all those mental activities we've just mentioned *underpin* creativity. I mean, look at Vygotsky, Piaget! Their understanding of these things is robust and they've never been seriously challenged on that.

AKOS: Although this whole definition thing is a massive question for me right now. It is really difficult for me to unsee that some of the foundations of ideas about creativity, ideas about English, ideas about teaching, Vygotsky, Piaget – they're by white males. So many other voices are missing.

ALEX: That's true.

(*Pause.*)

Maybe it's too simple to say it's *this,* and *this,* and *this,* it's so many factors. I suppose definitions like these are always changing because it's never going to be a perfect match or perfect fit, it all depends on the context of society and what's happening at a time and who's in charge.

(*Pause.*)

ISLA: I think that you position creativity slightly differently, Paul? I remember that you described a perspective that does not contradict the idea that creativity requires these cognitive skills, but yet simultaneously places it on a different plane.

PAUL: Yes, for me, it goes beyond developing the intellectual or the academic. There's a spiritual element too. I was talking to my A level students yesterday about creativity – it's our life blood and without it, people feel purposeless, despondent, and their life is just meaningless. Especially in a secular society which most of us inhabit.

SARA: I know what you mean. I think being educated in English is about being educated within your soul. It's about empathy and understanding of the human experience. I wouldn't be teaching English now if I didn't get that.

PAUL: Creativity is what makes life worth living. (*He looks around the circle; every eye is on him.*) Without it I would feel there was something missing. It's brought meaning to my life.

(*Pause.*)

JUDY: For me, creativity is the living of English: it's the opportunity for teachers and students to feel a happiness or a completeness or an excitement about living in the moment.

ISLA: That's also a beautiful notion. It reminds me of some of the separate conversations I had with you all: a number of you spoke of 'English' and 'creativity' interchangeably, as though they were synonymous. It suggests an intimate, inseparable, indelible bond between English and creativity.

Lights dim momentarily and come back up

I.4 People, processes and products

RUTH: (*Enters the discussion tentatively, thoughtfully, after a moment or two*) So yes, it's all these things; and it's about enjoyment. But the last thing I would want is for one of my students to be really passionate about a topic yet not be able to express that to others.

ALEX: A hundred percent. I'm from a black working–class family. In school we weren't really encouraged to challenge, to argue, to make a prolonged speech. So when I went to university, I felt like a fish out of water. I didn't want my students to feel like that: I wanted to give them the ability to speak, to articulate themselves in the best way possible, so that they don't feel a bit scared and apprehensive.

RUTH: (*Smiling*) So creativity is also what we're doing now, it's about speaking, communicating with other people.

ANNE: Even if they are on the same topic but have totally different views!

AKOS: Or different *emotions*. If my student is angry about something, because they are passionate about it, I want them to be able to express that! And I want to be able to engage with that and have a discussion about that. In a safe space.

ANNE: Me too. So yes, I'd say it's about collaboration, and talk, and experiment.

AKOS: And opportunities for teachers to actually engage with students as they do so. This might sound obvious, but I think it's really difficult to be creative in a classroom if you don't have a good relationship with your students.

GARY: (*Nodding vigorously*) Creativity is manifested through people who can work in teams: in classrooms, in schools and in the world beyond.

JUDY: (*Leaning over to pick up the card with the Summerfield quotation, an excerpt of which appears on the rear screen: "Creative English" … will involve us in talk about our selves* (sic)*, our language, our behaviour, our attitudes and beliefs.* (Summerfield, 1968: 44))

Look. When I read this, the word 'our' jumped out at me: 'Talking about our selves, our language, our behaviour.' That pronoun conveys the notion of *community*.

JACK: 'Our language' (*pause*). This reminds me of one of the ideas that Jimmy Britton[2] presented – that we can think of two wings of English activity. (*Flaps arms to illustrate the metaphor.*) One wing is a tendency towards *participant* use of language, using it to get things done. The other wing is *spectator*, we're reflecting on language, we're working on our representations of reality in order to make sense of the world. Both things go together. And in the centre (*touching his chest with both hands*), moving out to those two wings, is expressive language, the sort of ordinary language that's close to the self, that we use day in, day out. So we've got spectator, participant and expressive, those are the three things. In terms of creativity, expressive language is the kind of generative talk that helps make sense of everything. It's about understanding how having a view of language that's both generative and constitutive makes us who we are.

JUDY: I like that idea: creativity helps you fly. Individually and together.

The rear screen displays a video of starlings in murmuration.

SARA: (*Nodding*) So that suggests that creative English is about making yourself a better person *and* making yourself a more responsible member of *society*.

PAUL: I'd go further. To really move forward as an individual *and* to move forward as a society you need to use creativity as a *starting point*.

JUDY: That's interesting, because if we see it as fundamental, the starting point, we also need to remember that it's also about the end result. We haven't yet mentioned the idea of creativity as a product-driven notion.

That's what creativity is for a lot of people, as defined here (*picking up the card with the definition of creativity from* <u>All Our Futures</u> *(NACCCE, 1999: 30) which appears on the screen as she reads it aloud*): *Creativity is imaginative activity fashioned so as to produce outcomes that are both original and of value.'*

TONY: Yes, it's not *all* in the process, no (*chuckles*). The outcome is important, because you want to know it's real rather than just (*mimics*) 'We're messing around here'.

ALEX: Mmm, I'm thinking of creative activities such as art pieces or school productions or poetry anthologies that could be the tangible, tactile, valuable item at the end of it. This (*nodding at the quotation on screen*) is freeing – there is a sort of lucidity there that I really, really like.

JUDY: Perhaps. But would you accept that 'outcomes' – wretched word! – are not always necessarily tangible? You might live in the creative moment through shared reading or through talking; you might do it through just being together in a safe space and being able to suggest new things.

TONY: True. But another outcome of creativity is new knowledge. I worked in Singapore for a number of years. They realised there that a curriculum based on 'rote learn it, repeat it' resulted in only being able to repeat what they already knew. They realised they needed to be more creative to grow in knowledge.

LEON: And they were right. But why the focus on novelty? People seem to think that creativity is having bright ideas and thinking of new things, but that's extremely rare. Anyone you think about – any painter of the past, any poet of the past you think was brilliant – has built on the work of his or her predecessors. So, I'd say creativity is about development. I think that originality is *not* the most important thing.

GILL: But actually, I remember thinking when *All Our Futures* was published – and I still do think – that their definition of creativity is a helpful one in terms of education. They say it's not got to be original for the whole world, it's got to be original to the person generating whatever it is. If you've never thought of it, if it's new to you, it's therefore original.

TONY: There were one or two quite thoughtful people in New Labour back then, you know. You could feel on their wavelength. Creativity wasn't a bad word. It might not have been put into place often enough or fast enough, but it was seen as a positive thing.

PHIL: Huh! It's not now. Although maybe those who are nervous of creativity have a point. Don't forget that creativity can have dangerous outcomes.

The mushroom cloud of a nuclear explosion appears on the rear display screen.
Lights dim momentarily then come back up.

1.5 We're not building worker bees

JACK: Perhaps the important thing is not to define creativity, but to see what work creativity does – not just discursive work, but what work it does to organise sociopolitical commitments and understandings. What educational understandings does it help to organise? It's not simply about achieving something.

PHIL: (*Dryly*) Surely education is about finding out what is inherent in the child and what needs to be superimposed upon it.

Anne raises her eyebrows, questioningly

ISLA: I suspect that you are being deliberately controversial, Phil, in advocating a topdown view, given that you spoke previously about the importance of education going beyond the functional and materialistic. I think Jack is saying that creativity is a movement, something dynamic, which suggests that the impact it makes *in* the classroom has reverberations well beyond the classroom.

ANNE: Education is about opening doors! That's why I think the Nick Gibb statement you showed us is very narrow. (*Quotation appears on the rear screen: Education is the engine of our economy… most important of all, we must ensure that more people have the knowledge and skills they need to succeed in a demanding economy. (Gibb, 2015, n.p.)*)

It's Gradgrindian. It's only about skills they need to succeed in a 'demanding economy', not skills they need for life, not skills they need to be people.

JUDY: Considering the use of pronouns again, it's interesting Gibb is talking about 'we,' but using it in a way entirely alien from Summerfield's community-building 'our'. I suppose Gibb is trying to get some sense that we're all in this together, but he's apparently suggesting that there is something which is 'knowledge' and there is something which is a 'skill', bound and tangible, and that both are necessary to generate income. It's alarming.

ANNE: Exactly! Education should prepare them for work, of course – whether that be become a poet or go and work for a FSTE 100 company – but it's not all of it.

ALEX: Yeah! The economy is important, but where's the balance? We should focus on what we want holistically for students. Where is *fulfilment*? Where is *confidence*?

LEON: Agreed: an education system does have to educate people for the economic life of the country, but Gibb's definition is not sufficient.

TONY: It's fatuous. It's reductionist both about education and about economy.

SARA: It's a very capitalist viewpoint.

DOUG: And it's ironic. Britain is intensely creative, isn't it? The fashion industry, the music industry, film, literature, are of huge import. You do hear government ministers talking about that, but at the same time as they're introducing policies which threaten to utterly destabilise those creative industries.

PAUL: The emphasis is the wrong way round. The *by-product* of having creative, educated children who have a thirst for information and a thirst for knowledge is a more successful society and a more successful economy.

SARA: Yeah. I don't think we should say to students, 'This is what you need to go out into the world of work,' I think there's an argument to be made for education for education's sake. I think there has to be an understanding that education serves a purpose beyond just creating worker drones – we're not all working for the queen bee. Education is much more than that.

PAUL: (*Nodding vigorously*) Forget getting a good job, forget getting a wage and a house and all the other things that are held out as carrots to students. What about seeing the world in all its colours and variation, what about understanding when people are lying to you and when they're telling you the truth? What about being able to read sincerity in a friend?

He looks around the circle expressively.

These are the things that for me education is about. It's about enabling everyone to take a full and active part in their community – not about being the engine of the economy.

SARA: At the moment we are in a position where a lot of people feel quite disenfranchised.

PAUL: And society is attacking itself and attacking others who have a vital part to play in our society.

SARA: A creative education can change society. It can help people really feel that they're not disenfranchised any more.

(*Pause.*)

RUTH: This may sound naïve, but I didn't realise when I came into teaching just how much focus there would be on money and the economy. I came into teaching for the joy of learning.

GARY: And me – and, I suspect, the majority of us here. And I think at our peril should we lose that sense of this being a humane occupation. (*He picks up the card with the Gibb quotation and tears it in two.*) And it's *this* attitude that is causing the crisis we're experiencing and the haemorrhaging of teachers from the profession.

Notes

1 I previously cited Sara's words in Smith, 2018a.
2 James Britton. Jack's image is perhaps a reworking (or re-remembering) of the Transactional–Expressive/Expressive–Poetic image of modes of writing discussed by Bullock (1975: 164). Britton was a member of the Schools Research Council, which Bullock references, and was an active member of the committee contributing to the Bullock Report (1975); he wrote the Foreword for the third edition of Dixon's *Growth Through English*.

Act 2

Making sense of policy

II.1 Introduction and opening questions

Before reading the script, consider these quotations. Once again, to what extent do you agree or disagree with what is said? What opposing perspectives might be offered? Do these ideas build on or contradict anything raised in the previous scene? If possible, share your thoughts with your colleagues.

- *[T]here is the danger that a true instinct for humanism may be smothered by the demand for definite measurable results, especially the passing of examinations in a variety of subjects, and if those who are anxious to do justice to English find it so hard to carry out their desire, what is to be expected from those who will remain indifferent?* (Newbolt, 1921; 55)
- *Creativity: Pupils show creativity when they make unexpected connections, use striking and original phrases or images, approach tasks from a variety of starting points, or change forms to surprise and engage the reader. Creativity can be encouraged by providing purposeful opportunities for pupils to experiment, build on ideas or follow their own interests. Creativity in English extends beyond narrative and poetry to other forms and uses of language. It is essential in allowing pupils to progress to higher levels of understanding and become independent.* (DCSF/QCA, 2007: 63)

II.2 Reflections on policy

ISLA: I know we all understand Gary's frustration, given figures that suggest more teachers are leaving than ever before. Yet I noted from my conversations with some of you more – errr – experienced teachers (*smiles from Gill, Leon, Gary, Tony, Phil*) that even thirty years ago there was a sense of distrust within the profession about education policy imposed from above. Could you comment further, Gill?

GILL: I became Head of English when the National Curriculum was just being introduced – this was the very end of the 1980s – so it was a particularly fraught but interesting time. I was working in a really interesting department, with mixed ability teaching throughout, and fantastic other teachers. Testing was coming in; it was a stressful time.

LEON: (*Amused*) I recall how, back then, a colleague and I would chat and worry about how education was going!

GILL: But in my department we didn't want to conform, we wanted to do things differently.

DOI: 10.4324/9781003243311-10

LEON: (*Soberly*) And then remember the introduction of the National Strategies[1]? They brought in this teacher-led rather fast-paced, formulaic lesson: objectives, starter, episodes, evidence in writing, plenary. It was really rather deadly.

DOUG: It was what I could see the Literacy Strategy was doing to English teaching – the idea that a lesson should be in a certain number of chunks – that made me run for the hills. Or at least to the freedom of the independent sector: it was like coming back to something I felt I knew.

TONY: But at least back in the 2000s we were moving towards a much more creative curriculum. Granted, there was a sense of imposition, but at least New Labour were beginning to see that there were possibilities that could be developed. Look! (*He reaches to pick up the relevant quotation card, then points to the references to 'creativity' in the quotation when it appears on the screen.*)

Creativity: Pupils show creativity when they make unexpected connections, use striking and original phrases or images, approach tasks from a variety of starting points, or change forms to surprise and engage the reader. Creativity can be encouraged by providing purposeful opportunities for pupils to experiment, build on ideas or follow their own interests. Creativity in English extends beyond narrative and poetry to other forms and uses of language. It is essential in allowing pupils to progress to higher levels of understanding and become independent. (DCSF/QCA, 2007: 62)

But, as you know, that really has all gone by the board.

PHIL: (*Harrumphing – being deliberately provocative, gesturing towards the quotation*) That was merely a government attempt to provide token licence for more than rote learning.

ISLA: That's interesting. Are you suggesting that creativity was present in that policy document but not in classrooms of the day?

Phil makes a steeple of his hands and taps his ring fingers together, noncommittedly. Isla continues.

If that is the case, is the 2014 curriculum any different, in terms of opportunities for creativity? We know that the word 'creativity' is missing. Do you feel that its omission is an acknowledgement of the problem in defining it – perhaps it *is* present, in another guise – or is its absence more calculated?

JUDY: (*Looking directly at Phil; emphatic*) I'm sad that that statement is no longer in the present curriculum and I'm sad that the word 'creativity' isn't in there at all, or any words like it. It's a loss. I think that is a sign of the times, and it links in with the direction of travel.

GILL: Agreed. The current curriculum is not *supportive* of creativity and that (*nodding towards the DCSF/QCA (2007) quotation*) more holistic approach. I mean, when you look at the work of Newbolt and some of those big reports, they are explicitly arguing for creativity.

JACK: Neo-liberals shy away from creativity. They're allergic to it. (*Chuckles*)

GILL: So maybe your military metaphor *is* appropriate. (*She glances Jack; he smiles self-deprecatingly.*) Those in positions of power are looking for measurable outcomes, because they're in government for a short period of time. They need results (*snaps fingers*) quickly and are constantly looking for things that are quantifiable and measurable, so education discourse has become very driven. It is becoming dominated by 'impact' and 'outcomes'.

SARA: Exactly. Everything in schools has to be formalised, double-checked. It doesn't allow for creativity. The government is looking for *proof* of ability and attainment, but I think that creativity is separate from ability and separate from attainment. I can talk about the liquorish smell of the tarmac on a hot day, but there's no way you could write a mark scheme for that.

She raises her hands in a gesture of frustration.

ANNE: (*Sadly*) The system only measures what it wants to measure.

SARA: And *because* it's so difficult to measure, creativity is something of an afterthought.

LEON: Sadly, however, the data-drive won't go away because the government is worried about our poor productivity. It means that Progress 8^2 will be valuable…

PHIL: (*Jumping in dismissively*) …to those least qualified to have anything to do with education.

JUDY: Although they imply they have the moral high ground, which is worrying.

LEON: (*In a measured way, pressing on with his argument*) I think Progress 8 is with us permanently. There's cross-party political commitment to it. It will be very useful.

He pauses before introducing a contrasting point.

The *negative* of Gove's innovation in the current curriculum is the idea that knowledge is more important than skills. That is such nonsense. There's really very good evidence that that is simply not the case, that it's mistaken. Knowledge is redundant without understanding, being able to apply it. (*Pause*) And even though the English orders include the word 'enjoy', I fear that schools will lose sight of that.

GARY: And it results in a curriculum that is narrow and confining.

GILL: It is quite shocking what gets foregrounded on the schools' websites, what's in your face about spelling, punctuation and grammar for example, before you get to anything that really matters.

GARY: The current GCSE specification, in particular, is crushing. Lethal. Children are jumping through hoops – it's like dog training.

GILL: It means, I think, there are huge possibilities for being very *un*creative right now and I fear that.

ALEX: I do understand the importance of getting good GCSE results. Especially for those marginalized demographics of our society, I do understand that. But I don't want students to be *suffocated* by these specifications. But I think creativity can be the way in: if students have a love for subjects like English, then the results will follow, but we need to foster and harness that love first.

GARY: You're right. But the trouble is, as soon as you talk like that, people just assume you're part of some sentimental blob kind of thing[3].

RUTH: That makes me feel uncomfortable.

SARA: And the kids feel uncomfortable too!

Lights dim momentarily then come back up.

II.3 Uncomfortable, uncreative, ineffective?

SARA: I now find with year sevens is that they're almost afraid of creativity. Particularly with the new Key Stage two SATs[4] rubric: there's a real noticeable difference in year sevens this year, who had to do the new-style tests, and previous year seven cohorts.[5] This year they are almost fearful to try the creative things. In previous years it was (*in an enthusiastic tone*) 'Miss, is it all right if I do it this way?' and they'd try an experimental bit of writing. This year it's much more (*in an anxious tone*) 'Would it be all right if I did this? Will I still get the marks?' I really struggle with that. They clearly *want* to do the creative thing, but they understand what the expectations are of a school, and they don't see a school as necessarily a place where creativity should thrive.[6]

But if I set them a creative homework, they absolutely go with it: they really, really love it. I've had some amazing homeworks produced: the postcards sent to Martha in *Abomination*[7]; they've written them, made it look like they'd been through the post, all that stuff, they're amazing. Yet somehow, there's a marked difference when they're in the classroom, they just can't bring themselves to do it in the same way.

ANNE: I recognise that. I teach lots of children – mainly boys – who won't write things down in class because they're frightened of it being wrong. They'll *say* it to me in a conversation and then I'll say, 'Yeah, that's brilliant, that's a really good idea, go and write that down!' and only *then* will they write it.

PAUL: So the same thing is true of those very bright students you get at GCSE, who get fantastic A grades, they can do the analytical essay in the dark with their hands tied behind their back, but ask them to write a story or write poetry and dialogue and they're all at sea because they've been so used to writing what the teacher's told them to write, a PEE paragraph or extended PEE paragraph. They can do *that*, but when it comes to actually telling a story and writing convincingly about feelings or creating a sincere relationship, not a clue![8]

AKOS: I know, don't get me started about writing frames! If we only speak about analysis and not about *humanity*, there's something wrong, as far as I'm concerned. If we only speak about the transformation of Scrooge, but don't speak about the way that Dickens presents his joy, and presents his sorrow, and presents his pain, then I don't think we're really doing English, I think we're answering assessment questions.

PAUL: (*Nodding vigorously*) And I also find it a lot with A level students. I say, 'Right, tell me what you think about this text,' and their response begins, 'Is it about…?' And I say, 'No, no, no, *tell* me; talk your ideas aloud, take the chance of being wrong! Stop posing it as a question and tell me what *you* think!'

DOUG: And it means that A level students adopt a more perfunctory approach when writing too. I get that there's a desire for accountability in how marks are awarded, and that having a bunch of English teachers agreeing what was the best and what was not so good – as exam marking used to be – is not acceptable now. But I remember when more clear emphasis upon assessment objectives in curricula was brought in, such that an essay would be judged through the lens of say four or five assessment objectives, each one contributing a mark to the overall result. If there wasn't enough 'context', then an essay that was otherwise brilliant and insightful and beautifully structured and cogent, and *should* be getting a top grade, might not get a top grade because it had not hit all the assessment objectives.

Pause, musing.

Although, having said that, there is something creative in meeting the challenges of a particular examination essay structure.

PAUL: Possibly.

Now sits forward, with an urgent point to make.

I'm going to be controversial here. I'm not of the opinion that our National Curriculum or exam system necessarily has to smother our humanism as teachers. I think the greatest danger to creativity in the class is the teacher themselves.

(Pause.)

TONY: Of course. Uninspiring teaching is not just a result of current policy and the exam is not necessarily the killer. You can take a creative approach to passing the examination or a very Gradgrindy one.

(He flourishes an imaginary pen.) It's like sonnet writing! I work better when I write sonnets knowing there are those constraints to the form. You have the constraint you've got to work to, but you can interpret that creatively.

DOUG: Yes – having to deliver a brief to a deadline can create some really interesting work and push you into directions you wouldn't perhaps have gone in otherwise.

GARY: Sure, but the balance is wrong. We're growing a generation of teachers who have a *mindset* on criteria; at our peril we're losing sight of humane.

GILL: Please don't blame the teacher educators for that. There's a tangible disconnect between what we do *(nodding at Judy, Anne, Akos)* – training new teachers of English – and what they're experiencing in many of the schools they're practising in. And although a lot of our trainees aren't in schools where they're working with the National Curriculum, my sense is that colleagues in schools are under ferocious pressure. I am observing my own trainees teach and they are having to be in line – they are having to fit in.

JUDY: Me too – it's tragic. In a very data-driven, outcomes-driven curriculum, creative English isn't given the space it needs. It's something I encourage trainee teachers to explore, but I'm not sure it's something that we're seeing in schools. I don't think there's the space and capacity for that for that to happen. It's all 'quick fix' and intense stress.

GILL: So can we blame English teachers who might adopt a limited view of our version of creativity?

AKOS: You have to be a *really* creative person to be creative in schools today because there is so much that is constraining creativity.

ISLA: OK. It seems we're saying that, while the teacher is ultimately responsible for what happens in their classroom, the context in which that teacher works is particularly challenging at the moment. While creativity is not antipathetic to exam results, it is particularly hard for English teachers to work as they might want to because of the demands of the current curriculum and, in a market economy, a ferocious need for good grades.

RUTH: We're seeing that tension that Newbolt referred to played out (*picks up card as quotation is displayed on the screen*):

> *There is the danger that a true instinct for humanism may be smothered by the demand for definite measurable results, especially the passing of examinations... and if those who are anxious to do justice to English find it so hard to carry out their desire, what is to be expected from those who will remain indifferent?*

(Newbolt, 1921: 55)

ISLA: Sadly, yes. And it's even more worrying when students themselves are becoming fearful of being creative and (*nodding at Sara*) don't view a school as where creativity happens.

TONY: (*Thoughtfully*) It seems to me that you start getting *really* creative only when you get out of the box of 'the teacher' and 'the pupils' and you start involving the whole school, other disciplines, go beyond the school. If you're trapped in a three-way thing – you, the curriculum and the pupils – your creativity is limited.

ISLA: Yet it is the system in which we have to work. How can we square the circle? I'd like to think next about how this can be addressed: how can we create the climate we need to meet these challenges?

Notes

1 C.f. 6.2.1.
2 Progress 8 (and Attainment 8), first published in 2018, are school performance measures introduced to replace the percentage of students awarded GCSE A*-C as a performance measure. Student 'progress' between KS2 and GCSE is collated and averaged (www.gov.uk).
3 Michael Gove derided his critics as The Blob, a giant mutating world-threatening amoeba that featured in a 1950s Sci-Fi film (Robinson, 2014).
4 Standard Assessment Tests, sat by Year 6 pupils in maintained schools, used to measure a child's progress through primary school and as benchmark for secondary school.
5 The revised English SAT comprises a grammar, punctuation and spelling paper and a reading comprehension paper (*e.g.* www.gov.uk/.../primary-curriculum-key-stage-2-tests-and-assessments). The interview with Sara took place in autumn 2016; the revised SATs were first taken by Year 6 in May 2016.
6 Some of Sara's words are also cited in: Smith, 2018a.
7 Young Adult novel by Robert Swindells, published 2007.
8 The exchange between Anne and Paul is also cited in: Smith, 2018a.

Act 3

Creating the conditions and imagining the future

III.1 Introduction and opening questions

Before reading on, pause to think about these final two quotations. The first concerns the purpose of education itself and was written around 400 years ago – Wotton was a contemporary of Shakespeare. The second concerns creativity and is just 20 years old. To what extent do you agree or disagree with what is said? Do these ideas build on or contradict anything raised in the previous two scenes? If possible, share your thoughts with your colleagues.

- *First, there must proceed a way how to discern the natural inclinations and capacities of children. Secondly, next must ensue the culture and furnishment of the mind. Thirdly, the moulding of behaviour and decent forms. Fourthly, the tempering of the affections. Fifthly, the quickening and exciting of observations and practical judgement. Sixthly, and the last in order, but the principal in value, being that which must knit and consolidate all the rest, is the timely instilling of conscientious principles and the seeds of religion.*

  (Henry Wotton, n.d., *in* Board of Education, 1937: 8)
- *[C]reativity is a much a decision about and an attitude toward life as it is a matter of ability.*

  (Sternberg, 2003: 98)

III.2 Working within shapes and structures

JACK: To be provocative: 'twas ever thus? Let's take the long view. My research suggests that the picture of what English was like between 1945 and 1965 turns out to be very complicated. In one particular class I looked at from 1946 or 1947, there was this working-class Jewish kid – he turned out to be Harold Pinter!

Everyone laughs.

And a kid who became a professor of History at Cambridge! There was a huge amount of talent just in that room. There was a pocket of – to use the word – creativity. You know, kids absolutely galvanised, working well with teachers and doing all kinds of interesting things.

And then in the next room there was a teacher who was doing something straight out the text-book, doing pretty dull things. So, as we've said: creativity doesn't simply appear in a 40-minute period with a plenary at the end. It's in the hands of the teacher.

DOI: 10.4324/9781003243311-11

PHIL: Yes: one aiming for more than just mechanical training in cerebral performance.

DOUG: I've noticed lots of metaphorical models for teaching these days are mechanical or technological. They're about, 'Here's the tool which we want you to bolt onto this, which will then cause *this* to happen.'

AKOS: (*nodding at Jack*) But is doing it dully that teacher's fault? We haven't yet highlighted the fact that there is a lot of centralised planning and teaching because teachers are subject to so many lesson observations. This culture of observations – being Ofsted-ready – debilitate creativity, constrain, disable it. Like you *can* still move – but only very slowly.

GARY: Agreed. The National Curriculum and National Strategies implied that there's a set way of doing things, and an accountability culture which has – in some schools – reduced Heads of English to simply the people who implement management protocols. They have lost their vocation. We're being de-professionalised.

AKOS: Yeah – I've sat in the rooms where senior leadership and middle leaders are talking to each other about what how they're going to make the school (*mimics*) 'blah blah blah'. And that top-down message goes out to departments. And then creativity is cut short.

PAUL: (*Jumps in eagerly*) Which is why I'm no longer Head of Department. When our new Headteacher was appointed, he wanted a dictatorial Head of English. He said, 'Every lesson must look the same; if I go into classes, I want to see every teacher teaching this at the same time.'

I said, 'That's not how English works. Apart from everything else, all our classes are different. They have different dynamics, they have different students, and the teachers should be responding to the students in their class.' But to no avail. So I stepped down from that role.

GILL: I can understand that – although it's a shame, because the profession needs principled leaders. Classrooms are not groups of isolated individuals or clusters of thirty. They are about *relationships* – between the people in the class, and the teacher, and the texts, and so on and so forth.

PAUL: Creativity can be crushed in a classroom by a senior management team who interpret the word of Ofsted or word of the examination process in a particularly tight and stringent way.

ALEX: Creativity *can* happen, though. In my old school they had a passion for creativity, and when I was promoted, it was my job to reshape the Key Stage 3 curriculum. I wanted to have schemes of learning that were more representative of society, more contemporary, more reflective of the *ethnic makeup* of the school and the cohort of the group that we were teaching. And so one thing I did was to develop a scheme of learning which we called Diverse Little London, and it had Sam Selvon's *The Lonely Londoners*, it had Zadie Smith...

PAUL: Amazing!

SARA: That sounds great. An education in English should give everyone a better understanding of who they are *and* who other people are. Texts from different cultures give you much more of a human insight.

ALEX: (*Nodding, smiling*) All the experienced members of staff there gave me a lot of love and allowed me the responsibility to do this, and experiment. It was really well received – texts they hadn't seen before, or knew of, they were looking forward to sharing and teaching.

PAUL: That proves that, to make it work, senior management have to create an atmosphere in which teachers can take chances and not feel they are being penalised by the appraisal process or for the results that their children may – or may not – get. Teachers have to be given the safety and the freedom in which to be vital.

(*Pause.*)

DOUG: I like to think of an English classroom as being an organic thing, like creating a greenhouse or orangery in which the climatic conditions are such that things can spring to life and grow.

JACK: Put another way, you have to see creativity as something that has a *pre-history*.

ISLA: You mean by 'pre-history' the soil in which the creative seed is planted, and the tending of that seed once germinated, and the water and sunshine it gets – all those things?

JACK: Yes. I can give you an example. I've still got loads of records and kids' work going back to my earliest days in the classroom. I can look at a powerful poem produced by a black kid in about 1984, and by tracing back through the archive of video recordings and sound recordings and my lesson plans and bits of his writing and all the rest of it, I can put together the story of how that poem came to be.

What created that poem was partly the spark – the seed – from the kid, who happened to write poetry in his spare time but wouldn't say anything about it in school; and also the debates and discussions that went on in the class, sometimes organised by the teacher, sometimes not, about race, about identity, a whole load of stuff; and it all came out in the poem. So, you can't glamorise and celebrate his creativity as the moment when the poem was first read and recognised and valued; it came from all that went before.

Creativity comes from young adults being taken seriously, taking themselves seriously.

PHIL: (*Assertively*) Well, yes, that's all very well in an ideal world. But I'm in favour of a more interventionalist approach. I'm too concerned that leaving such vital development 'to grow for itself' risks failure under competition, diversion or lack of motivation.

JACK: I take your point. But I'm an optimist! I have learnt that, as a teacher, you have to give autonomy to kids and show regard for the language that they produce. I know this can easily be parodied and sentimentalised, but I think that at its best, it's a first principle of teaching: that you work with what the kids produce rather than constantly seek to intervene.

PHIL: OK. But as a matter of expedience? Expedience could drive creative solutions.

PAUL: It comes back to the teacher creating an environment in which kids can take chances

ALEX: … and the importance of exploration…

JUDY: … and fronting up the notion of experiment…

ALEX: … building off each other, learning off each other, bouncing ideas off each other…

GARY: … and giving students space to get things wrong.

JACK: I agree: teacher creativity is in the situation. The situation half creates itself. You are managing what is happening in your classroom, and it's the decision *not* to intervene that can be creative too. It's not easy. It can't be packaged, it can't be planned for in a very specific way.

GILL: But I would argue it *can* be on the planned for, or how would new teachers learn? How do we develop? That's why we do small scale research. You learn by doing it yourself, from talking about it with other people, researching your practice. Perhaps we could say it's about doing things differently. Not always majorly differently, just a bit differently, to see what happens.

JACK: Point taken; there's an element of preparation. But you have to work with the materials in the moment, in the classroom. It's like orchestrating something. And English teachers that are worth their salt – probably the majority of English teachers – know when it's happening. But now – with the league tables, assessment, all the kind of things they have to deal with in schools, they must ask themselves all the time, 'Can I afford to let the kids go on talking? Can I risk this blowing up? Am I allowed to do this?'

ALEX: Hopefully yes! Noisy is sometimes good! (*laughs*)

SARA: (*Soberly*) I think that teachers today do the absolute best that they can within the limitations they're working under, but if you've got five thousand and one expectations, and none of them really relate to creativity, then you have to do the ones that you're expected to do.

GARY: (*Shaking his head in mock disbelief*) I think we will look back on this era in education and think, how did we allow ourselves to underrate teachers?

PAUL: That's why I am fearful for the death of creativity in education – especially for those just starting out who must toe the line.

GARY: Until recently, if you worked in a great English department, you tended to be surrounded by fairly feisty, articulate, vociferous people who read a lot, went to the cinema a lot, argued a lot and drank red wine a lot.

Laughter and nodding.

Yet at the English conferences I speak at now, I've noted a palpable reduction of feistiness and confidence.

ISLA: And is that a result of the policy itself, or because even seasoned, experienced English teachers are somehow losing the agency to counter it? We've heard that you, Paul, opted to step down as Head of Department; Anne did the same. Doug moved out of the mainstream and into an independent school. Three committed, experienced and resilient teachers changed their role as a direct consequence of their dislike of curriculum-induced pressures in their schools. So how can new teachers develop their own professional autonomy?

Lights dim for a few second and come up again.

III.3 Creating an English teacher

GARY: I think what exemplifies an English teacher is the way they speak, the way they read, the way they explain things, and personal response stuff. But now there's a generation of teachers who were themselves brought through assessment foci and modularity and therefore that's their mindset, and a world of PowerPoint where the teacher sees preparation as buying some pre-package which you put onto a screen for the child can look at. At our peril we're losing that sense of this being a humane occupation.

AKOS: (*Smiling wryly*) It's because the curriculum has structured itself in a way that you just do what it says. (*Pause*) We're all happy to take on 'outstandingness', but we're not all ready to consider ourselves as a teacher that 'requires improvement' – to develop ourselves.

GILL: I agree that some teacher trainees coming through have lost what it means to enjoy reading and need to rediscover that.

AKOS: And discover what it is to enjoy reading different texts. Like that 'attitude not ability' idea we looked at? (Sternberg quotation is displayed on rear screen: *[C]reativity is a much a decision about and an attitude toward life as it is a matter of ability.* (Sternberg, 2003: 98))

Maybe creativity ends up not being encouraged as a result of our own lack of subject knowledge, if our attitude is not to go looking. Some new teachers don't have a breadth of subject knowledge because unwittingly they didn't seek it during their very white, male, canonical degree courses, even when it was available. They didn't seek for it because it was not taught when they were at school. It's a cycle. And so interpretation in classrooms is one sided – people are interpreting literature the way that they've been *told* to interpret it.

ISLA: Yes, that's true. Certainly some responsibility may lie with the unwitting 'non-seekers' you allude to, if I can phrase it like that. But I think there is now – finally – an awareness of the need for more inclusive readings of the canon as well as more diverse text choices?

SARA: I did study a range of cultures and texts in translation. That helped me see that, in a way, everything is part of the literary canon, everything is actually interrelated. And I think that thinking on that scale makes you much more creative because it makes you want to be a part of something.

ISLA: And that shows that you (*nodding at Sara*) – and Ruth and Alex – *do* have that creative attitude, to borrow Steinberg's phrase, despite being, arguably, recent products of the system. You are all independent-minded, thoughtful, committed and able young teachers. I'm going to embarrass you, but I could suggest that you are models of what we would wish all new English teachers to be.

SARA: I'm not sure about that… but I do want to be a lifelong learner. If I'm told something I didn't know before I'll go away and read about it and I'll try and find out about it and question it. You can effect enormous social change by having people that are inquisitive and people that don't just accept what they're told, people that ask questions.

RUTH: I'm a lifelong learner too. I was a student at the school I now teach at. Governments change and curriculums change, but the teachers I work with continue to instil that lifelong love of learning into today's students that they instilled in me.

ISLA: That's interesting! I don't doubt you, but wonder how you can be so sure of this? And what it looks like in practice?

RUTH: (*Smiles, shrugs*) We read! We talk! That's what excites me and that's the reason I teach. That really is it.

(*Pause.*)

ALEX: For me, it's about being malleable. Being nuanced.

SARA: Mmmm. Something I have been doing a lot of work on in my own practice recently is the idea that you need to be taught the rules before you can break them.

There is real import to that; Stephen Fry talks about it in *The Ode Less Travelled*[1] – he says that you have to learn the rules of poetry before you can go on to write free verse or adopt an ee cummings approach, whatever.

ISLA: Does that apply to English teaching more generally? Can you do it 'right' by deliberately doing it 'wrong'? We've already noted that creative teaching is possible, although the context is not encouraging of it; do English teachers need to be actively interventionist or subversive to teach in the way that they believe they need to?

RUTH: I'm not sure! But I don't think we can restrict the discussion to English. I often talk about creativity with my friend who's a Maths teacher. He argues that Maths is just as creative – if not more so! – than any other subject, and we've had plenty of discussion about *that*! (*Laughs*)

III.4 Imagining the future

ISLA: So how should we best respond to the situation in which we find ourselves? What messages do you have for policy makers and – or – teacher educators, in order to develop that broader, humanist vision of education we all seem to espouse?

GARY: We need boldness in our politicians. We need bold changes. If we just provide new teachers with tricks for the classroom largely – cheap gimmicks – they miss the philosophical intellectual underpinning they need.

JACK: That's why teachers need space as well as advice.

JUDY: A good advertisement for university-based PGCE courses.

GARY: And we need investment in the profession. I would build in a system of continuous professional development that builds on teacher knowledge – so if when you've done five years in this school, you then get to spend two weeks experiencing a different school, or in a university department, or have two weeks of reading time – a bit like the Shanghai model, where secondary teachers are given time to develop, to hone their craft.

LEON: It's the same in Finland. And even better in Alberta[2].

GARY: I think we will look back and see that the lack of proper professional development is the big omission of all government policy.

AKOS: And I'd add that an overload of observations, league tables and professional assessments have a negative impact as well.

GARY: Exactly. So getting good people, keeping good people, isn't through dangling financial carrots in front of them, it's about making the job more rewarding. Give them more time, more reflection, more opportunity to contribute more widely. I think it's pretty hard to argue that that wouldn't be beneficial to teachers.

TONY: Yes – it wasn't until I started working with Creative Partnerships that I saw creativity in a different way. Before that I thought more in terms of, 'It's just getting them to be creative with words', but I realised that it's much more a mindset.

AKOS: But a mindset that is different for everyone. I would say as a black teacher working alongside white teachers, there must be space for difference in individuals' creativity as well. There is not just one type. Teachers should be agentive and creative in their own way.

RUTH: (*Thoughtfully*) Yes, I do things now in the class I would never have done a couple of years ago. Recently I was doing poetry comparisons with a Year 10 class and just from nowhere I decided that I would get out a ball of string. The students would be poems; they'd each have a post–it note on their head. One would hold a piece of string and make a point about their poem, and to pick up the other end someone else needed to have a point that was either complementing or contrasting the first point. When they were writing about the poems they remembered to imagine the string. (*She laughs with pleasure at the memory.*)

GILL: Yes! That's a brilliant example of how you are shifting, even *transforming* your pedagogy through reflection.

GARY: Exactly (*nodding to Ruth*). So, thirdly, we need to enable school leaders to give teachers the freedom to make English the hottest subject on the curriculum, as your teachers did for you.

LEON: For that to happen, they need to resolve the extraordinary dislocation between what is taught and tested at Key Stage 1, which is not really preparing pupils for what is taught and tested at Key Stage 2, and so on. There's no continuity.

TONY: And they need to introduce more humane exams. Not necessarily continuous assessment, but a system that can better assess genuine attainment.

RUTH: I've heard that in some countries they have an oral exam, and I think that's an interesting way to check students' understanding.

TONY: You must be thinking of the International Baccalaureate. Yes, one assessment method used in the IB is a half hour oral examination with an external examiner. 'So let's talk about *King Lear*.' Terrifying in some ways, and expensive – so it has its disadvantages – but a good examiner can see through those who could just talk and those who needed to be brought out. It's got potential.

LEON: For that to happen, we'd need to abandon this notion of competitiveness which started under Margaret Thatcher. This competitive model – everybody out for themselves – doesn't work: we've been more or less flat-lining, according to PISA and PIRLS, since the nineteen-nineties – twenty five years. Much more valuable would be returning to groups, collaboration.

DOUG: Perhaps in ten years' time we might be looking at a kind of open market in qualifications whereby little consortia of schools are grouping together in differ-ent ways to offer alternatives? It's happening a little bit in independent schools with interesting results – I think these opportunities should be rolled out for *everyone*.

General nodding, agreement.

ISLA: (*Addressing everyone, checking notes made during the discussion*) We're nearly out of time, and I think Doug's point is a perfect place to pause. You clearly agree with him that creative English is a child's right; that such an approach can lead to the development of sensitive, empowered, inquiring individuals who will not become worker bees.

Further murmurs of assent.

III.5 Summing up: Isla's soliloquy

I admit to being surprised at the extent of consensus. As you know, when I invited you to take part in this project, I did not know in advance your views on creativity.

In fact, the level of synthesis in the discussion is extraordinary, especially given the range of your own educational and professional experiences.

It appears that, for you all, teaching is a vocation, and to fully achieve that vocation – whatever your experience and expertise – professional freedom is fundamental. But the conditions as enshrined in current policy might make achieving that freedom difficult today, with the dominance of the test all-enthralling and an apparent attempt to silence the debate around creativity leading to real and urgent pressures on subject English. And the dissonance between what the Curriculum tells us and what your training, reading and experience has led you to know is potentially unhelpful, particularly to new teachers. However, those of you with long professional memories suggest that the National Curriculum has had a contentious history, there has always been push-back, and English teachers have been able to work their way – creatively – around some of the restrictions.

What Ruth, Sara and Alex have said gives especial grounds for optimism. Young teachers, brought up within the Curriculum, and trained in schools feeling the pinch, they are – despite the odds – as creative in their practice as possible. They are inspired by the same things that many of you maturer colleagues were inspired by – the same things that have inspired good teachers for centuries, perhaps (*Extract from Wotton (n.d.) is displayed on the screen: "First, there must proceed a way how to discern the natural inclinations and capacities of children. Secondly, next must ensue the culture and furnishment of the mind…."*). They wish to celebrate the natural inclinations and capacities of children; they want to provide opportunities to furnish their minds with culture in its widest sense, and quicken and excite them with what they learn and experience; they want to instil conscientious principles – humanity – in our young people.

Your words today suggest that we need to continue working creatively and actively towards a curriculum that is constantly re-shaped and re-made, that opens up opportunity, that gives everyone a chance to grow. Furthermore, we need especially to keep new teachers safe, their heads above water. It is up to them to inspire their learners and the next generation of English teachers.

I'd like to thank you sincerely for your contributions.

Notes

1 Fry, 2007.
2 The literature demonstrates that CPD in Finland and Alberta is well-developed, centrally-funded and highly-valued (Government of Alberta, 2010; European Commission, 2020).

Part IV

Forging connections, creating change

Preface to Part IV

To recap, Part II of this book argues that although curriculum policy originally presented English as essentially a creative subject, rooted in a humane, child-centred pedagogy, this view has been 'turned on its head' (McCallum, 2012: 18) over the past century such that today's National Curriculum (DfE, 2014) appears *anti*-creative. In contrast, the playscript that makes up Part III demonstrates that representatives of the profession (the colloquists) are critical of aspects of the Curriculum that limit creative English and – contrary to fears expressed in the literature – espouse creativity where they can. This exposes contradictions: creative English currently has no official mandate but is understood by practitioners to be essential; academic and professional advice is often incompatible with policy (and sometimes openly hostile towards it); the humane tradition is not being fuelled.

Part IV now goes on to explore some of these tensions between the English policy and the practitioners in more depth and suggests that the way to resolve them is through forging connections. Threads drawn between past and present policy produce the warp; simultaneously, threads linking past and present English teachers form the weft. Together, they create a rich but unfinished tapestry, one that will continue to be woven into the future. It then highlights a growing consensus that education policy itself should be re-created if learners are to be sufficiently equipped to be able to re-create their world. English is as central to this effort (Facer, 2019) as it was when Newbolt positioned English as the 'keystone' over a century ago (1921: 5).

The book concludes with some practical, creative classroom activities recommended for today's classrooms, drawn from and inspired by English curriculum policy of the past.

DOI: 10.4324/9781003243311-12

5 To contest or comply? Creating change-makers

5.1 Introduction

This book was inspired by my unease at the removal of 'creativity' from the sixth iteration of the National Curriculum (DfE, 2014) for English in England, which is both a symptom and possible cause of the multi-layered crisis that English education is facing.

This penultimate chapter begins with a reflection on the playscript presented in Part III in the light of the literature seen in Part I and the policy documents in Part II, indicating how the dissonance between the current Curriculum and contemporary literature that promotes creative English is potentially unhelpful, particularly to new entrants to the profession and those conditioned to limited institutional practice. However, the chapter argues that a middle way is possible: as the colloquists demonstrate, if teachers have the confidence and ability to 'inhabit' the policy and make it their own, they can enact the Curriculum in creative ways. One way in which the knowledge and experience that allows creative practice to be reappraised, preserved and shared might be passed on is through communities of practice.

The chapter then makes further suggestions about how creativity and English can be properly reconnected. It argues that creative practice adapts in response to the context and needs, so that celebrating creative practice is not a romantic archival of the past, but necessary for on-going survival. It concludes by re-emphasising that enabling young people to be creative is essential for their own individual future well-being and – more broadly and more importantly – the future of humanity and the planet.

5.1.1 Opening questions

Before you continue your reading of this chapter, pause to reflect once more on your reading of this book so far and your own experience:

- Has your own definition of creativity changed or developed through your reading of this book? If so, try to define what the changes are and what prompted them.
- How might the relationship between the Curriculum and the English teachers who enact it be described?
- What ideas do you have to promote creative English practice on a personal, school, local and even wider level?

DOI: 10.4324/9781003243311-13

5.2 Weaving the tapestry: reflecting on the colloquies in the light of the policy documents

Let us start by drawing out the links between the colloquists' views and past and present policy. The colloquists see English as a unitary, creative subject, based on a wider view of personal growth, self-esteem, understanding of self and others, and a grasp of what makes us all better and worse human beings. The playscript includes discussion of the importance of collaborative, exploratory talk; of reading for pleasure; of expressive personal writing. This indicates that the personal growth view traced through Chapters 2 and 3 and promoted by Cox (1989) has remained the most popular of the five models amongst English teaching professionals, confirming suggestions by Marshall (2000) and Goodwyn (2016). They implicitly reject the cultural capital being pushed by the Curriculum and, with it, elitist notions of culture. As Jack notes, the unitary view of English does not separate language from literature. Rather, there is a sense that it is partly *through* engagement with literature that what Judy terms 'the living of English' (*op cit*) happens although, as Akos reminds us, we should consider carefully what literature we teach, and how.

Yet despite the colloquists' resistance, friction remains. Those currently in the mainstream classroom resent being part of the 'system' (Anne, Paul) and are frustrated that creativity is repressed due to the demands of accountability, while Doug, based in an independent setting and so less beholden to the letter of the Curriculum, still deplores its impact on the shape of examination specifications. The teacher educators are dismayed to observe their student teachers sometimes having to reduce potentially rich content to little more than feature-spotting.

The colloquists echo frustrations from the field (*e.g.* Jeffrey and Craft, 2004; Goodwyn, 2016; Perryman and Calvert, 2020) that an imposed Curriculum risks diminishing the English teacher's role. The older colloquists (Gill, Leon) concur with Stubbs (1989) and Cox (1991) that the erosion of a teacher's autonomy began as far back as the advent of the National Curriculum (and is something they fought against). This suggests that it is the *vehicle* of a mandatory curriculum that they challenge, since Gill and Leon implicitly admire the *content* of Cox's policy in terms of its positioning of English. Doug's experience shows how the National Literacy Strategy, introduced a decade after Cox, further undermined a teacher's professional freedom; but it is interesting that even after the demise of the Strategy in 2010, anxiety remains that teacher agency is ever more limited. Gary is scathing about 'deprofessionalisation', as are the critics (Cremin, 2016; Yandell and Brady, 2016; Bomford, 2018). However, despite the suggestions in the literature – reinforced anecdotally by the colloquists – that teachers are obliged to teach to the test, none of the colloquists admits to doing so; those who remain active in the classroom resist changing their own practice to conform to the accountability regime. Sara and Ruth give examples of both planned and spontaneous practices that are responsive to needs of their learners; and they see themselves as learners too. They understand that learning is iterative. Anne, Paul and Doug may have changed their roles to escape what they found to be unbearable pressures from management, but they did so to free themselves to continue to teach as they wish.

Further, Alex, Ruth and Sara's experiences demonstrate that even teachers who grew up with recent policy and have known nothing but the current Curriculum professionally are able to teach creatively, which suggests that – contrary to the fears expressed by Gary and others that collective memory of creative practice is diminishing – it has not disappeared altogether. Although new entrants to the profession (and interested others) are unable to rely upon the Curriculum to furnish themselves with a deep understanding of English in all its richness and complexity, it appears that this knowledge can be curated and passed on, including by the teacher educators who are 'living with contradiction' (Heilbronn, 2013: 35) in having both to prepare their trainees for the Curriculum and work around it. The testimonies suggest that new teachers can learn to work through the challenges of their training year as their understanding of English matures, which gives them the confidence to go on to practice as 'disruptive professionals' (Thomas, 2019, n.p.).

Together, then, the colloquists maintain a broad, varied, complex, humane view of creative English. Those who are classroom teachers seek to practice as creatively as possible within the constraints of the system, and the teacher educators are 'in solidarity' (Heilbronn, 2013: 35) in encouraging newcomers to do the same. Those in positions of responsibility (head teachers and those active in subject bodies) seek to promulgate creative practice as widely as possible. Far from being led by the Curriculum, they actively resist key aspects of it. Admittedly, the sample is exclusive and expert, and since it consists only of those who chose to remain in the profession, it excludes the voices of those who have left teaching because their creativity is stifled. However, it does indicate a common determination to be resilient and resist imposed agendas.

All this demonstrates that although policy-makers control the *wording* of the documents they publish, they cannot control their *reception*. Teachers are not, after all, 'empty vessels' even if they are 'silent voices' (Smit, 2005: 295) in terms of policy-making. They review policy in the light of their experience, and act accordingly, and we know from the colloquies that at least some choose to respond creatively. So how might we use what we know to reinvigorate disillusioned English teachers and to inform the next generation? What – and whom – might they trust? These questions are considered in this chapter, prompting reflection on agency and power in the wider sphere.

5.3 Addressing the teacher: from creative professionals to grocery boys (and girls)

Yet before considering the power of collective memory and the agency of teachers in more depth, I want to turn briefly to another theme that emerged from reading the policy documents and talking with the colloquists – how the policy documents themselves 'talk' to subject professionals.

Considering not so much *what* teachers are advised or told to teach, but *how*, is an indication of the extent to which the policy values the teachers and assumes them to be (or not to be) creative and agentive. Put simply, the documents written by those who consulted teachers extensively, actively involving them in the creation of policy (Newbolt, 1921; Bullock, 1975; Cox, 1989) are those that show respect to and trust in teachers; those that did not, apparently increasingly come to view teachers as cyphers.

The earliest policy documents present teachers as professionals, with authority to make choices: the formal title of the Blue Books series, <u>*Suggestions for the Consideration*</u>

of Teachers and Others Concerned in the Work of the Public Elementary Schools (my emphasis)
underlines that they were entrusted to take decisions in the best interests of their students, a point emphasised in the Introduction:

> The only uniformity in practice that the Board of Education desire to see… is that
> each teacher shall think for himself (sic), and work out for himself, such methods
> of teaching as may use his powers to the best advantage and be best suited to the
> particular needs and conditions of the school.

> (BoE, 1905/1912: 3)

This indicates that the productivity of learner is based on creativity of teacher: the
teacher's role is to respond (creatively) to the needs of students.

For Newbolt, teaching is a noble, even heroic calling: teachers are part of an 'army'
(Newbolt, 1921: 25) – albeit an army Newbolt states to be underpaid, insufficiently
resourced and inadequately trained. In another powerful metaphor, he presents the
teacher as a mighty 'lever', without which it is impossible to 'raise the mass' (*ibid*). The
imagery indicates that Newbolt is encouraging his readership to appreciate that teachers should be respected and have power vested in them. The Bullock Report shows a
similar respect to teachers. The Foreword, written by the then Education Secretary,
requests that 'teachers at all levels will look carefully at the recommendations' (1975: iii),
implying a confidence that teachers will act accordingly. The agency is with the teacher
to develop their practice in the light of what they read.

This trusting tone changes with the arrival of the Curriculum. By its very existence,
a statutory Curriculum does not offer 'suggestions', but obligations: according to one
view, the advent of the Curriculum and the associated semantic field of 'delivery' rele-
gates teachers from curriculum innovators to grocery boys (Armstrong, 1988), an exag-
gerated image which nonetheless emphasises the extent to which teachers' standing had
been reduced since Newbolt's day. It is only Cox (1989) who explicitly discusses of the
role of the teacher, as he attempted to keep the profession onside after what had been a
particularly turbulent time and unsympathetic treatment by the press (Aldrich, 2005).
Echoing its predecessor policies, his National Curriculum states that teachers are autonomous professionals, free to make decisions on behalf of their pupils. He encourages
teachers to go beyond the specified targets: 'we would not wish teachers to feel limited
by them' (1989: 54) – which implies he is advocating that teachers extend their practice
wherever possible. He gives advice – 'Pupils should see adults writing. Teachers should
write alongside pupils, sharing and talking about their writing.' (1989: 44). Very occasionally he could be construed as patronising: '*Using sensitivity and tact*, teachers should
help pupils to tackle texts of increasing difficulty.' (1989: 29, my emphasis): it is not clear
here whether Cox is guiding teachers or instructing them.

In subsequent Curriculum documents, one difficulty in considering the way teachers
are addressed is the ambiguity of the modal verb 'should': it can denote both advice and
imperative. 'Pupils should be taught' is a phrase borrowed from Cox (1989) and used
repeatedly in the next two iterations of the Curriculum (DfE/WO, 1995; DfEE/QCA
1999a). Cox generally offers a guiding hand when he uses 'should', yet because the curriculum documents from 1995 (DfE/WO) onwards are sparer, the repeated 'shoulds',
often introducing a series of bullet points laying down what 'should' be taught, suggest
a sense of command. While Cox gives advice, his immediate successors appear to give
teachers instructions.

The 2007 Curriculum is slightly more nuanced. It uses 'Pupils should *be able to…*' (*e.g.* DCSF/QCA, 2007: 64, my emphasis): such wording implies a more facilitatory teacher role (albeit, as suggested in Chapter 4, with limited real licence for creativity). Yet a facilitatory role was something to which Gove objected: in a speech to a teacher conference (2008), he blamed pupil-centric policy for 'dethroning' teachers. His Curriculum returns to listing what 'should be taught' and, to reiterate the point, also turns the passive into active, putting the teacher at the forefront: there is frequent reference to 'Teachers should…' (*e.g.* DfE, 2014: 2, 3). But if such wording is intended to 're-throne' teachers by putting them explicitly in control of their pupils, it also emphasises their subjugation to higher powers and policy.

This lexical point reinforces the notion that the Curriculum is imposed upon teachers by dominant others. Such imposition, almost by definition, denies them agency and impedes (or even prevents) creativity; it also helps explain the unpopularity of the Curriculum as presented in the contemporary literature. However, the colloquists' confident agency indicates that even if this is the intention, it has not wholly succeeded: English practitioners are able to practice creatively notwithstanding. (It could even be suggested that their dislike of the Curriculum is a reaction to the assertive way they are addressed.)

5.4 Questions of agency: inhabiting the curriculum and maintaining the maps

It is interesting that in cases where there is 'mismatch' (Biesta *et al.*, 2015: 624) between teachers' beliefs and wider institutional cultures and policy, it is usually assumed that practice *suffers* as a result of dominant policy, as implied by Biesta *et al.*: they suggest that the growth of prescriptive curricula and oppressive testing have not only deprofessionalised teachers and removed their agency, but narrowed teachers' beliefs and values commensurately. However, as the colloquists demonstrate, teachers can hold considerable influence because it is *they* who ultimately control the lesson-to-lesson classroom experiences of their students. Accordingly, English teachers in the current climate are more powerful than they might imagine.

It is a combination of teachers' thoughts, beliefs and assumptions that have strong implications for how curriculum policy appears in practice (Hargreaves, 1994). These are inspired by a combination of powerful forces: a teacher's own experiences of education and wider life experience, collaborative practice and the tradition of creative English teaching. These deep professional reservoirs act as a prism through which they can view, critique and respond agentively to policy. The parameters within which they work may have been set by the policy-makers, but are inhabited by living actors, who can take it, re-create it and find their own way through it.

In illustration, it is helpful to consider an essay entitled *Walking in the City* (De Certeau, 1984). De Certeau recalls looking down with a near bird's-eye view from the original World Trade Centre onto the streets of New York, watching pedestrians making their way around the city. He noted that some navigated the grid of streets and squares and parks in ways the planners might not have intended (or even imagined); they inhabited the cityscape creatively, making it their own. De Certeau realised that while planners have power in designing a layout consisting of rigid structures, they have little control over how that framework is *actually* used. This metaphor illustrates the reach and impact of English teachers' agency within policy strictures. While teachers did not design the Curriculum, they can 'inhabit' it. Although constrained by its framework, they are free to choose any route through it, travel by any appropriate mode, spend as long or as little time in any one place as they like, potentially finding as they go unplanned opportunities. Granted, in many schools there are additional structural layers imposed by academy or departmental strictures, and, of course, not all journeys through the city will be true explorations: some will need to be direct (and possibly uninspiring) trips from A to B, perhaps as envisaged by the planners. The freedom of the journey depends on the pedestrian – on whether they are confident to explore, feel they have permission to do so, the time, the resources. It is, perhaps, partly a matter of manoeuvring tactically through the 'uneven distributions' (Ball *et al.*, 2012: 97) of a school's layout, staffing, timetabling and scheduling, and capitalising where they can.

The image implies that the Curriculum can simultaneously constrain *and* open things up – just as the limitations of the sonnet form might inspire the creation of a poem, as suggested by Paul, Doug and Tony (*op cit*). Having an external structure such as a Curriculum can even be helpful (and appreciated by teachers) in enabling teacher agency (Erss, 2018), *as long as* the teacher is sufficiently confident, prepared and empowered to make appropriate choices, knowing when it is necessary or expedient to take the direct route and when taking the long way round might be more interesting and enriching.

The colloquists' testimony indicates that they are denizens of the Curriculum city, and can set out with assurance. However, it may be harder for newcomers to feel acclimatised with only the 'official' map or a satnav to help them. Any traveller knows that you need the Rough Guide to help you properly navigate a new place, and then you need to hook up with locals who can show you alternative routes, teach you the tactics and tell you what the neighbourhood was like before the new ring road sliced through it, until you *really* begin to feel at home. Equally, teachers conditioned to the current Curriculum, teaching very prescriptive courses – unused to independent travel – may need guidance when a more enlightened policy comes in and frees them to be more agentive (Erss, 2008).

Preserving the collective memories of those who know well not only the streets of the current National Curriculum for English but its previous layouts – designed by planners with different agenda – is therefore crucial in ensuring that life and spirit within the city survive into the future. The examples of practice provided by the colloquists – the knowledgeable 'locals' – are cumulatively powerful because their stories reinforce each other. The playscript is more than the sum of the individual parts – it is a composite of many single images, *bilds*, that create the 'bildung' or 'culture' (Gadamer, 1975/2004: 9) of English teaching. It is an impression of their *collective* memory, a charting of tradition.

Sustaining and building collective memory keeps the conversation alive. To lose the connection now, allowing the ley lines of English to disappear and so open up impenetrable 'gaps' (Biesta, 2004: 19), could be particularly damaging. Although developments in teacher education suggest that new teachers are increasingly critical (in the reflective and reflexive sense) of both policy and their own practice (Morgan, 2014), the restrictions of the Curriculum and accountability frameworks have created a generation of English teachers who have had little experience of curriculum innovation, of what it is to explore in an arguably arid context. English separated from its creative, agentive, humane history risks becoming 'deracinated' (Bleiman, 2020: 187), rootless – and 'routeless'. It could therefore be said to be the *responsibility* of those active in the profession to actively maintain and develop collective memory, ensuring that their knowledge of the past combined with an understanding of their potential agency can enlighten classrooms of the future.

5.5 Creating change-makers: some practical proposals

One means of capturing and building on the collective memories of experienced practitioners like these – those who are powerful forces in their own classrooms, have deep knowledge of their subject and valuable stories to tell – is through building communities of practice. A community of practice is a coming-together of individuals connected through their role (Lave and Wenger, 1991); a community can therefore support English teachers to enhance their individual agency through collaboration.

Accordingly, this section – which proposes practical ways in which the theories in this book might be made flesh – begins by outlining the development of subject English communities of practice as an easily-achievable action. It goes on to offer two more ambitious proposals: that the term 'creativity' should explicitly be re-incorporated in the National Curriculum for English, and that expert English teaching professionals should be involved in the creative process of re-imagining and re-writing the policy as part of a principled Curriculum review.

5.5.1 Creating communities of practice

A community of practice affords cross-generational connections that support the maintenance of professional memory by creating and affirming personal relationships between one teacher and another. A community is typically made up of both experts and novices (Lave and Wenger, 1991), although these demarcations should not be used in a limited way (*e.g.* one individual English teacher might be an 'expert' in their classroom but a novice head of department, or an 'expert' in English Literature A Level but a novice in English Language). Membership of a community involves sharing real situations and solving problems with others. People offer and receive guidance, understanding and support; they celebrate and pass on what they know to their colleagues. As such, communities have the potential to increase teacher agency, contribute to teacher wellbeing and ultimately improve learning outcomes. They have been used in educational settings for some time (Kimble and Hildreth, 2008), including in teacher education (Paton and Parker, 2017), and this book has already charted the founding of English-specific communities, including the original English Association in 1906 and the London Association for the Teaching of English in 1947. But there is room for more to be created where they are absent. They might be established and supported through university partnerships, formal and informal Teach-Meets, academy chains and local authority hubs. Social media platforms such as Twitter offer powerful potential too.

In the short term, I hope that this book will encourage all English teachers to regard themselves as part of a community of practice and, if they are not already, become active participants, perhaps even establishing a group. As living links in the history of creative English teaching, they will inspire others to forge their own links too. The metaphor is not of a single, heavy, restrictive chain, but a mesh of delicate golden rings – flexible, strong. Connected thus to colleagues past and present, each is a tiny yet crucial part, protecting the precious heart of English for the future.

It is particularly important to welcome newcomers to the profession to this community and to help them understand that although they will spend much of their time practising as individuals in their separate classrooms, they are part of a wider body, each a link that strengthens the golden mail. This may give new teachers, particularly those trained to deliver a knowledge-based curriculum and are sceptical of creative English pedagogy, the confidence to experiment and take creative risks in a way that they might not otherwise feel mandated to do.

5.5.2 Rewrite 'creativity' into the English curriculum

My second proposal is that 'creativity' must be rewritten into English policy. As Jack noted, the inclusion of the term provides, at least, something around which debate can pivot. Ofsted recently described English as having a 'strong creative and expressive dimension' (2022: n.p.), which hints that creativity might be inching back into political favour. Yet, given the contentious history of 'creativity' regarding English, any definition needs to be carefully constructed: the most recent attempt at defining creativity in the Curriculum (DCSF/QCA, 2007) is, as I have shown, limited, in that it assumes creativity always to have a *written* outcome; and prior to that, Cox (1989) makes a clear and impassioned argument for creative English without reference to the term itself. It may be that the adoption of 'creativities' (McCallum, 2012: 20) is apposite. Yet for any definition to serve a useful purpose in curriculum policy, English teaching professionals must be involved in its construction.

5.5.3 Involve expert English professionals in re-imagining and re-writing the curriculum

Thirdly, education policy going forward should be informed by a consultative process between representatives from across the field of subject English and policy-makers, a 'collective development' (Biesta *et al.*, 2015: 624). Although the worlds of today's policy-makers and teaching professionals are very different – the one based on data at a macro level, the other concerning people and relationships on a micro level – a solution may lie in bringing these two worlds together. Here it is important to stress that it is not the Curriculum alone that causes tension: as discussed, a curriculum structure can be helpful; and the academisation programme ensures that the majority of maintained secondary schools in England are not *explicitly* bound by the Curriculum until Key Stage 4. The problem is rather the combination of the Curriculum and the examination and accountability system to which it is tethered. Both the Curriculum and the assessment regime must be *recreated* simultaneously: to revise the one without the other would have little effect.

Ofsted's current Inspection Framework (2019) already requires that teachers justify their curriculum design on a school level; this conversation should be opened up more broadly and is perhaps something to which the new Institute of Teaching could attend. To welcome the contribution of subject experts to policy development would be to go full circle and return to the organic process through which the earliest policy documents such as Newbolt (1921) were written. If those who are to enact the policy are involved in its co-creation – or, to return to de Certeau's (1984) analogy, co-design their ideal city – it is more likely to be embraced and celebrated in classrooms (Smit, 2005). Further, such a move would indicate a restoration of trust in the experts by the policy-makers which might lead, in turn, to teaching professionals renewing their confidence in the authorities.

There are various models that might be researched towards the creation of a new Curriculum. For instance, one approach would be to dispense with a 'National' curriculum altogether and develop an area-based or local curriculum (Facer and Thomas, 2012; Dutaut, 2018), as used successfully in international jurisdictions such as Finland (Lähdemäki, 2018). Additionally, or alternatively, is the notion of a co-created Curriculum, already proving successful in higher education in parts of the UK, Ireland and the United States (Bovill, 2014) as better able to meet local and regional needs.

An even more radical option is to devolve the Curriculum entirely to teaching professionals, alongside a devolved assessment system. Technological advances such as anti-plagiarism software could be used to prevent unethical practice that dogged this system in the past. Such an approach would allow teachers to be curriculum innovators and develop a curriculum in which *'creativity and English* link to learning' (McCallum, 2012: 32) according to need and interest. Research into these possibilities is overdue.

5.6 Conclusion: creating the agentive child

The importance of teacher creativity and agency is evidently not an end in itself: the creative, agentive teacher produces the creative, agentive child, equipped to respond to the challenges faced by society today and the changes of tomorrow.

To practice creatively is not to react uncritically to direction, but to have the flexibility to collaborate, solve problems, be imaginative with content and style, innovate – and have the freedom to be radical if need be – albeit within the limitations of the official structures. Children who learn from creative practitioners learn to be creative themselves and 'grow' personally; young people are thereby prepared to 'assume joint responsibility for the world' (Arendt, 1954: 10) and respond agentively to the unprecedented issues of the 2020s and beyond. It is not hyperbole to suggest that if our children do not grow up to be agentive adults, capable of dealing with ever-increasing pressures of war, population and climate change, the future of humanity is at stake. Education should prepare them to know what they can take with them on their journey (and what should be left behind) to enable them to create something 'radically new' to 'accompany us into the future' (Osberg, 2010: 168).

Subject English is particularly important in helping children imagine and articulate the ideas that will enable them to answer these challenges because it is concerned with creating and engaging with stories. Through story they can imagine responses to challenging situations and consider complex 'what ifs'. Such activities are therefore not frivolous, but 'deadly serious' (Facer, 2019: 11): it is crucial that students are practised in envisaging, experimenting and developing flexible responses. All the elements of English – speaking, listening, reading and writing – are needed to equip students for the global problems already upon us; indeed, they are vulnerable without them. Through actively rehearsing English in school, students develop the agency to take the stories they make off the page and into the world. It is when the stories are enacted and performed that they will have an impact. Malala Yousafzai and Greta Thunberg are examples of young people who have not only the creativity to imagine the future, but the agency to act.

Ultimately, therefore, the nurturing of personal growth through child-centred, creative English might lead to the growth of a better future, in a world curated by fair-minded, mutually supportive and caring inhabitants. It should, at the very least, prevent a worse future. The importance of maintaining the tradition of radical, creative English in the here-and-now is strengthened by emphasising that it is the basis to all our tomorrows.

In summary:

This book has sought to underline the essential connections between creativity, English and learning because English, thus conceived, is fundamental in enabling the humane education Biesta describes – '*a human event of communication, meaning making and interpretation*' (2015: 11).

English is *all about* language and communication with 'our selves' (Summerfield, 1968: 44), with texts, with others. To decouple English and creativity jeopardises opportunities for genuine conversation and, with it, the development of new knowledge and opportunities both for individuals and society to *make* and be (*re*)*made*. To this end, Chapter 5 has advocated encouraging teacher agency, developing communities of practice and reconnecting the Curriculum with those who teach it.

I have begun a creative conversation that I hope they, as I, will continue.

6 Historical perspectives to future directions

6.1 Introduction

This book is not intended to be a handbook of creative practice, although ways to foster creative teaching and learning are often explicit and, I hope, always implicit. Nevertheless, it would not be out of place to devote this final chapter to a selection of my own favourite classroom strategies; and doing so by going back to the future is an appropriate coda to the theme that has run throughout: that understanding history can help us plan the way forward. What follows are ideas that connect policies and practice of the past with classrooms of the present, aimed at inspiring English teachers on their onward journeys.

The 11 suggestions are drawn directly from the policy and advisory documents discussed in Chapters 2–4, up to and including Cox's Curriculum (1989). Together, they cover the requisites of a subject English education; but crucially, they are creative, adaptable, effective and enjoyable, and easy to set up. In tune with earlier sections of this book, activities for speaking and listening, reading and writing are offered in that order, although of course there are overlaps – for instance, drama-based activities are included under Speaking and Listening to highlight the mode, although given the exercises are text-based, they would be just as relevant under Reading.

In each case, I provide the full quotation from the relevant policy document, then an explanation of how and why its message is still relevant, valid and valuable for contemporary creative English teaching.

6.2 Speaking and listening

6.2.1 The importance of oracy: groupwork

> We wish very strongly to insist that training in continuous oral expression should be brought to the front as the most indispensable part of the school course. Without it the junior classes will fail in their object of 'grounding' the children. The senior classes, also, will find that their teaching of English will have but ill-balanced results if all the speaking is done out of school, all the reading and writing in school. Here, in addition to dramatic work, debates and brief 'lectures' by the pupils themselves may be helpful. Oral work is, we are convinced, the foundation upon which proficiency in the writing of English must be based. More than that, it is a condition of the successful teaching of all that is worth being taught.
>
> (Newbolt, 1921: 71)

DOI: 10.4324/9781003243311-14

Given the wealth of research on the topic (*e.g.* Alexander, 2008; Burgess *et al.*, 2022; voice21.org), it is near indisputable that Newbolt was right and classroom talk promotes learning.

The phrase 'classroom talk' encompasses pair-work, groupwork and whole class discussion. Pair-work, often in the form of 'Think – pair – share' is widely practised in schools, often as a precursor to class discussion, but groupwork is less common. Here the value of groupwork is emphasised, not only as a suitable context for the drama, debates and lectures that Newbolt recommends, but also for discussion-based talk.

Working in groups allows learners to explore, weigh up, investigate, experiment; they can listen to each other's arguments and rehearse their own (something particularly helpful to less confident learners); they can test out tentative thoughts and have their ideas embraced and extended by others. Depending on the learning goal, the question under discussion can be targeted and precise, or more open.

To encourage all to contribute (and prevent some individuals dominating a discussion), a teacher might:

i) allocate roles within each group (*e.g.* chair, speakers for/against the motion, time-keeper, etc.) or use De Bono's 'Thinking Hats' (n.d);
ii) offer Talk Tokens – each learner has a given number of counters which they 'spend' whenever they contribute to the discussion. This encourages more confident speakers to consider carefully when to enter the discussion, while less confident speakers know that their contribution is expected;
iii) provide slips with sentence-starter stems to encourage learners to respond to each other's points, such as 'But have you thought of…?', 'On the other hand…', 'I understand the point you are making, however…'. Indeed, a useful activity might be to prepare for a discussion by getting the class to create banks of such sentence-starters.

6.2.2 Drama for understanding language and literature

In the Senior School dramatic activity [begun in the Junior School] should be vigorously continued. Classroom productions, the dramatisation of longer stories of more complex ballads, discussion, criticism and school production, all have their place.

(BoE, 1937: 392)

As this edition of the Blue Books emphasises, embodied learning can be as effective with older learners as the young. These specific suggestions focus on how drama approaches can be used at any stage of literary study, from (i) introducing a new collection of poems to (ii) revising longer texts.

i) Offer an unseen poem to groups of 4–6, a different poem per group. Invite the groups to devise a performance of their poem. Challenge them to do so in different ways, if appropriate. For example:
   • *Pass the punctuation*: Everyone in the group participates by reading the poem from punctuation mark to punctuation mark, passing on the meaning with a suitable gesture.

- *Sound Studio*: One or two key voices read the poem aloud, with others creating appropriate sound effects using their voices or props.
- *ECHO echo echo*: One or two key voices read the whole poem aloud, with other voices echoing important words or phrases, with appropriate gestures.
- *Be daring with dynamics*: Learners work out where the dynamic drama needs to come to best emphasise key messages from the poem. For instance, they might start by reading the poem very quietly, build up to strong, loud voice(s) and recede again. Volume can be increased or decreased by adding/taking away different voices, or by individuals modulating their voices.

  Each group rehearses and then presents its performance. When going on to exploring the poems in more detail, discussion might be opened by inviting the relevant group to comment on the poem in the light of their experience.

ii) When revising a novel or a play, allocate a different chapter/scene to different groups. Ask them to recreate its key events, and present them within a very tight time frame (*e.g.* 20 seconds). All members of the group should be involved, whether as characters or part of the set. This requires that the group recall the main events, agree on significant moments, and work out how to present them in a meaningful way (perhaps including key quotations). Performing the presentations consecutively summarises the whole narrative within minutes. Film them, so that they can be revisited and compared to focus on aspects such as theme, characterisation and structure.

6.2.3 Drama for understanding drama texts

Drama is both a creative art form in its own right and also an instrument of learning.... At secondary school level, pupils will be involved in the study of plays and dramatic texts. As actors, audience or directors (all three, we hope) they will be the interpreters of plays written by others... Pupils should approach plays through the dramatic medium. This exploratory and performance-based approach will not only lead to a deeper understanding of the text in question (a dramatic exploration of a speech in Shakespeare, for instance, will show how the placing of different emphases can alter fundamentally one's interpretation of character or meaning) but will also lead to an understanding of the play as theatre. Performance-based activity may, of course, take place at classroom level, in small-scale improvisational sessions or in text work.

(Cox, 1989: 101)

There is a wealth of advice available (*e.g.* www.rsc.org.uk; Cambridge School Shakespeare series) on how to play with the plays of Shakespeare in class to create meaningful learning. Some time-efficient approaches that do not require re-arranging the classroom include:

- When reading a playscript – or listening to an audio production – display a background image via the whiteboard or visualiser to 'set the scene' and turn the classroom into a theatre at a stroke. Offering learners a choice of backdrops and getting them to decide and justify which is most appropriate is a powerful starter task, requiring that they recall prior learning.

- Allocate key lines or extracts to pairs or groups as appropriate. Invite them to produce freeze-frames to demonstrate relationships between characters, bearing in mind proximity, facial expression, gesture, blocking, etc. Take photos of each freeze-frame; these can then be displayed on the board and annotated, or used in an interactive display.
- Not all drama activities need to be 'active'. At-seat performance and improvisation using very basic puppets (figures made with pencils and pipe-cleaners) can be very effective in helping learners consider mood, tone, pace and emphasis, all of which support textual understanding.

6.2.4 Poetry recitation for poetic understanding:

Individual children should be encouraged to choose their own poetry for repetition, and to this end they must not only constantly hear good poetry read aloud, but they must have frequent opportunities to read it for themselves. They may well be encouraged, where circumstances are favourable, to read and learn poetry at home. The pieces selected for recitation may properly be read aloud by the teacher, who, however, should be chary of imposing on the child either his own conception of the poem or his own rendering of it. And insomuch as the recitation of poetry implies an audience, a child should be required to recite what he has learnt by heart to the rest of the class, who may be allowed to criticise his own rendering.

(BoE, 1914: 35–36)

As Gillian Clarke poignantly illustrates in *Miracle On St David's Day* (1982), a poem learnt by heart as a child can stay in the memory forever. The successful Poetry by Heart project (www.poetrybyheart.org.uk) builds upon the Board of Education's recommendations by encouraging schools to enter a national recitation competition, providing learners with opportunities to take poems and make them their own. Its website showcases 1,000 years of literature, from Beowulf to the present; a high proportion is by women and poets from the global majority. Not only is the competition engaging and builds oral confidence, but it develops close reading skills and understanding as learners consider the deep meaning of words and phrases to nuance their performance (Whitley, 2017).

6.3 Reading

6.3.1 Promoting reading for pleasure

It is a particularly effective device for a teacher to stir demand by reading out arresting passages from new books. Television programmes likely to arouse a keen interest can be anticipated, and the teacher can have ready and waiting the appropriate books to catch the wave. There is almost no limit to the 'publicity' devices that might be conceived. For instance, in the display of dust jackets of new books arrows can lead off to large illustrations and short offprints of associated material. Pupils can be given a board on which to pin up extracts calculated to make the curious want to know more. The teacher might tape trailer passages on cassettes for children to listen to on headsets. Some pupils might produce advertisement posters or design alternative dust jackets from their knowledge of the book. And always the children should be encouraged to talk about what they have read, to the teacher and among themselves. By keeping a note of what children read he could bring three or four together who had had common experience of a particular book and let them explore one another's reactions to it. This is so much more productive and so much less forbidding than the obligatory written book review, where the pupil knows that his pleasure has inevitably to be followed by a chore.

(Bullock, 1975: 128)

In its Research Review: English, Ofsted make the unsourced claim that activities to promote reading might be a 'distraction' (Ofsted, 2022: n.p.), using up time and energy that should be better spend on reading practice. However, research (*e.g.* Becker *et al.*, 2010; Cremin *et al.,* 2014; Cremin, 2019) suggests the opposite. World Book Day is a popular annual initiative that offers books for £1:00 and invites learners to dress up as their favourite book character, but its success can arguably be ascribed as much to the freedom it provides learners to talk about their own favourite reads (Picton *et al.*, 2021), and so such activity should not be restricted to one day a year. Through reserving a prominent wall in an English classroom for displays such as Bullock describes, or making an interactive virtual equivalent prominent on the school's website through apps such as www.pinterest.com or Padlet.com – and then making time every so often to talk about the recommended books in class and updating the displays – teachers can galvanise excitement about reading, keeping it at the forefront of learners' minds. It is when books are discussed *away* from English lessons, in the lunch queue and the playground, that a school's reading culture is embedded.

6.3.2 *Reading a range of literature*

7.4 The concept of "range" extends also – and very importantly – to social and cultural diversity. Pupils should gain increasing understanding that texts may be related to interests of different groups – such as women or men, adolescents or minorities of different kinds – and that critical thinking about existing stereotypes and values can be stimulated by studying literature which expresses alternative points of view: for example, on the family, nature and industrialisation, the nation or literature itself. The recognition that there are authors who have not traditionally formed part of the literary "canon" in the past may also lead to discussion that can form part of an equal opportunities policy across the curriculum. For example, authors writing in dialect and authors from certain social groups have been under-represented.

7.5 Today, literature in English in the classroom can – and should – be drawn from different countries. All pupils need to be aware of the richness of experience offered by such writing, so that they may be introduced to the ideas and feelings of cultures different from their own. English teachers should seek opportunities to exploit the multicultural aspects of literature. Novels from India or Caribbean poetry might be used for study of differing cultural perspectives, for example. Not only should this lead to a broader awareness of a greater range of human "thought and feeling", but – through looking at literature from different parts of the world and written from different points of view – pupils should also be in a position to gain a better understanding of the cultural heritage of English literature itself.

(Cox, 1989: 94)

Here, Cox makes a powerful argument for diversifying the reading diet. Like Elliott (2020), he emphasises that good practice is not to jettison valued canonical texts written by and about male able white authors, but to read them alongside other texts – a 'both/and' approach. For inspiration, try Lit in Colour (https://litincolour.penguin.co.uk/), a comprehensive website providing racially and ethnically diverse book recommendations and accompanying resources. Sources such as Goodreads.com and booksellers' and publishers' websites offer lists of recommended feminist and LGBTQ+ fiction, and texts featuring disabled and differently abled characters. Short stories offer huge potential: *Diverse Shorts* (EMC, 2018) and *The Iridescent Adolescent* (EMC, 2021) are anthologies of powerful and beautiful writing.

Where possible, involve learners in the choice of their shared class reader. Give over a lesson to exploring several options. Read the blurbs; consider the covers; look at online reviews; check out author websites where relevant; make a list of how each might support or challenge stereotypes (different groups might take on each of these responsibilities and feed back). Read the first few pages of each to consider initial themes, plotlines, and what we learn about characters. Hold a vote.

If you have no control over which text to teach, acknowledge this, and invite the class to recommend a book they would like you to read. When you have read it, spend some time in class sharing your thoughts. The same arguments apply to non-fiction texts.

6.3.3 Fast reading of whole books

It is a very good plan for the teacher from time to time to take one book with the whole class, though it should not as a rule be read round by the scholars in turn, and to use it as material for conversation lessons and written exercises. Frequent reading-aloud by the teacher… cannot be too strongly recommended as a means of enforcing the appeal of literature.

(BoE, 1927: 87)

Recent research echoes this argument. Westbrook *et al.* (2019) demonstrate that what is now called 'fast reading' or 'cold reading', whereby a class text is read in its entirety by the teacher, very fluent readers, or through an audiobook *before* detailed discussion, is more effective than a slower chapter-by-chapter-interleaved-with-activities plod, and that the benefits are felt by learners of all attainment levels. The sustained, uninterrupted approach engenders enthusiasm for the narrative, retains momentum and is thus better remembered; accordingly, once the text is completed, richer discussion can be facilitated. A lesson might start with a shared recap of the plot to date, be punctuated with brief pauses for observation and questions, and end with prediction. Such a method is 'creative' because the teacher is creating the lesson in the moment. It is not pre-planned; they may not know exactly how much will be covered, but they respond to the responses of the learners and the tension of the narrative. Furthermore, the avoidance of manufactured activities helps to prevent the teacher unintentionally directing the learners' opinions on the text, ensuring that their experience is authentic rather than manufactured (Giovanelli and Mason, 2015).

6.3.4 *Exploring short texts or extracts of texts*

> *Cloze*: Methodology: An extract represented with deletions in text in order to focus on author's style and vocabulary. In groups the class make suggestions about deleted words by drawing on their understanding of style and language used in text so far.
>
> Learning Features: Highlighting stylistic/linguistic features of text, drawing attention to syntax. Encouraging hypothetical/speculative talk as well as problem-solving activity. Developing reflective awareness of how a text is constructed, encouraging awareness of selection and alternatives.
>
> (Cox, 1989: 135)

Appendix 6 to the first National Curriculum offers 29 'Approaches to the class novel', but many activities suggested are appropriate for the exploration of any text, literary or otherwise, with cloze – or word deletion – one of the simplest yet most effective. While the deleted words might be randomly selected, it is often valuable to choose related words, such as all the nouns or adjectives, or words belonging to a particular semantic field; alternatively, when exploring a poem, the deleted words might be used to highlight structural features, such as the rhyme scheme. Depending on the intended level of challenge, options for the missing words can be provided (if offering electronic resources, use drop-down lists available in word-processing packages), or suggestions might be inspired by reference to a thesaurus, so providing opportunity for wider vocabulary development. The class could work in pairs, groups or as a whole to weigh and justify options, enabling in-depth consideration of word class, tone, mood and so on, before the author's choice of lexis is revealed and then further discussed.

For examination revision, pairs might select the words to be deleted for their classmates, thereby reinforcing their understanding of key vocabulary, connotation, ambiguity, etc.

6.4 Writing

6.4.1 *Writing poetry as a way into reading poetry*

> A class of 10-year-olds have been reading limericks and the teacher has asked them to try writing some themselves. She is writing too. She knows that the metrical form works through a fixed pattern, involving a given number of lines, length of lines, rhyme, rhythm and stress, positioning of subject, and joke in the last line. She understands the clear patterns of reader-listener expectation. Ear well attuned, the teacher may be able to produce several good limericks without engaging in further analysis. But it is unlikely that the children will be able to do this. They will need help in discovering the essentials of the verse structure and they may need to count syllables and beat stresses and mark rhyme schemes as well as think of a good joke line. Reading and writing ballads involves the same attention to form as well as content.
>
> (Kingman, 1988: 38)

A thread that runs throughout the policy and guidance is that encouraging learners to write poetry is a fruitful means of enabling them to read poetry. Whereas this exploration of the limerick is for older primary-aged learners, the sonnet form might be explored in a similar way by secondary learners:

- Provide the class with a selection of sonnets and ask them to establish the 'rules' of a sonnet. (The selection might be limited to Petrarchan, Spenserian or Shakespearean sonnets if relevant.)
- Once the rules have been identified, introduce a 'faulty' sonnet (perhaps written or adapted by the teacher) containing the wrong number of lines or irregular metrical pattern. Ask learners for suggestions to improve it, based on the rules. This is an effective means of supporting them 'discover the essentials of the verse structure'.
- Then, ask learners to write their own sonnet according to the rules identified, on a topic of their choosing, with access to a rhyme-finder website such as www.rhyme-zone.com for support. Parody sonnets can work very well!

Similarly, creating a poem in the style of a poet is an effective means of exploring structure, tone, lexis and style. In the following example from 'Fragments from a Modernised Version of "The Canterbury Tales"', a 1950s schoolgirl describes her science teacher in a style unmistakably Chaucerian:

> A man there was who in the field of science
> Would set all opposition to defiance,
> And when he spake boys might his orders hear
> Rolling reverberations through the head as clear
> And eek as loud as doth the chapel bell,
> With warning to obey those orders well.[1]

6.4.2 Collaborative composition

> In the hands of a good teacher, composition is an admirable way of exercising a child's imagination... Class teaching lends itself especially well to work of this kind. If the subject, for instance, chosen for the day's practice to be a harvest scene, some children can be made to write their description from the point of view of the farmer, others from that of the labourers, each of whom has his particular part to play in the process; others, again, can describe the whole scene as it appears to a passer-by. Afterwards, specimens of these exercises can be read aloud, and each group learns something from the other's attempt as well as from its own. A good deal, also, is done by methods such as these to mitigate the monotony of revision...

> Nor must the teacher forget that he can do much more than teach English by the judicious use of exercises of this type; by developing the imaginative powers of his children he is teaching them to put themselves in other people's places, to realise that there are more sides than one to every question, and by so doing he can help to lay the foundations of sympathy, tolerance, justice and other essentially social virtues.
>
> (BoE, 1914: 38)

In this example, learners' ideas are combined to create a class panorama to inform individual writing. The 'everyday' harvest scene might be updated to a busy supermarket or bus station or sports centre – anywhere involving the coming together of people (a photo or painting of such a setting might provide additional stimulus). After some discussion to establish details of the setting – the time of day, the weather – learners either choose or are allocated an actor in the scene, then are asked to briefly describe the scene from that person's perspective. Sharing the mini-monologues within a small group or the class – and imagining conversations that might have taken place between the individual voices – then provides inspiration for a more developed piece of writing, whether narrative or non-fiction (a persuasive piece arguing for improved employee rights; a travel blog describing a recent trip). The involvement of all learners in this way also leads to more informed peer assessment.

6.4.3 *From role-play to writing*

> For some children, including the less confident and less gifted, [activities based on actualities] can provide a firm base from which to undertake expeditions into imagined worlds. In once school we saw a class absorbed in a project which involved all the activities to be found in the formal 'speech lesson', but provided them with a context that gave them meaning. The children were asked to study the problem of the siting of a new airport and produce their solutions. The teacher had planned it meticulously, producing photographs, documents and large-scale maps. Within their groups the students played the roles of interested parties and prepared for these roles by tape-recording conversations with a number of local people, e.g. museum curator, planning officer and shop-keepers, and by writing personal profiles. All the group activity culminated in a sharing of the work, in which some pupils gave talks, some were interviewed, and other presented round table discussions. Throughout the project they had been given the opportunity to test hypotheses and solve problems and at the same time to project themselves into the feelings of others.
>
> (Bullock, 1975: 148)

In oracy as well as in written work, having a real audience can be a strong motivator. Since it is often not practical or possible to arrange 'real' contexts within a school day, role-play can be an effective alternative, as this extract from the Bullock Report illustrates. The project described is complex, involving canvassing people out of school, but role-play works well too on a smaller scale. A GCSE-style non-fiction extract is a good starting point. Get learners to identify the writer's perspective or viewpoint on a topic, then challenge them to create characters with different or opposing viewpoints. Combing the text for clues to inform a character's choice of register, vocabulary and rhetoric is an effective means of supporting learners' explorations of the writer's craft as well as their message. They might then – after some time for preparation – take part in a discussion in role, perhaps with one representing the writer.

Note

1 I am indebted to Dr James Ogden who sent me this extract written by a student, taken from his school magazine, *Quid Non*, Salt High School, Shipley, No. 9, July 1951.

Bibliography

Abrams, F. (2012) *US Idea of 'Cultural Literacy' and Key Facts a Child Should Know Arrives in UK* in: *The Guardian* 15.10.2012. Available online at: https://www.theguardian.com/education/2012/oct/15/hirsch-core-knowledge-curriculum-review [last accessed 26.10.2020]

Aldrich, R. (2005) *Lessons from History of Education: The Selected Works of Richard Aldrich* London: Taylor and Francis

Alexander, R. (2008) *Towards Dialogic Teaching: Rethinking Classroom Talk* (4th edition) York: Dialogos

Amsler, S. (2015) *The Education of Radical Democracy* London: Routledge

Anderson, G. (2013) *Exploring the Island: Mapping the Shifting Sands in the Landscape of English Classroom Culture and Pedagogy* in: *Changing English: Studies in Culture and Education* 20 (2) pp. 113–123, DOI: 10.1080/1358684X.2013.788291

Anning, A. (1996) *Being the Best in the Worst of Times* in: *Oxford Review of Education* 22 (1) pp. 113–117

AQA (2018) *GCSE English Language Paper 1. Explorations in Creative Reading and Writing. Report on the Examination.* Available online at: https://filestore.aqa.org.uk/sample-papers-and-mark-schemes/2018/june/AQA-87001-WRE-JUN18.PDF [last accessed 05.07.2020]

Arendt, H. (1954) *The Crisis in Education.* Available online at: https://www.normfriesen.info/files/ArendtCrisisInEdTable.pdf [last accessed 06.07.2020]

Armstrong, M. (1988) *Popular Education and the National Curriculum* in: *Forum* 30 (3) pp. 74–76

Arnold, M. (1851) *On Dover Beach.* Available online at: http://www.victorianweb.org/authors/arnold/writings/doverbeach.html [last accessed 26.11.2015]

Arnold, M. (1869) *Culture and Anarchy* [ebook] Oxford: Oxford World's Classics

Arnold, M. (1880) *The Study of Poetry.* Available online at: http://www.bartleby.com/28/5.html [last accessed 20.07.2015]

Aynesley, S., Brown, C. and Se, J (2012) *Opening Minds: An evaluative literature review.* Available online at: https://www.thersa.org/discover/publications-and-articles/reports/opening-minds-an-evaluative-literature-review [last accessed 22.04.2019]

Baker, M. (2005) *Why Tomlinson Was Turned Down.* Available online at: http://news.bbc.co.uk/1/hi/education/4299151.stm [last accessed 08.09.2020]

Ball, S.J., Maguire, M. and Braun, A. (2012) *How Schools Do Policy: Policy Enactments in Secondary Schools* London: Routledge

Banaji, S. and Burn, A. (2010) *The Rhetorics of Creativity: A Literature Review* Newcastle: Creativity, Culture and Education

Bannerman, C. (2008) *Creativity and Wisdom* in: Craft, A., Gardner, H. and Claxton, G. (eds) *Creativity, Wisdom and Trusteeship: Exploring the Role of Education* Thousand Oaks: Corwin Press pp. 133–142

Barron, F., Montuori, A. and Barron, A. (1997) *Creators on Creating: Awakening and Cultivating the Imaginative Mind* New York: Tarcher/Penguin

BBC (2007) *Your 1950s: School Life.* Available online at: http://news.bbc.co.uk/1/hi/magazine/6687549.stm [last accessed 26.10.2020]

Beadle, P. (2014) *Thirty Years on, How Have GCSEs Performed?* in: *The Guardian* 30.12.2014 https://www.theguardian.com/commentisfree/2014/dec/30/gcse-coursework-qualification-education-margaret-thatcher [last accessed 09.09.2020]

Becker, M., McElvany, N. and Kortenbruck, M. (2010). *Intrinsic and extrinsic Reading Motivation as Predictors of Reading Literacy: A Longitudinal Study* in: *Journal of Educational Psychology* 102 (4), pp. 773–785

Benson, C. (2004) *Creativity, Caught or Taught? Professor John Eggleston Memorial Lecture* in: *Journal of Design and Technology Education* 9 (3) pp. 138–144

Biesta, G. (2004) *Mind the Gap! Communication and the Educational Relation* in: Bingham, C. and Sidorkin, A. (eds) *No Education without Relation* New York: Peter Lang pp. 11–22

Biesta, G. (2006) *Beyond Learning: Democratic Education for a Human Future* London: Routledge

Biesta, G. (2015) *On the Two Cultures of Educational Research, and How We Might Move ahead: Reconsidering the Ontology, Axiology and Praxeology of Education* in: *European Educational Research Journal* 14 (1) pp. 11–22

Biesta, G. and Osberg, D. (2008) *The Emergent Curriculum: Navigating a Complex Course between Unguided Learning and Planned Enculturation* in: *Journal of Curriculum Studies* 40 (3) pp. 313–328. Available online at: https://dspace.stir.ac.uk/bitstream/1893/464/1/emergent-curriculum%20jcs%202008.pdf

Biesta, G., Priestley, M. and Robinson, S. (2015) *The Role of Beliefs in Teacher Agency* in: *Teachers and Teaching* 21 (6) pp. 624–640, DOI: 10.1080/13540602.2015.1044325

Blair, T. (1996) *The Great Debate.* Available online at: http://www.educationengland.org.uk/documents/speeches/1996ruskin.html [last accessed 08.08.2022]

Blake, J. (2019) *What Did the National Curriculum Do for Poetry? Pattern, Prescription and Contestation in the Poetry Selected for GCSE English Literature 1988–2018* Doctoral thesis, University of Cambridge

Blake, J. and Shortis, T. (2010) *Who's Prepared to Teach School English?* London: CLIE

Blamires, M. and Peterson, A. (2014) *Can Creativity Be Assessed? Towards an Evidence Informed Framework for Assessing and Planning Progress in Creativity* in: *Cambridge Journal of Education* 44 (2) pp. 147–162, DOI: 10.1080/0305764X.2013.860081

Bleiman, B. (2020) *What Matters in English Teaching?* London: English and Media Centre

Board of Education (1905/1912) *Suggestions for the Consideration of Teachers and Others Concerned in the Work of Public Elementary Schools* London: His Majesty's Stationery Office

Board of Education (1914) *Suggestions for the Consideration of Teachers and Others Concerned in the Work of Public Elementary Schools* London: His Majesty's Stationery Office

Board of Education (1923) *Suggestions for the Consideration of Teachers and Others Concerned in the Work of Public Elementary Schools,* revised edition London: His Majesty's Stationary Office

Board of Education (1924) *Some Suggestions for the Teaching of English in Secondary Schools in England* London: His Majesty's Stationary Office

Board of Education (1927) *Handbook of Suggestions for Teachers* London: HMSO

Board of Education (1937) *Handbook of Suggestions for Teachers* London: HMSO

Boas, F.S. (1914) *Wordsworth's Patriotic Poems and Their Significance Today* in: English Association, The (1907–21) *Pamphlets on the Teaching of English.* Available online at: https://archive.org/details/pamphletsonteach00engl [last accessed 08.08.2022] p. 238

Boas, F.S. (1919) *Teachers of English* in: English Association, The (1907–21) *The Teaching of English in Schools.* Available online at: https://archive.org/details/pamphletsonteach00engl [last accessed 08.08.2022] pp. 246–252

Bomford, K. (2018) *What Are (English) Lessons for?* in: *Changing English* 26 (1) pp. 3–15 https://www.tandfonline.com/doi/full/10.1080/1358684X.2018.1519370?src=recsys

Bovill, C. (2014) *An Investigation of Co-Created Curricula within Higher Education in the UK, Ireland and the USA* in: *Innovations in Education and Teaching International* 51 (1) pp. 15–25, DOI: 10.1080/14703297.2013.770264

Bowen, L., Bradley, K., Middleton, S., Mackillop, A. and Sheldon, N. (2012) *History in the UK National Curriculum: A Discussion* in: *Cultural and Social History* 9 pp. 125–143, DOI: 10.2752/147800412X13191165983114

Brindley, S. (2015) *Knowledge in English Teaching – The Naming of Parts?* in: Brindley, S. and Marshall, B. (eds) *MasterClass in English Education: Transforming Teaching and Learning* London: Bloomsbury

British Council (2010) *Mapping the Creative Industries: A Toolkit.* Available online at: https://creativeconomy.britishcouncil.org/media/uploads/files/English_mapping_the_creative_industries_a_toolkit_2-2.pdf [last accessed 09.10.2019]

British Library (n.d) *About Us.* Available online at: https://www.bl.uk/about-us [last accessed 07.08.2019]

Britton, J. (1975) *The Development of Writing Abilities: Ages 11–18* London: Macmillan/ Schools Council Research Studies

Bruner, J. (1996) *The Culture of Education* Cambridge, MA: Harvard University Press

Bullock, A. (1952) *Hitler: A Study in Tyranny* New York: Harper Collins

Bullock, A. (1960) *The Life and Times of Earnest Bevin* London: Heinemann

Bullock, A. (1975) *A Language for Life: Report of the Committee of Enquiry Appointed by the Secretary of State for Education and Science under the Chairmanship of Sir Alan Bullock F.B.A.* London: HMSO

Burdett, N. (2015) *What Is Good Assessment?* in: *The Future of Assessment, 2025 and beyond,* Manchester: AQA pp. 10–17

Burgess, S., Rawal, S. and Taylor, E. (2022) *Characterising Effective Teaching.* Nuffield Foundation. Available online at: https://www.nuffieldfoundation.org/wp-content/uploads/2022/05/Burgess-Characterising-Effective-Teaching-Full-Report-April-2022.pdf [last accessed 12.08.2022]

Burnard, P. (2006) *Reflecting on the Creativity Agenda in Education* in: *Cambridge Journal of Education* 36 (3) pp. 313–318, DOI: 10.1080/03057640600865801

Burns, R. (2018) *Applying the 'powerful knowledge' Principle to Curriculum Development in Disadvantaged Contexts.* Available online at: https://impact.chartered.college/article/applying-powerful-knowledge-principle-curriculum-development-disadvantaged-contexts/ [last accessed 15.09.2019]

Calaprice, A. (ed) (2000) *The Expanded Quotable Einstein* Princeton, NJ: Princeton University Press

Cambridge School Shakespeare www.cambridge.org/wf/education/subject/english/shakespeare/cambridge-school-shakespeare

Carter, R. (2004) *Language and Creativity: The Art of Common Talk* London: Routledge

Chappell, K. (2018) *From Wise Humanising Creativity to (post-humanising) Creativity,* in: Harris, A., Thomson, P. and Snepvangers, K. (eds) *Creativity Policy, Partnerships and Practice in Education* London: Palgrave Macmillan pp. 279–306

Chappell, K. and Craft, A. (2011) *Creative Learning Conversations: Producing Living Dialogic Spaces.* Available online at: https://ore.exeter.ac.uk/repository/bitstream/handle/10871/9765/Creative%20learning%20conversations.pdf?sequence=2 [last accessed 28.08.2020]

Chappell, K., Hetherington, L., Ruck Keene, H., Wren, H., Alexopoulos, A., Ben-Horin, O., Nikolopoulos, K., Robberstad, J., Sotiriou, S. and Bogner, F.X. (2019) *Dialogue and Materiality/Embodiment in Science|Arts Creative Pedagogy: Their Role and Manifestation* in: *Thinking Skills and Creativity* 31 pp. 296–322

Chappell, K., Pender, T., Swinford, L., *et al* (2016) *Making and Being Made: Wise Humanising Creativity in Interdisciplinary Early Years Arts Education* in: *International Journal of Early Years Education.* Available online at: https://ore.exeter.ac.uk/repository/handle/10871/20372 [last accessed 20.07.2020]

Chaucer, G. (c.1390) *The Parson's Prologue and Tale.* Available online at: https://chaucer.fas.harvard.edu/pages/parsons-prologue-and-tale [last accessed 14.07.2022]

Childs, W.M. (1919) *Chairman's Address* in *The Teaching of English in Schools* pp. 30–32. Available online at: https://archive.org/details/pamphletsonteach00engl/page/n241/mode/2up (pp. 272–274) [last accessed 24.10.2000]

Chitty, C. (1989) *Towards a New Education System: The Victory of the New Right?* London: Falmer Press

Clarke, G. (1982) *Miracle on St David's Day*. Available online at: https://www.poetrybyheart.org.uk/poems/miracle-on-st-davids-day/ [last accessed 09.08.2022]

Claxton, G. (2006) *Thinking at the Edge: Developing Soft Creativity* in: *Cambridge Journal of Education* 36 (3) pp. 351–362

Coleridge, S.T. (1817) *Biographia Literaria*. London: Best Fenner. Available online at: https://www.bl.uk/collection-items/biographia-literaria-by-samuel-taylor-coleridge [last accessed 01.04.2020]

Collins, M. (2020) *The Beatles and Sixties Britain*. Cambridge: Cambridge University Press

Compton, A. (2007) *What Does Creativity Mean in English Education?* in: *Education 3–13: International Journal of Primary, Elementary and Early Years Education* 35 (2) pp. 109–116

Conway, E. (2015) *The UK, Germany and France: GDP over History*. Available online at: http://www.edmundconway.com/2015/02/the-uk-germany-and-france-gdp-over-history/ [last accessed 26.10.2020]

Cooper, I. (1981) *The Politics of Education and Architectural Design: The Instructive Example of British Primary Education* in: *British Education Research Journal* 7 (2) pp. 125–136 https://doi-org.bris.idm.oclc.org/10.1080/0141192810070202

Couldry, N. (2012) *Media, Society, World: Social Theory and Digital Media Practice* London: Polity Press

Cox, B. (1989) *English for Ages 5 to 16: Proposals of the Secretary of State for Education and Science and the Secretary of State for Wales* London: Department of Education and Science and the Welsh Office

Cox, B. (1991) *Cox on Cox: An English Curriculum for the 1990s* London: Hodder & Stoughton

Cox, B. (1995) *Cox on the Battle for the English Curriculum* London: Hodder Education

Cox, B. and Dyson, A. (eds) (1969a) *The Crisis in Education: Black Paper 2* imprint unknown

Cox, B. and Dyson, A. (eds) (1969b) *The Fight for Education: Black Paper 1* imprint unknown

Craft, A. (2001) *An Analysis of Research and Literature on Creativity in Education: Report Prepared for the Qualifications and Curriculum Authority*. Available online at: http://www.creativetallis.com/uploads/2/2/8/7/2287089/creativity_in_education_report.pdf [last accessed 14.07.2022]

Craft, A. (2005) *Creativity in Schools: Tensions and Dilemmas* London: Routledge

Craft, A. (2006) *Fostering Creativity with Wisdom* in: *Cambridge Journal of Education* 36 (3) pp. 337–350 https://doi-org.bris.idm.oclc.org/10.1080/03057640600865835

Craft, A., Gardner, H. and Claxton, G. (eds) (2008) *Creativity, Wisdom and Trusteeship: Exploring the Role of Education* Thousand Oaks: Corwin Press

Cremin, T. (2016) *Introduction – Creativity and Creative Pedagogies: Exploring Challenges, Possibilities and Potential* in: Cremin, T. (ed) *Creativity and Creative Pedagogies in the Early and Primary Years* London: Routledge pp. xvii–xxvii

Cremin, T. (2019) *Reading Communities: Why, What and How?* https://cdn.ourfp.org/wp-content/uploads/20210301105855/Reading_Communities_TCremin_2019.pdf?_ga=2.143626037.1047564709.1632085596–2008111907.1613423023.

Cremin, T. and Barnes, J. (2018) *Creativity and Creative Teaching and Learning* in: Cremin, T. and Burnett, C. (eds) *Learning to Teach in the Primary School* (4th edition) London: Routledge pp. 428–442

Csikszentmihalyi, M. (1990) *Flow* New York: HarperCollins

Cremin, T., Burnard, P. and Craft, A. (2006) *Pedagogy and Possibility Thinking in the Early Years* in: *International Journal of Thinking Skills and Creativity* 1 (2) pp. 108–119

Cremin, T., Mottram, M., Powell, S., Collins, R. and Safford, K. (2014) *Building Communities of Engaged Readers: Reading for pleasure*. London and New York: Routledge.

Cremin, T. and Myhill, D. (2019) *Creative Writers as Arts Educators* in: Noblit, G. (ed) *Oxford Research Encyclopedia of Education*. New York: Oxford University Press, DOI: 10.1093/acrefore/9780190264093.013.394

Cremin, T. and Oliver, L. (2017) *Teachers as Writers: A Systematic Review* in: *Research Papers in Education* 32 (3) pp. 269–295

Darling, J. (1982) *Education as Horticulture: Some Growth Theorists and Their Critics* in: *Journal of Philosophy of Education* 16 (1) pp. 173–185

Davison, J. (2009) *Battles for English* in Davison, J. and Dowson, J. (eds) *Learning to Teach English in the Secondary School* London: Routledge pp. 20–43

DCSF/QCA (2007) *The National Curriculum: Statutory Requirements for Key Stages 3 and 4* London: DCSF/QCA

De Bono Six Thinking Hats – De Bono Group https://www.debonogroup.com/services/core-programs/six-thinking-hats/

De Certeau, M. (1984) *Walking in the City* in: *The Practice of Everyday Life* (Translated by Steven Rendall) Berkeley: University of California Press pp. 91–110

Dearing, R. (1994) *The National Curriculum and Its Assessment: Final Report* London: HMSO. Available online at: http://www.educationengland.org.uk/documents/dearing1994/index.html [last accessed 26 October 2020]

Defoe, D. (1791/1992) *Robinson Crusoe* London: Wordsworth Classics

Delors, J. (1996) *Learning: The Treasure within. Report to UNESCO of the International Commission on Education for the Twenty-first Century* Paris: UNESCO

Demopoulos, K. (2005) *Exam Board Surprise at 'obvious plagiarism' in Coursework* in: *The Guardian* 3 November 2005. Available online at: https://www.theguardian.com/education/2005/nov/03/gcses.secondaryschools [last accessed 9 September 2020]

Dewey, J. (1916) *Democracy and Education*. Available online at: https://www.gutenberg.org/files/852/852-h/852-h.htm [last accessed 20 October 2020]

DES (1959) *Suggestions for the Consideration of Teachers and Others Concerned with the Work of Primary Schools* London: HMSO

DfE (2010) *The Importance of Teaching: The Schools White Paper 2010*. Available online at: https://www.gov.uk/government/publications/the-importance-of-teaching-the-schools-white-paper-2010 [last accessed 12.05.2020]

DfE (2011) *Teachers' Standards: Guidance for School Leaders, School Staff and Governing Bodies*. Available online at: https://assets.publishing.service.gov.uk/government/uploads/system/uploads/attachment_data/file/665520/Teachers__Standards.pdf [last accessed 20.10.2020]

DfE (2012) *Expert Panel: Terms of Reference*. Available online at: https://webarchive.nationalarchives.gov.uk/20130108065205/http://www.education.gov.uk/schools/teachingandlearning/curriculum/nationalcurriculum/a0073091/expert-panel-terms-of-reference [last accessed 15.09.2019]

DfE (2013) *English Programmes of Study: Key Stage 3*. Available online at: https://assets.publishing.service.gov.uk/government/uploads/system/uploads/attachment_data/file/244215/SECONDARY_national_curriculum_-_English2.pdf (publishing.service.gov.uk) [last accessed 13.07.2022]

DfE (2014) *National Curriculum in England: English Programmes of Study*. Available online at: https://www.gov.uk/government/publications/national-curriculum-in-england-english-programmes-of-study [last accessed 13.07.2022]

DfE (2019a) Initial Teacher Training (ITT): Core Content Framework. Available online at: https://www.gov.uk/government/publications/initial-teacher-training-itt-core-content-framework [last accessed 13.07.2022]

DfE (2019b) Early Career Framework. Available online at: https://www.gov.uk/government/publications/early-career-framework [last accessed 13.07.2022]

DfE (2019c) *Tests and Assessments (Key Stage 2)*. Available online at: https://www.gov.uk/education/primary-curriculum-key-stage-2-tests-and-assessments [last accessed 04.05.2020]

DfE (2020) *Secondary Accountability Measures (Including Progress 8 and Attainment 8)*. Available online at: https://www.gov.uk/government/publications/progress-8-school-performance-measure [last accessed 26.10.2020]

DfE&WO (1993) *English for ages 5 to 16 (1993)* London: DfE

DfE&WO (1995) *English in the National Curriculum* London: HMSO

DfEE (1998) *The National Literacy Strategy: Framework for Teaching* London: DfEE

DfEE/QCA (1999a) *The National Curriculum for England: English* London: DfEE/QCA

DfEE/QCA (1999b) *The National Curriculum Handbook for Primary Teachers in England* London: DfEE/QCA

DfES/QCA (2004) *The National Curriculum: Handbook for Secondary Teachers in England (Revised)* London: DfES/QCA

Dickens, C. (1854) *Hard Times*. Available online at: http://www.gutenberg.org/ebooks/786 [last accessed 24.03.2015]

Dixon, J. (1967) *Growth through English: A Report Based on the Dartmouth Seminar, 1966* OUP/National Association for the Teaching of English

Donoghue, B. (2008) *Downing Street Diary: With James Callaghan in No. 10* London: Jonathan Cape

Dover Wilson, J. (1916) *Poetry and the Child* in: English Association, The (1907–21) *Pamphlets on the Teaching of English*. Available online at: https://archive.org/details/pamphletsonteach00engl [last accessed 12.01.2016] p. 238

Dover Wilson, J. (1919) *English in the New Continuation Schools* in: *The Teaching of English in Schools*. Available online at: https://archive.org/details/pamphletsonteach00engl/page/n241/mode/2up (pp. 272–274) [last accessed 24.10.2000] pp. 30–32

Dover Wilson, J. (1932) *Editor's Preface* in: Arnold, M. (ed) (1869/1932) *Culture and Anarchy* Cambridge: Cambridge University Press. Available online at: https://archive.org/stream/matthewarnoldcul021369mbp/matthewarnoldcul021369mbp_djvu.txt [last accessed 26.10.2020]

Dryden, J. (1700) *Preface to Fables Ancient and Modern*. Available online at: https://www.bartleby.com/39/25.html [last accessed 14.07.2022]

Dutaut, J.L. (2018) *The National Curriculum Is Dying RIP* in: *TES 30.06.18*. Available online at: https://www.tes.com/news/national-curriculum-dying-rip [last accessed 06.07.2010]

Dymoke, S. (2011) *Creativity in English Teaching and Learning* in: Davison, J., Daly, C. and Moss, J. (eds) *Debates in English Teaching* London: Routledge pp. 142–156

Eaglestone, R. (2021) *'Powerful knowledge', 'cultural literacy' and the Study of Literature in Schools*. Available online at: https://onlinelibrary.wiley.com/doi/10.1111/2048-416X.2020.12006.x [last accessed 13.07.2022]

EEF (2021) *Cognitive Science Approaches in the Classroom: A Review of the Evidence*. Available online at: https://d2tic4wvo1iusb.cloudfront.net/documents/guidance/Cognitive_science_approaches_in_the_classroom_-_A_review_of_the_evidence.pdf?v=1629124457 [last accessed 08.08.2022]

EMC (2018) *Diverse Shorts* London: English & Media Centre

EMC (2021) *The Iridescent Adolescent* London: English & Media Centre

Eliot, T.S. (1923) *The Function of Criticism*. Available online at: https://fortnightlyreview.co.uk/2018/08/eliot-function-of-criticism/ [last accessed 14.07.2022]

Elliott, J. (1998) *The Curriculum Experiment* Buckingham: OUP

Elliott, V. (2020) *Knowledge in English: Canon, Curriculum and Cultural Literacy* London: Routledge

English Association, The (1907–21) *Pamphlets on the Teaching of English*. Available online at: https://archive.org/details/pamphletsonteach00engl [last accessed 07.09.2022]

Erss, M. (2018) *'Complete freedom to choose within limits' – Teachers' Views of Curricular Autonomy, Agency and Control in Estonia, Finland and Germany* in: *The Curriculum Journal* 29 (2) pp. 238–256, DOI: 10.1080/09585176.2018.1445514

European Commission (2020) *Finland: Continuing Professional Development for Teachers Working in Early Childhood and School Education* 29.01.2020. Available online at: https://eacea.ec.europa.eu/national-policies/eurydice/finland/continuing-professional-development-teachers-working-early-childhood-and-school-education_en [last accessed 26.10.2020]

Facer, K. (2019) *Storytelling in Troubled Times: What Is the Role for Educators in the Deep Crises of the 21st Century?* in: *Literacy* 53 (1) pp. 3–13

Facer, K. and Thomas, L. (2012) *Towards an Area-Based Curriculum? Creating Space for the City in Schools* in: *International Journal of Educational Research* 55 pp. 16–25

Feldman, D.H. (2008) *Creativity and Wisdom: Are They Incompatible?* In: Craft, A., Gardner, H. and Claxton, G. (eds) *Creativity, Wisdom and Trusteeship: Exploring the Role of Education* Thousand Oaks, CA: Corwin Press pp. 77–83

Fleming, M. (2010) *Arts in Education and Creativity: A Literature Review* (2nd edition) London: Creativity, Culture and Education

Fleming, M. and Stevens, D. (2010) *English Teaching in the Secondary School* (3rd edition) Abingdon: David Fulton

Forster, E.M. (1908) *A Room with a View.* Available online at: https://gutenberg.org/files/2641/2641-h/2641-h.htm

Fowler J.H. (1910) *The Teaching of English Composition* in: English Association, The (1907–21) *Pamphlets on the Teaching of English*, pp. 1–12. Available online at: https://archive.org/details/pamphletsonteach00engl [last accessed 12.01.2016] pp. 108–122

Fowler, J.H. (1915) *School Libraries* in: English Association, The (1907–21) *Pamphlets on the Teaching of English*, pp. 1–14. Available online at: https://archive.org/details/pamphletsonteach00engl [last accessed 12.01.2016] pp. 186–200

Friere, P. (1968/2017) *Pedagogy of the Oppressed* London: Penguin

Fry, S. (2007) *The Ode Less Travelled: Unlocking the Poet within* London: Arrow

Fryer, M. (1996) *Creative Teaching and Learning* London: Paul Chapman Publishing

Fryer, M. (2012) *Some Key Issues in Creativity Research and Evaluation as Seen from a Psychological Perspective* in: *Creativity Research Journal* 24 (1) pp. 21–28

Gadamer, H.G. (1975/2004) *Truth and Method* (3rd edition) London and New York: Continuum

Gallagher, K. (2009) *Readicide: How Schools Are Killing Reading and What You Can Do about It* Portland: Stenhouse Publishers

Gibb, N. (2015) *The Purpose of Education.* Available online at: https://www.gov.uk/government/speeches/the-purpose-of-education [last accessed 13.07.2015]

Gibbons, S. (2013) *The London Association for the Teaching of English 1947–67: A History* London: Trentham Books

Gibbons, S. (2017) *English and Its Teachers* Abingdon: Routledge

Gibbons, S. (2019) *'Death by PEEL?' The Teaching of Writing in the Secondary English Classroom in England* in: *English in Education* 53 (1) pp. 36–45, DOI: 10.1080/04250494.2019.1568832

Gill, J. (1909) *The Early Stages in the Teaching of English* Available online at: https://archive.org/details/pamphletsonteach00engl/page/n241/mode/2up [last accessed 08.08.2022] pp. 96–106

Gillard, D. (2018) *Education in England: The History of Our Schools* Available online at: http://www.educationengland.org.uk/ [last accessed 20.10.2020]

Giovanelli, M. and Mason, J. (2015) *'Well I don't feel that': Schemas, Worlds and Authentic Reading in the Classroom* in: *English in Education* 49 (1) pp. 41–56, DOI: 10.1111/eie.12052

Goodwyn, A. (2016) *Still Growing after All These Years? The Resilience of the Personal Growth Model of English in England and also Internationally* in: *English Teaching: Practice and Critique* 15 (1) pp. 7–21, DOI: 10.1108/ETPC-12-2015-0111 (28.04.2019)

Gove, M. (2008) *Michael Gove to Brighton College Teacher Conference* 08.05.2008. Available online at: http://childlink.co.uk/ [last accessed 12.05.2020]

Government of Alberta (2010) *Background Paper: Professional Learning for Teachers in Alberta's K-12 Education System.* Available online at: https://open.alberta.ca/dataset/f28d7e18-891e-4107-b63e-867e7127e4a9/resource/55d48d8a-9196-4d9a-8196-6c3cf15bf5cc/download/5456292-2010-09-Background-Paper-Professional-Learning-for-Teachers-in-Alberta-Eduaction-System.pdf [last accessed 16.10.2019]

Green, B. and Cormack. P. (2008) *Curriculum History, 'English' and the New Education; or, Installing the Empire of English?* in: *Pedagogy, Culture & Society*, 16 (3) pp. 253–267, DOI: 10.1080/14681360802346648

Hall, C. and Thomson, P. (2013) *Creative Partnerships? Cultural Policy and Inclusive Arts Practice in One Primary School* in: *British Educational Research Journal* 33 (30) pp. 315–329, DOI: 10.1080/01411920701243586

Hall, D. and Hewings, A. (2001) *Innovation in English Language Teaching: A Reader* London: Open University Press

Han, K.S. and Marvin, C. (2002) *Multiple Creativities? Investigating Domain-Specificity of Creativity in Young Children* in: *Gifted Child Quarterly* 46 (2) pp. 98–109, DOI: 10.1177/001698620204600203

Hargreaves, A. (1994) *Changing Teachers, Changing Times: Teachers' Work and Culture in the Postmodern Age* London: Cassell

Haste, H. (2008) *Good Thinking* in Craft, A., Gardner, H. and Claxton, G. (eds) *Creativity, Wisdom and Trusteeship: Exploring the Role of Education* Thousand Oaks, CA: Corwin Press pp. 96–104

Hattenstone, S. (2008) *Who Wants to be a Drug Addict at 41?* in: *The Guardian 6 December 2008.* Available online at: http://www.theguardian.com/music/2008/dec/06/noel-gallagher-oasis [last accessed 4 November 2015]

Heilbronn, R. (2013) *Wigs, Disguises and Child's Play: Solidarity in Teacher Education* in: *Ethics and Education* 8 (1) pp. 31–41, DOI: 10.1080/17449642.2013.793960

Herbert, T. (2018) *WW1 Facts and Numbers: Remembering How Many Died, WW1 Soldiers and the Mind-Blowing Scale of the War This Armistice Day.* Available online at: https://www.standard.co.uk/lifestyle/ww1-soldiers-in-numbers-how-many-died-world-war-one-facts-for-armistice-day-a3986761.html [last accessed 08.04.2020]

Hirsch, E.D. (1988) *Cultural Literacy: What Every American Needs to Know* New York: Vintage Books

Hodgson, J. and Harris, A. (2022) *The Genealogy of 'Cultural Literacy'* in: *Changing English*, DOI: 10.1080/1358684X.2022.2081530 Pre-print.

Hodgson, J. and Wilkin, S. (2014) *English in Education* in: *English in Education*, 48 (3) pp. 196–229, DOI: 10.1111/17548845.2014.11912518

Holbrook, D. (1968) *Creativity in the English Programme* in: Summerfield, G. (ed) *Creativity in English: Papers Relating to the Anglo-American Seminar on the Teaching of English (Dartmouth College, New Hampshire, 1966): The Dartmouth Seminar Papers* Champaign, IL: NCTE pp. 1–20

Huddleston, P. (2015) *How Should We Assess Vocational and Practical Learning?* in: Bassett, D. (2015) *The Future of Assessment, 2025 and beyond* Manchester: AQA pp. 26–35

Hughes, T. (1857) *Tom Brown's Schooldays* London: Harper and Brothers. Available online at: https://www.gutenberg.org/files/1480/1480-h/1480-h.htm [last accessed 26.10.2020]

Jeffrey, B. (2006) *Creative Teaching and Learning: Towards a Common Discourse and Practice* in: *Cambridge Journal of Education* 36 (3) pp. 399–414, DOI: 10.1080/03057640600866015

Jeffrey, B. and Craft, A. (2004) *Teaching Creatively and Teaching for Creativity: Distinctions and Relationships* in: *Educational Studies* 30 pp. 77–87, DOI: 10.1080/0305569032000159750

Jessop, T. (2019) *Poetry in Research: Authentic or Sentimental Representation?* [PowerPoint presentation] School of Education, University of Bristol, 23.10.2019

Jewell, S. (2007) *Bigger Picture: Flexibility and Freedom* in: *The Guardian n.d.* Available online at: https://www.theguardian.com/education/curriculumreform/story/0,2048557,00.html [last accessed 08.09.2020]

John-Steiner, V. (1997) *Notebooks of the Mind: Explorations of Thinking*, Revised Edition Oxford: Oxford University Press

John-Steiner, V. (2006) *Creative Collaboration* Oxford: Oxford University Press

Jones, K. (2009) *Culture and Creative Learning: A Literature Review* London: CCE Literature Reviews

Joubert, M. (2010) *The Art of Creative Teaching: NACCCE and beyond* in: Craft, A., Jeffrey, B. and Leibling, M. (eds) *Creativity in Education* London: Continuum pp. 17–34

Kaufman, J.C. and Beghetto, R.A. (2009) *Beyond Big and Little: The Four C Model of Creativity* in: *Review of General Psychology* 13 pp. 1–12, DOI: 10.1037/a0013688

Kimble, C. and Hildreth, P. (2008) *Communities of Practice: Creating Learning Environments for Educators, Volume 1.* Charlotte: Information Age Publishing

Kingman, J. (1988) *Report of the Committee of Inquiry into the Teaching of English Language* London: HMSO

Kingsley, C. (1863) *The Water-Babies, A Fairy Tale for a Land Baby* London: Macmillan & Co.

Knight, C. (1990) *The Making of Tory Education Policy in Post-War Britain 1950–1986* London: Falmer Press

Knight, R. (1996) *Valuing English: Reflections on the National Curriculum (Quality in Secondary Schools & Colleges)* London: David Fulton

Knoop, H.H. (2008) *Wise Creativity and Creative Wisdom* in: Craft, A., Gardner, H. and Claxton, G. (eds) *Creativity, Wisdom and Trusteeship: Exploring the Role of Education* Thousand Oaks, CA: Corwin Press pp. 119–132

Kogan, M. (1987) *The Plowden Report Twenty Years on* in: *Oxford Review of Education* 13 (1) pp. 13–21. Retrieved from http://www.jstor.org.bris.idm.oclc.org/stable/1050507

Kress, G., Jewitt, C., Bourne, J., Franks, A., Hardcastle, J., Jones, K. and Reid, E. (2004) *English in Urban Classrooms: A Multi-Modal Perspective on Teaching and Learning* London: Routledge

Lähdemäki, J. (2018) *Case Study: The Finnish National Curriculum 2016—A Co-created National Education Policy* in: *Sustainability, Human Well-Being, and the Future of Education* pp. 397–422 https://link.springer.com/chapter/10.1007%2F978-3-319-78580-6_13

Last, J. (2017) *A Crisis in the Creative Arts in the UK?* Available online at: https://www.hepi.ac.uk/wp-content/uploads/2017/09/A-crisis-in-the-creative-arts-in-the-UK-EMBARGOED-UNTIL-7th-SEPTEMBER-2017.pdf [last accessed 09.10.2019]

Lave, J. and Wenger, E. (1991) *Situated Learning. Legitimate Peripheral Participation* Cambridge: University of Cambridge Press

Lawson, A. and Silver, H. (1973) *A Social History of Education in England* London: Methuen

Lit in Colour. Available online at: https://litincolour.penguin.co.uk/ [last accessed 08.08.2022]

Littleton, K. and Mercer, N. (2013) *Interthinking: Putting Talk to Work* London: Routledge

Logan, P.M. (2012) *On Culture: Matthew Arnold's Culture and Anarchy, 1869* in: *BRANCH: Britain, Representation and Nineteenth-Century History.* Available online at: http://www.branchcollective.org/?ps_articles=peter-logan-on-culture-matthew-arnolds-culture-and-anarchy-1869 [last accessed 26.10.2020]

Loi, D. and Dillon, P. (2006) *Adaptive Educational Environments as Creative Spaces* in: *Cambridge Journal of Education* 26 (3) pp. 363–381, DOI: 10.1080/03057640600865959

Londesborough, M., Partridge, L., Bath, N. and Grinsted, S. (2017) *Learning about Culture* London: RSA. Available at https://www.thersa.org/globalassets/pdfs/reports/rsa-learning-about-culture-report.pdf [last accessed 12.03.2020]

Lytton, H. (1971) *Creativity and Education* London: Routledge

Malaguzzi, L. (1996) *The Hundred Languages of Children: The Reggio Emilia Approach to Early Childhood Education* Norwood, NJ: Ablex Publishing Corporation.

Mansell, W. (2012) *The New National Curriculum: Made to Order?* in: *The Guardian* 12.11.2012. Available online at: https://www.theguardian.com/education/2012/nov/12/primary-national-curriculum-review [last accessed 11.09.2019]

Marshall, B. (2000) *English Teachers – The Unofficial Guide: Researching the Philosophies of English Teachers* London: Routledge

Marshall, B. (2001) *Creating Danger: The Place of the Arts in Education Policy* in: Craft, A., Jeffrey, B., and Leibling, M. (eds) *Creativity in Education* London: Continuum pp. 116–125

Matisse, H. (1954) *Is Not Love the Origin of All Creation?* Available online at: https://artreview.com/henri-matisse-love-origin-creation-1954-archive-looking-life-eyes-child/ [last accessed 14.07.2022]

McCallum, A. (2012) *Creativity and Learning in Secondary English* Abingdon: Routledge

McKendrick, M. (2004) *Statement from Professor Melveena McKendrick, Pro-Vice-Chancellor with Responsibility for Education, in Response to the Final Report from the Working Group on 14–19 Reform (the Tomlinson report)*. Available online at: https://www.cam.ac.uk/news/response-to-the-tomlinson-report [last accessed 26.10.2020]

Medway, P., Hardcastle, J., Brewis, G. and Crook, D. (2014) *English Teachers in a Postwar Democracy: Emerging Choice in London Schools, 1945–1965* New York: Palgrave Macmillan

Morgan, J. (2014) *Michael Young and the Politics of the School Curriculum* in: *British Journal of Educational Studies* 63 (1) pp. 5–22, DOI: 10.1080/00071005.2014.983044

Morgan, K. (1984) *The Oxford Illustrated History of Britain* Oxford: Oxford University Press

Moules, N.J., Mccaffrey, G., Morck, A. and Jardine, D. (2011) *On Applied Hermeneutics and the Work of the World* in: *Journal of Applied Hermeneutics* 1 pp. 1–5

NACCCE (1999) *All Our Futures: Creativity, Culture and Education*. Available online at: http://sirkenrobinson.com/pdf/allourfutures.pdf [last accessed 17.03.2015]

National Archives (n.d.). *Aftermath: Britain after the War*. Available online at: https://www.nationalarchives.gov.uk/pathways/firstworldwar/aftermath/brit_after_war.htm [last accessed 08.04.2020]

NationMaster (n.d.) *Economy > GDP. Countries Compared*. Available online at: https://www.nationmaster.com/country-info/stats/Economy/GDP#1980 [last accessed 26.10.2020]

Negus, K. and Pickering, M. (2004) *Creativity, Communication and Cultural Value*. London and Thousand Oaks, CA: Sage

Newbolt, J.H. (1897) *Vitai Lampada*. Available online at: https://www.poemhunter.com/poem/vita-lampada/ [last accessed 13.09.2020]

Newbolt, J.H. (1910) *Drake's Drum*. Available online at: https://www.poemhunter.com/poem/drake-s-drum/ [last accessed 13.09.2020]

Newbolt, J.H. (1921/1934) *The Teaching of English in England (being the Report of the Departmental Committee Appointed by the President of the Board of Education to Inquire into the Position of English in the Educational System of England)* London: HMSO

Newsom, J. (1963) *Half Our Future: A Report of the Central Advisory Council for Education (England)* London: HMSO. Available online at: http://www.educationengland.org.uk/documents/newsom/newsom1963.html [last accessed 26.10.2020]

Noble, J. (2022) *Changes to GCSE Blamed for 'crisis' drop in A-level English Exam Entries*. Available online at: https://feweek.co.uk/changes-to-gcse-blamed-for-crisis-drop-in-a-level-english-exam-entries/ [last accessed 13.07.2022]

OED (2022) *Oxford English Dictionary*. Available online at: https://www.oed.com [last accessed 13.07.2022]

Ofsted (2010) *Learning: Creative Approaches That Raise Standards*. Available online at: https://www.creativitycultureeducation.org/publication/learning-creative-approaches-that-raise-standards/ [last accessed 13.07.2022]

Ofsted (2019) *The Education Inspection Framework*. Available online at: https://assets.publishing.service.gov.uk/government/uploads/system/uploads/attachment_data/file/801429/Education_inspection_framework.pdf [last accessed 14.09.2020]

Ofsted (2022) *Research Review Series: English*. Available online at: https://www.gov.uk/government/publications/curriculum-research-review-series-english [last accessed 08.08.2022]

Ofsted and Spielman, A. (2017) *HMCI's Commentary: Recent Primary and Secondary Curriculum Research*. Available online at: www.gov.uk/government/speeches/hmci-commentary-october-2017 [last accessed 21.10.2020]

Osberg, D. (2010) *Taking Care of the Future? The Complex Responsibility of Education & Politics* in: Osberg, D. and Biesta, G. (eds) *Complexity Theory and the Politics of Education* Rotterdam: Sense Publishers pp. 157–170

Oxford Dictionaries (2015) *Creativity*. Available online at: http://www.oxforddictionaries.com/definition/english/creativity [last accessed 17.03.2015]

Pahl, K. and Pool, S. (2019) *Arts Activities and the Curriculum: Listening to the Noise of the Worm* in: *Research Intelligence* 138 pp. 24–25

Pappas, N. (2014) *Politics and Philosophy in Plato's Menexenus: Education and Rhetoric, Myth and History* London and New York: Routledge

Patton, K. and Parker, M. (2017) *Teacher Education Communities of Practice: More Than a Culture of Collaboration* in: *Teaching and Teacher Education* 67 pp. 351–360.

Perry, D.R. (1974) *Creativity in Writing: A Sequence of Readings for Secondary English Teachers and Departments* Washington, DC: US Dept of Health, Education and Welfare; National Institute of Education

Perryman, J. and Calvert, G. (2020) *What Motivates People to Teach, and Why Do They Leave? Accountability, Performativitiy and Teacher Retention* in: *British Journal of Educational Studies* 68 (1) pp. 3–23, DOI: 10.1080/00071005.2019.1589417

Pestalozzi, J. (n.d.) The Johann Heinrich Pestalozzi Society. https://www.jhpestalozzi.org/

Piaget, J. (1953) *The Origin of Intelligence in the Child* London: Routledge and Kegan Paul

Picton, I., Goodwin, H. and Clark, C. (2021) *Exploring the Impact of World Book Day on the Reading Lives of Children in the UK 2019–2021: Helping Children to Feel Part of the World of Reading and That Reading Is Part of Their World.* National Literacy Trust. Available online at: Exploring-the-impact-of-World-Book-Day-on-childrens-reading-2019–21-final.pdf (worldbookday.com) [last accessed 10.08.2022]

PISA (2019) *PISA 2018 Results (Volume III): What School Life Means for Students' Lives* 3 December 2019. Available online at: https://www.oecd.org/publications/pisa-2018-results-volume-iii-acd78851-en.htm [last accessed 26 October 2020]

Plowden, B. (1967) *Children and Their Primary Schools: A Report of the Central Advisory Council for Education (England)* London: Her Majesty's Stationery Office

Poetry by Heart. Available online at: https://www.poetrybyheart.org.uk/ [last accessed 08.08.2022]

Pullman, P. (2003) *Isis Lecture to Oxford Literary Festival* Available online at: http://www.philip-pullman.com/other-writing-recent-talks-and-lectures/the-worlds/education/ [last accessed 17.03.2015]

QCA (2000) *Curriculum Guidance for the Foundation Stage* Sudbury: QCA. Available online at: http://www.educationengland.org.uk/documents/foundationstage/2000-curriculum-guidance.pdf [last accessed 21.10.2020]

QCA (2005) *Creativity: Find It, Promote It* London: QCA. Available online at: http://archive.teachfind.com/qcda/www.qcda.gov.uk/resources/publication560a.html [last accessed 21.10.2020]

Quiller Couch, A. (ed.) (1912) *The Oxford Book of English Verse 1250–1900* Oxford: Clarendon Press

Qur'an. Available online at: https://corpus.quran.com/translation.jsp?chapter=35&verse=1 [last accessed 14.07.2022]

Ribbins, P. and Sherratt, B. (1997) *Conservative Secretaries of State and Radical Educational Reform Since 1973* London: Cassell

Robinson, K. (2007) *Do Schools Kill Creativity?* Available online at: https://www.youtube.com/watch?v=iG9CE55wbtY [last accessed 18.09.2019]

Robinson, K. (2008) *Changing Education Paradigms.* Transcript available online at: https://www.thersa.org/globalassets/pdfs/videos/2010/10/rsa-animate---changing-paradigms/rsa-lecture-ken-robinson-transcript.pdf [last accessed 08.08.2022]

Rosen, M. (2015) *Guide to Education.* Available online at: http://michaelrosenblog.blogspot.co.uk/2015/04/guide-to-education.html [last accessed 15.07.2015]

Rosenshine, B. (2012*) Principles of Instruction: Research-Based Strategies That All Teachers Should Know.* Available online at: https://www.aft.org/sites/default/files/periodicals/Rosenshine.pdf [last accessed 08.08.2022]

Rowson, J. (2008) *Are We Disposed to Be Creative?* in: Craft, A., Gardner, H. and Claxton, G. (eds) *Creativity, Wisdom and Trusteeship: Exploring the Role of Education* Thousand Oaks, CA: Corwin Press pp. 84–85

RSC www.rsc.org.uk/shakespeare-learning-zone

Runco, M. and Jaeger, G. (2012) *The Standard Definition of Creativity* in: *Creativity Research Journal* 24 (1) pp. 92–96, DOI: 10.1080/10400419.2012.650092

Russell, B. (1919) *The Study of Mathematics: Mysticism and Logic: And Other Essays* London: Longman

Sampson, G. (1918/2017) *Cambridge Readings in Literature* Location unknown: Palala Press

Sampson, G. (1922) *English for the English* Cambridge: Cambridge University Press. Available online at: https://archive.org/stream/englishforenglis00samprich#page/n9/mode/2up [last accessed 28.11.2017]

Scruton. R. (2000) *An Intelligent Person's Guide to Modern Culture* South Bend: St Augustine's Press

Seltzer, K. and Bentley, T. (1999) *The Creative Age: Knowledge and Skills for the New Economy* London: Demos

Sharwood Smith, E. (1919) *English in Schools* in *The Teaching of English in Schools* pp. 29–30. Available online at: https://archive.org/details/pamphletsonteach00engl/page/n241/mode/2up [last accessed 24.10.2020] pp. 270–271

Shaw, G.B. (1913) *Pygmalion*. Available online at https://gutenberg.org/

Shayer, D. (1972) *The Teaching of English in Schools 1900–70* London: Routledge & Kegan Paul

Sherratt, Y. (2006) *Continental Philosophy of Social Science: Hermeneutics, Genealogy and Critical Theory from Ancient Greece to the Twenty-First Century* Cambridge: Cambridge University Press

Simon, B. (1991) *Education and the Social Order 1940–1990* London: Lawrence & Wishart

Slocum, D. (2014) *The Relevance of Vulgar Creativity*. Available online at: https://www.berlin-school.com/blog/relevancy-vulgar-creativity [last accessed 14.07.2022]

Smit, B. (2005) *Teachers, Local Knowledge, and Policy Implementation: A Qualitative Policy-Practice Inquiry* in: *Education and Urban Society* 37 (3) pp. 292–306 https://doi-org.bris.idm.oclc.org/10.1177/0013124505275426

Smith, L. (2017) *Coming up for Air: GCSE, Progress 8, Assessment and Survival* [PowerPoint] NATE ITE symposium, King's College, London 18.11.2017

Smith, L. (2018) *'We're Not Building Worker Bees.' What Has Happened to Creative Practice in England Since the Dartmouth Conference of 1966?* in: *Changing English* 26 (1) pp. 48–62, DOI: 10.1080/1358684X.2018.1532786

Smith, L. (2019) *The Role of English in the Conversation of Humankind: Humanism and Creativity in Newbolt (1921) and the National Curriculum (2014)* in: *English in Education* 53 (3) pp. 253–265, DOI: 10.1080/04250494.2019.1643233

Smith, L. (2020a) *All the Nines: Creativity in English Curricula in England in 1919, 1989 and 2019 as a Reflection of Britain's Place in Europe* in: *Changing English* 27 (3) pp. 305–320, DOI: 10.1080/1358684X.2020.1716688

Smith, L. (2020b) *Top Ten Texts: A Survey of Commonly-Taught KS3 Class Readers* in: *Teaching English* 23 pp. 30–33

Smith, L. (2021) *Colleagues in Collaboration: The Members of Newbolt's Committee* in Green, A. (ed) *The New Newbolt: One Hundred Years of the Teaching of English in England* London: Routledge pp. 22–40

Snell, J. and Cushing, I. (2022) *'A lot of them write how they speak': Policy, Pedagogy and the Policing of 'nonstandard' English*. Literacy, pre-print. Available online at: https://onlinelibrary.wiley.com/doi/epdf/10.1111/lit.12298 [last accessed 11 August 2022]

Stein, M.I. (1953) *Creativity and Culture* in: *Journal of Psychology* 36 pp. 311–322, DOI: 10.1080/00223980.1953.9712897

Sternberg, R.J. (1999) *Handbook of Creativity* Cambridge: Cambridge University Press

Sternberg, R.J. (2003) *The Development of Creativity as a Decision-Making Process* in: Sawyer, R.K., John Steiner, V., Moran, S., Sternberg, R., Feldman, D., Nakamura, J. and Csikszentmihalya (eds) *Creativity and Development* New York: Oxford University Press pp. 91–138

Sternberg, R.J. (2005) *Creativity or Creativities?* in: *International Journal of Human-Computer Studies* 63 (4–5) pp. 370–382

Sternberg, R.J (2008) *Leadership as a Basis for the Education of Our Children* in: Craft, A, Gardner, H. and Claxton, G. (eds) *Creativity, Wisdom and Trusteeship: Exploring the Role of Education* Thousand Oaks, CA: Corwin Press pp. 143–157

Stevens, D. (2011) *Cross-curricular Teaching and Learning in the Secondary School: English* Abingdon: David Fulton

Stubbs, M. (1989) *The State of English in the English state: Reflections on the Cox Report* in: *Language and Education* 3 (4) pp. 235–250, DOI: 10.1080/09500788909541265

Sugrue, C. (2010) *Plowden: Progressive Education – A 4-Decade Odyssey?* in: *Curriculum Inquiry* 40 (1) pp. 105–124. Available online at: http://www.jstor.org.bris.idm.oclc.org/stable/40602917

Summerfield, G. (1968) *Creativity in English: Papers Relating to the Anglo-American Seminar on the Teaching of English (Dartmouth College, New Hampshire, 1966): The Dartmouth Seminar Papers* Champaign, IL: NCTE

Sure Start (2003) *Birth to Three Matters: A Framework to Support Children in Their Earliest Years* London: DfES/Sure Start

Taylor, J. (2015) *Response to the Withdrawal of Creative Writing at A Level.* Available online at: https://www2.le.ac.uk/offices/english-association/news-1/response-to-withdrawal-of-creative-writing-at-a-level [last accessed 09.10.2019]

TES (2019) *Exclusive: England opts out of new Pisa Creativity Test.* Available online at: https://www.tes.com/magazine/archive/exclusive-england-opts-out-new-pisa-creativity-test [last accessed 08.08.2022]

Thomas, D. (1934) *The Force That through the Green Fuse Drives the Flower.* Available online at: https://www.poetrybyheart.org.uk/poems/the-force-that-through-the-green-fuse-drives-the-flower [last accessed 21.10.2020]

Thomas, H. (2019) *English Teaching and Imagination: A Case for Revisiting the Value of Imagination in Teaching Writing* in: *English in Education* 53 (1) pp. 49–60, DOI: 10.1080/04250494.2018.1557856

Thomson, P., Hall, C. and Jones, K. (2012) *Creativity and Cross Curriculum Strategies in England. Tales of Forgetting and Not Knowing* in: *International Journal of Educational Research* 55 6–15, DOI: 10.1016/j.ijer.2012.06.003

Tomlinson, M. (2004) *14–19 Curriculum and Qualifications Report: Final Report of the Working Group on 14–19 Reform* Annesley, DfES

UCAS (2022) *Monthly Statistics on Initial Teacher Training (ITT) Recruitment 2022–23.* Available online at: https://www.gov.uk/government/publications/monthly-statistics-on-initial-teacher-training-itt-recruitment [last accessed 13.07.2022]

UNESCO (1990) *World Conference on Education for All: Meeting Basic Learning Needs.* Available online at: http://www.unesco.org/education/pdf/11_93.pdf [last accessed 18.09.2019]

UNESCO (2019) *Futures of Education.* Available online at: https://en.unesco.org/futuresofeducation [last accessed 13.07.2022]

Videbaek, S. (2020) *PISA: Beyond the League Tables and the Headlines.* Available online at: https://www.seced.co.uk/best-practice/pisa-beyond-the-leaguetables-and-the-headlines/ [last accessed 26.10.2020]

Voice 21 – The National Oracy Education Charity https://voice21.org/

Wallas, G. (1926/2014) *The Art of Thought* Tunbridge Wells: Solis Press

Watson, A. and Newman, R. (eds) (2022) *A Practical Guide to Teaching English in the Secondary School* London: Routledge

Westbrook, J., Sutherland, J., Oakhill, J. and Sullivan, S. (2019) *'Just reading': The Impact of a Faster Pace of Reading Narratives on the Comprehension of Poorer Adolescent Readers in English Classrooms* in: *Literacy UKLA* 53 (2) pp. 60–68

White, J. (2012) *Powerful Knowledge: Too Weak a Prop for the Traditional Curriculum?* Available online at: https://www.newvisionsforeducation.org.uk/about-the-group/home/2012/05/14/power-ful-knowledge-too-weak-a-prop-for-the-traditional-curriculum/ [last accessed 15.09.2019]

Whitley, D. (2017) *Poetry and Memory: Project Report* Cambridge: University of Cambridge. Available online at: http://www.poetryandmemory.com/uploads/2/6/1/9/2619440/poetry_and_memory_project_report_march_2017.pdf [last accessed 10.08.2022]

Whittemore, R. (1968) *A Caveat on Creativity* in: Summerfield, G. (ed) *Creativity in English: Papers Relating to the Anglo-American Seminar on the Teaching of English (Dartmouth College, New Hampshire, 1966): The Dartmouth Seminar Papers* Champaign, IL: NCTE pp. 45–49

Whitty, G. (2010) *Revisiting School Knowledge: Some Sociological Perspectives on New School Curricula* in: *European Journal of Education* 45 (1) Part I pp. 28–45

Williams, R. (1961/2011) *The Long Revolution* Cardigan: Parthian Books

Wilson, J. (1972) *Philosophy and Educational Research* Slough: National Foundation for Educational Research in England and Wales

Wintour, P. (2012) *Michael Gove Accused of Major Gaps in Draft National Curriculum for English* in: *The Guardian* 31.10.2012. Available online at: https://www.theguardian.com/politics/2012/oct/31/michael-gove-draft-national-curriculum [last accessed 14.09.2019]

Wordsworth, W. (1798) *Lines Composed a Few Miles above Tintern Abbey, On Revisiting the Banks of the Wye during a Tour* 13.07.1798. Available online at: https://www.poetryfoundation.org/poems/45527/lines-composed-a-few-miles-above-tintern-abbey-on-revisiting-the-banks-of-the-wye-during-a-tour-july-13-1798 [last accessed 21.10.2020]

Wyse, D., Hayward, L., Livingston, K. and Higgins, S. (2014) *Editorial: Creating curricula: Aims, Knowledge & Control* in *The Curriculum Journal* 25 (1) pp. 2–6, DOI: 10.1080/09585176.2014.878545

Wyse, D. and Spendlove, S. (2007) *Partners in Creativity: Action Research and Creative Partnerships* in: *Education 3–13* 35 (2) pp. 181–191, DOI: 10.1080/03004270701312034

Yandell, J. (2003) *Thoughtless Language, or the Death of Child-Centred Education* in: *Changing English* 10 (1) pp. 5–12, DOI: 10.1080/1358684032000055091

Yandell, J. (2008) *Mind the Gap: Investigating Test Literacy and Classroom Literacy* in: *English in Education* 42 (1) pp. 70–87

Yandell, J., and Brady, M. (2016) *English and the Politics of Knowledge* in: *English in Education* 50 (1) pp. 44–59, DOI: 10.1111/eie.12094

Young, M. (2009) *Education, Globalisation and the 'voice of knowledge'* in: *Journal of Education and Work* 22 (3) pp. 193–204

Index

Note: **Bold** page numbers refer to tables; *Italic* page numbers refer to figures and page numbers followed by "n" denote endnotes.

Printed in Great Britain
by Amazon

22870049R00099